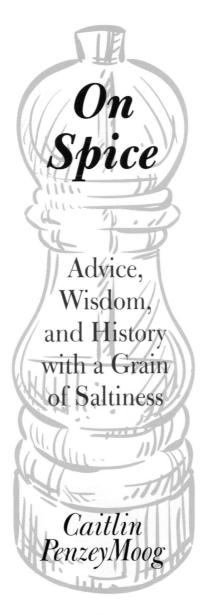

On Spice

Advice, Wisdom, and History with a Grain of Saltiness

Caitlin PenzeyMoog

Skyhorse Publishing

Skyhorse Publishing books may be purchased in bulk at special discounts for sales promotion, corporate gifts, fund-raising, or educational purposes. Special editions can also be created to specifications. For details, contact the Special Sales Department, Skyhorse Publishing, 307 West 36th Street, 11th Floor, New York, NY 10018 or info@skyhorsepublishing.com.

Published by Skyhorse Publishing, Inc. 307 West 36th Street, 11th Floor, New York, NY 10018. Skyhorse® and Skyhorse Publishing® are registered trademarks of Skyhorse Publishing, Inc.®, a Delaware corporation.

www.skyhorsepublishing.com

10 9 8 7 6 5 4 3 2 1

Names: PenzeyMoog, Caitlin, author.
Title: On spice: advice, wisdom, and history with a grain of saltiness / Caitlin PenzeyMoog.
Description: New York, New York: Skyhorse Publishing, 2018. | Includes bibliographical references and index.
Identifiers: LCCN 2018023556 (print) | LCCN 2018026516 (ebook) | ISBN 9781510735262 (ebook) | ISBN 9781510735255 (hardcover: alk. paper)
Subjects: LCSH: Spices. | Herbs.
Classification: LCC TX406 (ebook) | LCC TX406 .P46 2018 (print) | DDC 641.6/383—dc23
LC record available at https://lccn.loc.gov/2018023556

Cover design by Brian Peterson
Cover photograph by iStockphoto
Interior phography by Jimmy Hasse

Print ISBN: 978-1-5107-3525-5
eBook ISBN: 978-1-5107-3526-2

Printed in China

For Grandma, who is salt,
and Grandpa, who is pepper.

Contents

Preface

I grew up working for my family in our spice shops. There were occasional stints at my aunt's store in downtown Milwaukee, and some summers in college spent at the Penzeys Spices warehouse. Mostly, I worked and learned at my grandparents' small store in a suburb of Milwaukee, Wisconsin. It didn't look like much from outside: a squat rectangle, a triangular roof (like a child's drawing) with bricks painted red and cracked pavement forming a three-car parking lot. Once you opened the door, though, something remarkable happened. A blast of aroma hit, pungent and overwhelming, sweet and savory, a thousand smells commingling until they blended into the smell of the Spice House.

My grandparents started that humble store in 1957, the same year they married. They nurtured it over decades, then their children took up the business, and eventually their grandchildren came to pass through its doors on their own journeys, sifting and stirring and smelling from the time they were so young they could hardly hold the scoops. The red brick faded and was repainted, the price of vanilla rose and fell and rose again, and us three grandkids who worked the store on weekends and over summer breaks grew up among family and spice. The wares on the shelves remained mostly the same: the vanilla beans tall and proud behind glass, saffron tucked safely into the corner, a hundred apothecary jars lining shelves in long, tidy rows. A giant-old fashioned register emitted its shrill *ca-ching* when the cash drawer sprung open. Behind the counter hid a back room, where the mess sprawled across worktables and the shelves were lined with yet more spices, in giant burlap bags and big plastic barrels. You needed a scoop bigger than your hand to shovel out the salt. Tiny tins from Spain, still smelling of the saffron they transported, shone in the light, while the noisy cinnamon grinder stood at the ready, dusty with cinnamon powder and bulky, several decades old but looking like something that sprung out of the Industrial Revolution.

That's all gone now: the cinnamon grinder and the burlap and the old-fashioned cash register. It's been cleared out of the building, which may stand empty but is forever imbued with the smells of a thousand spices. I last worked there four years ago, just before I moved from Milwaukee to Chicago for a new and exciting career. The future was such a strong pull that I didn't mark that occasion, the ending of my time at the Spice House. The morning was spent simply, drinking coffee with my grandma while we filled jars of cinnamon at the front counter, where the soft surface made it safer to tap them down. *Tap tap tap*, and the cinnamon would settle a centimeter lower in the jar as the air escaped with a soft *phut*, and we'd fill the newly created space with more cinnamon. This is the method my grandfather taught me. He said that spices had music in them, if you knew how to listen. He had died several years before, and I hadn't marked the last time I spoke with him any more than I did that last time I closed up the store and locked the finicky old door behind me.

Writing this book has, in many ways, been my attempt to get back to that place. Its potent spice smell was the most familiar in the world to me and my brother and sister, growing up amongst its wares. We'd crowd in the sugary warmth of the vanilla room to read books about mysticism, then go to the tiny kitchen where my grandfather would cook us pork chops with some mysterious combination of spices. Grandma would make coffee for herself and cassia tea for my grandfather. I never liked cassia tea then, but now I drink it almost every day.

I've had to relearn much of what I'd forgotten: the origin of nutmeg and the different kinds of peppercorns, the nuanced difference between Turkish thyme and Mexican thyme, how to make dried mustard hot again. I grew up with spices, but they had been like air to me: I was surrounded and took it for granted. Informal lessons were applied over a thousand different customer interactions, wondering if we had a spice that could make broccoli taste good or whether grinding a nutmeg was really necessary for their holiday drink. Sometimes I knew the answer, and sometimes I'd run back to where someone older was working, seeking the answers I should have already had. *Remind me the difference between Malabar and Lampong pepper. Do we sell any pepper hotter than jalapeño? How long does a vanilla bean last?*

As you'll see in the coming pages, to write about spices is also to write about my family. This book addresses the questions I heard, over and over again, while working in their shop. Much is information I picked up over the course of a childhood spent among the spices. I hope the practical information and advice serves well anyone interested in spices and cooking. This book addresses the unasked questions, too, the type customers didn't know to raise, like whether more expensive spices are superior (only in certain cases), and the efficacy of miracle spices (highly doubtful), and when it's worth the effort to toast and hand-grind spices (whenever you have the time).

Spices also act as a window to other subjects—history, myth, cooking, culture, science, food production—and when I thought it of interest, I included discussion on these topics. Sometimes, thinking I knew the answer but finding my explanation lacking, I consulted the old books on spices kept at my grandparents' house. This research led me down some avenues I hadn't anticipated, but part of the education my grandparents tried to impart is to always follow your curiosity. When I heard the spices singing, I stopped to listen.

This guide is not technical or scientific. It is not a history of spices. In a way, it's a decent approximation of what it was like to grow up in a spicemonger family. Between the dos and don'ts, the explanations and pointers, is something more personal, and that's in keeping with how my grandparents ran their shop. Their store and story were always about so much more than spices.

THERE'S NO RIGHT WAY TO SPICE

Many customers had questions about the *right* way to use a spice, and many more were happy to provide firm statements in reply. These statements usually reveal more about the speaker than about the spice. Simply put: Anyone emphatically stating that you *must* use a certain spice in a certain way (or must *never* use a certain spice in a certain way) is wrong. Spices cannot be neatly categorized down clean lines.

Like recipes, spices should be tinkered with. You may add whatever you want to a curry sauce, even if it's not a traditional curry spice. You can decide to put black pepper on literally everything—even a pale sauce, which food writers love to assert is the realm of white pepper only. Taco seasoning's jurisdiction goes well beyond tacos. Cumin is more than a Mexican flavor, and can be added to much more than you'd think.

I'd like everyone to see their spice racks as wide-open vistas of culinary possibilities, instead of Tetris shapes you struggle to make fit. Have you ever tried pouring cinnamon into a jar? If you're not careful, it explodes like a mushroom cloud. Spices are messy. It doesn't matter how tradition, history, or celebrity chefs says they're to be used. Spice usage has been flexible since humans first started harvesting them, so why would that change now?

Spices make food tasty; there's really nothing more complicated to it.

What is a spice?

A chef, a botanist, an economist, and a scientist get together for dinner. They all love spices and, being argumentative types, they start to break it down. The chef calls the salt at the table a spice. The botanist, offended, says it's not a *plant*, but a *mineral*, and therefore is not a spice at all. The scientist challenges the botanist, asking them to define exactly which part of a plant is the spice: is it volatile oils that matter, or can spices only come from certain parts of the plant? The economist interjects that the bodies governing trade don't care if it's a mineral or a plant.

A geographer at the next table overhears and insists that there's a big difference between herbs grown locally and in the Mediterranean. The chef, already sorry he started this conversation, can't stand for that—herbs aren't spices, but a different category altogether. Although, he ponders out loud, if coriander leaf in an herb, what does that make coriander seed?

I am not a chef, botanist, economist, scientist, or geographer. I am a cook, and I define spices as those powders, seeds, leaves, liquids, and, yes, minerals that I add to food to make it taste better. It's a very broad definition, and it would never pass muster in the Dewey Decimal System. Lucky for spices, they belong in the kitchen, and food itself keeps mum on the difference between an herb or a spice or where salt belongs. Only recently have we even bothered to consider the issue. For a long time, *spice* simply meant wares rare and usually expensive: *spice* shares a root with *special*. Around the time of the Hundred Years' War, when the Black Death swept through Europe, Europeans considered sugar and oranges to be spices. Like pepper and cassia, they were hard to acquire, delicious, and came from faraway places.

I am interested in how we use dried powders, barks, leaves, seeds, flowers, stamens, extracts, nuts, pods, fruits, and minerals in the kitchen, where little else matters except making tasty food. Rather than create an elaborate and complicated detective board with bay leaf connected to cinnamon by red string, I consider all those goods to be spices. I've found that categorizing spices according to rigid principles is seldom helpful in understanding how we can use them to improve our cooking.

Without further ado, let us explore this wild and aromatic world.

My grandfather teaches my sister, me, and my brother about spice.

Salt

Pepper is the king. He's the gaudy royalty, the Emperor Caligula, the Marie Antoinette, the Elvis of spices. But while pepper rules by divine right, it is salt who *is* divine. The Greek Helios, maybe, who brought the sun across the Earth in his chariot. Or Huixtocihuatl, an Aztec fertility goddess who also oversaw salt and salt water. People can make do without pepper if they must, but they cannot live without salt.

Hyponatraemia is the medical term for sodium deficiency, a condition that might be familiar to marathon runners, who know that if they sweat too much and only drink water, they're at risk of their bodies shutting down. Sodium plays a crucial role in the body by managing blood pressure, helping the central nervous system, and maintaining the right amount of fluids in blood cells. Some scientists theorize that this need for salt is why we love it so much: We need it to survive, so we love its taste.

We can get it through consuming animal flesh, or by ingesting it directly. Even thousands of years ago, it seems, people knew that salt was not optional. Pliny the Elder, a Roman naturalist whose extensive writing gives us much of what we know about ancient Rome's plant life (and who created the model of the encyclopedia), wrote "Heaven knows, a civilized life is impossible without salt." A few hundred years later, fellow Roman Cassiodorus said, "Mankind can live without gold . . . but not without salt." Whether they knew they *literally* needed salt in their bodies to function is almost beside the point. Salt is in every civilization's history, sprinkled lovingly on food by people around the world (except, it seems, by certain Native American populations, who didn't harvest salt but consumed sodium chloride by eating animal meat). There is even evidence of humans using salt to preserve food during the last ice age.

For many people who eat meals with saltshaker at the ready, like me, salt seems necessary for what it does to food, not its role in the body. For years my apartment had two saltshakers: one for the kitchen and one for the dining room table. Then, and I'm not sure how it happened (except perhaps it's the organic way spices flow for members of my family), there was a saltshaker in every room. Now there's a salt-shaker *and* a salt cellar in my kitchen, giving me the option to either shake or pinch salt onto foods while I'm cooking.

I know my family can't be the only one repeatedly asking "can you pass the salt?" at dinnertime. I wonder, though, if salt's high demand led anyone else's aunt to show up to Christmas one year, like a goddess out of myth, with a saltshaker for every member of the family, each with our names embossed in glitzy gold lettering. But, like disappearing socks or pens, saltshakers seem destined to vanish into the void. Of the dozen saltshakers my aunt doled out like Santa Claus, only a few remain today. That (so I tell myself) is why I have a shaker in every room: they're in such high demand that they never stick around for long.

SALT IS SALT

My grandfather had a mantra: "salt is salt." What he meant was that salt can be broken down into many groupings, but such distinctions hardly matter. The broad catego-ries are rock salt, kosher salt, and the color salts: gray sea salt, Himalayan pink salt, Hawaiian red salt, etc. These *are* different, but when it comes to salting your food, well, they're all just salt. It's an adage that's served me well when it comes to the seduc-tion of the small batch, the rare, the expensive. Luckily with salt, it doesn't matter if you buy the processed stuff off the grocery store shelf or are able to procure a pinch of brown salt from Japan, where only 600 pounds are mined every year. The expensive salts will not make your food taste any better than the cheap salts. Salt is salt.

My favorite salt is among the cheapest: kosher salt. Growing up, my family used little else. Though it is traditionally used for preparing kosher foods, the salt itself is not necessarily kosher. Rather, nearly all salt is kosher and *may* be religiously cer-tified as such (check the box), but not all "kosher salt," of the distinctive size and shape, has been certified. It's not the color or origin or religious affiliation that makes salt culinarily different, but the surface area.

The differences can be understood through the example of ice, snow, and rain. A grain of rock salt is like a chunk of ice: it falls on a surface and dissolves very slowly.

Kosher salt, on the other hand, is like a snowflake: it lands on the surface and immediately dissipates, spreading out to cover more ground. Table salt is like smaller pieces of ice, or a hard rain. It falls in tiny bits, bouncing around the food and into cracks and crevices like rain in a gutter. That's why kosher salt is preferred for salting foods at the table: it covers more surface and melts more evenly. My dad, a chef, also likes it for the thick texture, which makes it easy to pinch and disperse. A year or two ago, when I had lost yet another saltshaker and didn't have any replacement jar and shaker lids on hand, I dumped kosher salt into a small ramekin bowl. With this makeshift salt cellar, I realized what my dad was talking about. Using salt this way results in much more direct contact between your fingers, the salt, and the food. You feel how much salt you're using when you pinch it and, by extension, how much salt you're actually putting on your food. Now I primarily use the salt cellar in the kitchen, and save the shakers for the other rooms. (Plus, it's much harder to lose a small bowl of salt than a shaker that may be tucked away out of sight and accidentally disappear into the contours of the house.)

ALL SALT ISN'T JUST SALT, CHEMICALLY

All cooking salts are sodium chloride, but many contain other minerals that were added naturally or artificially. Pure sodium chloride is white, so if you have a salt that isn't white, it's fair to assume there's a lot more stuff mixed up in the salt than just sodium chloride. Mass-produced table salt is purified to get rid of these naturally occurring additives that are highlighted in other salts, and thus it has little of the flavor that comes with colored salts.

Those colored salts contain minerals, like magnesium, and also sulfates, soil sediments, algae, and bacteria. These additives run the risk of carrying pollutants, especially when the product is manufactured from sea salt.[1] Such salt is very old, and has had centuries or more to pick up all sorts of junk that's been wafting in the air, floating in the water, and sinking into the soil.

---

[1] I wouldn't worry about that too much, though. Plenty of food carries such risks, and you can't live your life worrying too much about them.

TYPES OF SALT

Table salt: This is the most common salt found in shakers on dinner and diner tables across the country. It has small, round, and refined granules. Sometimes rice or an anticaking agent are added, to keep the salt from clumping. Generally, I avoid it on food, though it's fine to use to salt the pot of water before adding pasta, or pouring on your carpet if you get a flea infestation. Table salt does do one important thing, though: it contains iodine, an important supplement.[2]

Gray sea salt: I use kosher salt for everything except fresh garden tomatoes. For that, I want gray sea salt. Gray sea salt is large and damp, making the grains cluster together in chunks. It has a minerally tang that goes excellently with fresh produce like tomatoes,[3] watermelon, and peaches. Because the moistness forms large granules, gray sea salt can also be a good finishing salt raw on meats, like beef tartare or seafood crudo, and some desserts, where you want the salt to sit on top of the dish without dissolving.

Pink salt: There are several kinds of pink (or red) salts. The most common are Himalayan and Hawaiian. They get their pretty color from nearby minerals or, in the case of true Hawaiian salt, from proximity to volcanic clay that's rich in iron oxide. It's important to remember that these minerals are not within the salt itself. Pink and red salts are a case of style over substance. Of all the gourmet salts that come at a high price, none is so strangely worshiped and fetishized as pink salt. Himalayan salt lamps look like big crystals of pink salt that glow from within and tout benefits from silly (cleansing the air and improving energy, mood, and sleep) to downright nutty (curing seasonal affective disorder and reducing allergens in

---

[2] Iodine deficiency can cause goiters in adults and mental problems in newborns, so, in the 1920s, a goiter-prevention program was launched that added this necessary supplement to salt. It was a stroke of brilliance to add it to table salt: Everyone in the US consumes salt, regardless of income or geography. Scientifically, it was easy to add iodine to salt, too.

[3] Tomatoes and salt go so well together because the salt breaks down the tomato membrane and draws out its juices, making the tomato far more flavorful than without the salt. Plus, the salt adds its usual salty flavor.

the air).[4] While some palates can pick up the subtle flavors of colored salts, what matters is the texture. Often the grains are large, so in recipes that call for colored salts, using any large-grain salt will do.

Black salt: Black salt might be black because of a high amount of charcoal in it, or it might actually be pink or white salt that's been cooked with spices to darken its color. Black salt recipes can include pretty much any spice you want, from herbs to cinnamon to chili flakes. Some types of colored salt grow darker when cooked.

Fleur de sel: Like other delicacies from France, this salt has traditionally been harvested in a specific spot: Grérande, Brittany. "Flower of salt" in French, it's a delicately flavored salt that's usually expensive. The minerals in fleur de sel are clean and bright. This is a good salt to get a big crunch on your food, used as a finishing salt. The crunch factor is the only reason I choose this salt, as I like the big, structural crystals to sit on top of warm foods like wilted spinach, and rich, fatty foods like a good butter.

Rock salt: This is not the salt you put on roads to make ice melt, but it does come in big, roundish chunks. It's produced to be put in grinders, which will make the salt smaller for no reason.

Slab salt: If you've ever been served food on a slab of pink salt, it's Himalayan salt from Pakistan, known for its minerals and an aura of specialness. It glows. It's very pretty. Restaurants add a wow factor by serving hot or cold dishes on slabs of it, since it will retain both hot and cold temperatures for a long time.

Smoked salts: A great many more salts are one of the above that's been smoked, sometimes with additional spices added for more flavor. Smoked salts can have

---

[4] A *New York Times* article from August 2017, "Now at Saks: Salt Rooms, a Bootcamp and a Peek at Retail's Future," describes "salt rooms," small, enclosed rooms lined with pink Himalayan salt where vapors consisting of 99 percent sodium chloride are misted into the room in and inhaled for 10 minutes. Customers beware: These treatments are bullshit. Salt is salt.

different flavors depending on what they're smoked over, just like the difference you taste cooking a steak over charcoal versus wood. Fancy smoked salts can be smoked using barrels wine has aged in, for example, which supposedly impart the wine flavor and, more importantly, can be sold at a premium price.

SALT WELL

For most of humanity's existence, getting our hands on salt wasn't as easy or as cheap as it is nowadays. Salty, fatty foods were rare but necessary. So why are people supposed to cut back on salt? Isn't it bad for you? Doesn't it increase your risk of stroke and heart attacks?

It's true that the majority of people in the United States eat more salt than they need to.[5] The World Health Organization and the United States' Centers for Disease Control (CDC) have an initiative to reduce the average salt intake by 30 percent. In other words: to lower worldwide salt consumption by a third. Interestingly, salt intake is roughly the same the world over; it's not just the US population that overdoes it. Wherever salt is easily available, people will eat more than they need to, which suggests that we as a species share a universal love of salt, that our palates evolved to always desire salt when available. Average sodium intake in the United Kingdom is roughly the same as in the United States. Japan, meanwhile, has higher average sodium intake than the US, thanks to cultural preferences for soy sauce and pickling.[6]

But if you want to lower your sodium intake, don't bother throwing out your salt-shaker. The majority of the salt we eat is in prepackaged, prepared food, and it is abundant in those foods we regularly buy from the grocery store. Pre-made bread is responsible for a lot of our sodium intake, as are bottled sauces and salad dressings, deli meats, processed cheese, and salty snacks. When you eat fast food or at a restaurant, chances are high that it tastes so good because the food is packed to its

---

[5] More than 90 percent of the US population consumes too much salt, according to a 2013 CDC study. The US Department of Health and Human Services puts the daily max for salt at 2,300 mg. The study found the average American's daily intake to be 3,592 mg.
[6] This according to the World Health Organization, in a study done to discuss reducing salt intake.

breaking point with salt. These are the real vehicles that deliver too much sodium into the average person's diet.[7]

If you want to cut back on salt, cut back on those foods. Reducing sliced bread, replacing bottled salad dressing with homemade oil and vinegar, and cutting out salty snack foods will decrease your sodium intake far more than altering the relatively minimal amount you add at the table. You might as well add that (relatively tiny) amount of salt to your diet to enjoy your pork chops and green beans; the damage is already done by the boxes of cereal and bags of potato chips. And if anyone gives you grief for heavily salting your food at the table (I've been told to slow down more times than I can count), calmly inform them that more than two-thirds of the average American's salt intake comes from premade foods, fast food, and restaurant meals. Or just use the reply my grandma, a prodigious salter, has on standby: "I'll reduce my salt when my *doctor* tells me to."

However, salt enthusiast that she is, you'll never catch my grandma bringing her own salt to a restaurant (though she does keep a shaker in the glove compartment of her car, just in case she stops for fast food on a road trip and deems the fries insufficiently salted). Growing up in a family where talking shop meant discussing the virtues of kosher salt gave me an appreciation for perfectly salted foods, but no one in my family would dare use their own saltshakers in a restaurant. I've witnessed others do so in steak houses and can only assume that the people who bring their own stuff (usually in grinders, of course) are sadly insecure about themselves, enough to believe that bringing in equipment makes them connoisseurs. There is a lot of insecurity around food and spices, and capitalists would have you believe that all you need to do to cook well is buy more things. By extension, you must *really* know your

---

[7] The CDC estimates 71 percent of the average American's sodium intake comes from a combination of processed foods and restaurant foods. (Source: CDC, "Sodium and Food Sources.") Levels are getting lower, though. According to a June 2017 study in the *Journal of the American Medical Association*, "Salt levels in store-bought packaged foods and drinks decreased by around 18% between 2000 to 2014" (*JAMA*, "Sodium Reduction in US Households' Packaged Food and Beverage Purchases, 2000 to 2014").

stuff if you bring a salt grinder to a fancy steak joint. But you can leave the salting to the chef or, if you don't trust them, find a different restaurant.

SALT GRINDERS ARE RUBBISH

I've used the word *shake* to describe adding salt to food and I will never say *grind*.

Grinding pepper makes very good sense, as it is physically breaking open the peppercorn. The result is fresh pepper. Look closely at a whole peppercorn, and you'll see a black, wrinkly surface. This outer hull has been dried hard, acting like a natural container for the vibrantly flavored inner meat of the peppercorn. It's just like an avocado, or a banana. By removing the outer protective layer, you reveal the tasty fruit within. Fruits oxidize the moment you cut into them, turning avocados and apples brown the longer they sit out in the open air. If you grind pepper in advance, it oxidizes, too. Therefore, you should grind the whole peppercorn just as it's going onto food, breaking the outer shell and using the resulting cracked pieces to flavor food. The outer shell, though hardened, also brings flavor.

Salt, on the other hand, can only be broken down into smaller pieces. It's not making the salt fresher to grind it at the table, because there is nothing inside to release. It only goes from a large piece of salt to several smaller pieces of salt. My guess is that salt grinders arose because people like symmetry, and a handsome wood pepper grinder doesn't match the squat saltshaker at the table. But ask yourself: Do you favor unnecessary symmetry for no real reason? If the answer is yes, a salt grinder may be right for you. Just know that it's unnecessary.

Another reason salt grinders are bullshit: salt is moist. Have you ever had to pound a saltshaker on the table to disperse the clumps? Salt does that naturally because it is hygroscopic, a fancy word which means salt attracts water particles to the point that it semi-dissolves and, thus, clumps together. Putting salt in a grinder will often corrode the grinding mechanisms as moisture in the air is drawn to the salt crystals. As you know if you've ever left a bicycle or wrench out in the rain for too long, metal rusts. One caveat to all this: If you insist on grinding salt, be sure to buy a grinder specifically created for that purpose. Most pepper grinders have mechanisms made of carbon steel, which will be corroded by the salt and destroyed, but you *can* find salt grinders with ceramic mechanisms if you absolutely must grind your salt.

SALT GENEROUSLY

It seems almost unnecessary to describe salt's many uses. Unlike, say, caraway seed, salt's applications are obvious and endless. You already know when to add salt at the table: whenever you think you need it. Home cooks know that adding salt to a boiling pot of water before throwing in pastas and grains helps to bring out their flavor. And salt, often along with pepper, is added at many steps of the cooking process. Consider humble roasted vegetables. They're diced and mixed with salt, pepper, and oil. After they're roasted in the oven, more salt and pepper is added. It seems like this would be enough, but even more is added once the vegetables make it to the table.

I'm a proponent of salting food on the plate, just before eating, where I can decide the amount for myself and where salting results in a stronger flavor than if it was done in the kitchen. Of course, you have to salt the water for rice or noodles, but I'd argue for less overall salting of vegetables and meats during the cooking process. Still, salt is the single most important spice for making foods taste good, but it can be so ubiquitous that it's almost forgotten about.

Salt is a flavor "potentiator," meaning it brings out the best-tasting flavors already present in the food. Sweet foods taste sweeter, meatier foods taste meatier, fried foods taste fried-ier. It's second nature to shake salt onto foods at the dinner table, because you can taste the difference it makes. The salt is right there on the surface. But we use salt to improve the flavor of foods all the time, even when it's not obvious. There's a reason virtually all baked goods require a teaspoon or two of salt. Cakes, cookies, brownies, and the like have a weaker overall flavor if salt isn't added. Salt is crucial in bread baking, as it not only enhances the flavor but subdues the yeast, necessary for a good crumb.

MSG

Salt has nothing on MSG as a "misunderstood white particle that makes food delicious." Unlike salt, MSG has few defenders. Monosodium glutamate, a product of glutamic acid, is a naturally occurring substance found in mushrooms, tomatoes, and especially robust cheeses like Parmesan. The quality these foods have in common is their abundance of *umami*, the hard-to-describe, impossible-to-miss aspect of foods that combines taste and mouthfeel.

MSG isn't bad for you: it isn't an allergen and it's not responsible for headaches. It has gotten a lot of bad press over the years, and the scientific community has all but shrugged off further studies to demonstrate its harmlessness. But if you've ever enjoyed mushrooms, cheese, or tomatoes, you've had MSG. The Food and Drug Administration deemed it "generally recognized as safe," and the European Union (whose stances on food are generally much better and up-to-date than those of the US government) classifies MSG as a "food additive" safe within certain limits and in certain foods. The few studies that were done could prove no link between MSG and the headaches said to be caused by it.

MSG intensifies the flavor of foods. It acts like salt, but it doesn't replace salt. Whereas salt can be easily detected, MSG cannot. MSG does have its own distinctive taste: the unmistakable flavor of chicken soup. But that taste is only apparent when eaten plain, or when way too much is used. When the proper amount of MSG is added to foods, its taste goes unnoticed. It only leaves behind an enhanced version of what the food was before. It intensifies the flavors already present, and diminishes flavors like sourness and bitterness. It even makes salt taste saltier.

A simple taste test can demonstrate the power of MSG. Make two soup broths however you want. If you have premade broth or stock, that will do. Or you can add bouillon cubes or stock paste to hot water. Divide into two bowls. Into one, sprinkle some MSG. Taste the two broths, and you'll taste one that's infinitely better than the other. MSG makes this simple soup more soup-like. MSG is typically dissolved into dishes, like soups and stews, but I add it as a straight seasoning as well.

One evening, some friends and I ordered delivery pizza. I set out my standby seasonings: crushed red pepper flakes and a blend we called North Face, a cheesy mix of sweet bell peppers, shallot, and herbs. Two of my friends went to explore the spice cabinet, experimenting with different spices and seasonings on their own. They came out of the kitchen to ask what "M56" was, for they had found a mysterious-looking pure white powder with the enigmatic hand-written scrawl on the label. This, they concluded, was the most delicious spice of all, adding an instant burst of flavor to their pizza. It was simply MSG, written in my grandfather's messy hand.

CREAM OF TARTAR

Cream of tartar is mostly used to help eggs "stabilize" when beating air into them for meringues, whipped cream, angel food cake, and pies. It's a key ingredient in snickerdoodles because of the effect cream of tartar has on sugars, keeping the dough soft so the baked cookie is chewier than it would be without the cream of tartar.

Cream of tartar is created by purifying the potassium crystals that precipitate when making wine.[8] The crystals form crusts on wine casks from the grape's tartaric acid, which is where the cream, which is actually a powder, gets the name. It's sometimes called *acid salt* and is a key ingredient in sodium-free salt substitutes and baking powder. You can also use it to make homemade playdough that won't harm kids when they inevitably eat some.

TAKE IT WITH A GRAIN OF SALT

Salt is perhaps the foodstuff most at home in our colloquialisms: "take it with a grain of salt," "salt of the earth," "worth your weight in salt"—not to mention old superstitions many still adhere to today, like throwing salt over your left shoulder after you spill some, and the story of Lot's wife turning into a pillar of salt (which doesn't sound so bad to me). Throwing salt over her shoulder is something my grandma always did when I was growing up, one of those benign habits done to avoid bad luck, like never naming the Scottish play out loud in a theater or saying "God bless you" after a sneeze. Theories on *why* you're supposed to throw spilled salt over your left shoulder tend to focus on the left-sinister-devil connection. According to my grandma, it "stops the devil cold." In her book *Salt & Pepper*, Michele Anna Jordan writes that the demons are said to hover at our left, "awaiting the moment of weakness that would give them access to our souls, clumsiness apparently a chief means of entry. Throwing salt, it seems, stopped them in their invisible tracks."[9]

---

[8] *The Oxford Companion to Food*, 225.

[9] *Salt & Pepper*, 3.

MAKING MIDDLE-EARTH FOOD TASTE BETTER

Life is so inconceivable without salt that it regularly makes an appearance even in fantasy worlds. These alternate universes show us impossible magic, extraordinary creatures, advanced technology . . . and salt. From classic fantasy literature to modern video games, authors and artists don't want to deprive their creations of salt. Salt as symbol for hospitality and friendship may have its origin in *One Thousand and One Nights*, which contains a tale wherein a thief breaks into the sultan's treasure room to steal a sack of jewels. But, in the darkness, he happens to lick a salty stone. So, he leaves the jewels alone, for, "One cannot steal from those whose salt one has tasted."

Game of Thrones fans know the same lesson, thanks to the HBO show's infamous Red Wedding, where the devious Frey family invited the Stark family over for a wedding celebration, then brutally murdered them. Readers and viewers were shocked that several major characters died in one blood-soaked scene, and characters within the fictional world of Westeros were equally shaken, for the Freys had broken the tradition of "guest rights," a sacred practice of hospitality wherein salt and bread are representative of the safety granted by your host.[10] Catelyn Stark tells her son, "Once you have eaten of his bread and salt, you have the guest right, and the laws of hospitality protect you beneath his roof." Breaking guest rights angers the old gods. Indeed, the Frey patriarch (and all of his many sons) eventually came to a most gruesome end.

In Patrick Rothfuss's *The Kingkiller Chronicle*, a townsman complains reflexively about the high price of salt. The series' protagonist, Kvothe, even procures salt for a friend for whom food is scarce, telling her there's trace minerals in it (including iodine—perhaps added by the local university to ward off goiters).

One of my favorite uses of salt is in *The Legend of Zelda: Breath of the Wild*, a recent open-world video game where your playable character, Link, regularly cooks meals from ingredients gathered as you explore. There are local meats and vegetables and fruits, but also herbs and salt and a spicy mix that resembles curry. Adding rock salt to a meal increases its value and changes the composition of the foods, yielding

---

[10] The idea of guest rights is not the product of a fantasy world, but dates back to ancient Greece and the concept of *xenia*, or hospitality.

different benefits when eaten. (The mountains Link mines the salt from must be heavy in the same minerals that gives Himalayan salt its distinctive color, for his salt can also be used to dye his clothing pink.)

Fictional characters far and wide, old and new, understand the necessity and value of salt. Salt is all over pop culture, sometimes signifying something crucial—like guest rights and the consequences of betrayal in *Game of Thrones*—or simply available despite unclear necessity. Long before George R. R. Martin shocked with the Red Wedding, J. R. R. Tolkien used salt to symbolize home and fond memories of simple pleasures, like a meal of meat and salt, for the homesick Hobbits. Samwise Gamgee *is* right: You never know when you'll need salt, so it's best to keep it near and be prepared for unexpected journeys.

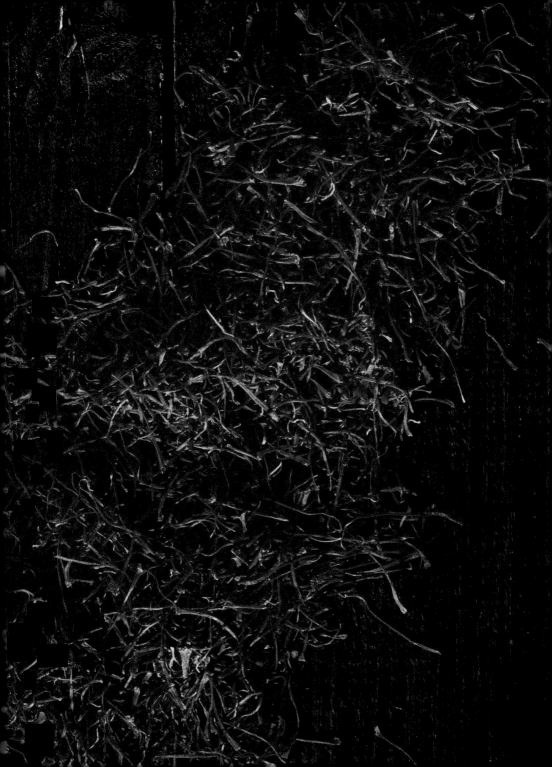

Saffron

In some ways, saffron is salt's opposite. Salt is cheap; saffron is the world's most expensive spice. Salt is everywhere; saffron grows in only a few spots on the globe. Salt is not grown, but simply there, waiting to be mined; saffron is the result of an astonishing amount of work, from planting bulbs to harvesting the flower's stigmas to drying them into the familiar dark red threads.

My grandfather wanted to make his hometown, Wauwatosa, Wisconsin, the "saffron capital of the world." Every spring, from when I was 4 years old until about 10, we would make saffron growing kits and hand them out to homeowners or leave the packets in mailboxes.[1] These kits included several (expensive) saffron bulbs and hand-written instructions laboriously copied and folded according to my grandfather's specifications. We would plant our own saffron bulbs too, both at the Spice House and at my grandparents' home, just around the corner. Once, while digging the earth next to their house, my grandma snapped a photo of my siblings and me that seemed to show a ring of magical figures above our heads. Grandpa wrote about it later, explaining shutter speeds and refraction, though he mentioned old Irish lore, too, which holds that the world is really divided into just two classes of people: those who have been visited by the fairies and those who haven't.

The photo of us planting saffron is special, but not out of the ordinary for a trio of kids who grew up around spices that imbued the mundane with the magical and

---

[1] During this mission, we learned it's illegal for anyone but a postperson to put mail in mailboxes. As far as I know, we were never turned into the authorities.

mystical. The Spice House held its own kind of alchemy that could take over when we retreated into its depths. The front of the store was lively and cheerful with customers. Old-fashioned apothecary jars lined the walls, and we used a balance scale to weigh spices to order. The back was much more lived in, given over to projects (new spice blends concocted in huge metal bowls) and interests (the writings of the mystic George Gurdjieff), which my grandfather would try to draw me into with varying levels of success. For a small shop, it seemed to hold the whole world: names of foreign ports printed on faded burlap, metric measurements, bright tins from around the globe. Countertops and shelves were given over to books, with thick spines and embossed leather covers, grimoires of food or magic tales like in *The Neverending Story*. The Spice House was like a physical manifestation of my grandparents. It was a place of business, but it was also a place for the two of them to explore other interests, without much distinction between hobbies and work, as we read my grandfather's favorite poem over batches of cinnamon sugar and discussed philosophical texts we were too young to understand while keeping our hands busy bottling seasonings.

We never did make Wauwatosa into the saffron capital of anywhere. The owners of those large old houses with their big square lawns probably preferred flowers that were bright and splashy, and the saffron bloom is a modest thing. While I assumed it was silly to try to grow saffron at all in the climate of Wisconsin (warm enough in the summer but bitingly cold in the long winter months), I was wrong. Saffron is one of the few spices that doesn't originate in hot climates, and it can be—and has been and is—cultivated in the United States. Just not by us.

I think my grandfather wanted to bring his hometown into the tradition of the traveling saffron bulb. Its story begins in the Fertile Crescent thousands of years ago before sweeping around the Mediterranean and eventually popping up in places like Austria and England. Now that I've read some of the same books he did about the spice's history, I wonder if he wanted to connect the time line of saffron to Wauwatosa, and to him, so that one day his project would be recorded in the books alongside other saffron stories.

THE FLOWER

Saffron is the only spice that is the stigma of a flower, making it as unique botanically as it is singular in flavor. The saffron flower is a crocus, in the iris family, notable for its unusually long stigmas and large petals. Like a tulip, saffron is grown from bulbs (called *cormlets* or *corms*). The saffron flower, while a pretty purple color, looks similar to other crocuses. Peer inside, though, and you'll see three bright red stigmas. The stigmas are part of the flower's female sex organs, though in the case of the saffron flower, these sex organs are sterile, as saffron propagates via the corm.

Like wine, the conditions of the landscape heavily affect the quality of saffron. Soil and irrigation influence the flavor and strength of the stigmas, as do the harvesting and drying processes. These three stigmas must be harvested during the small window the flower is in bloom, just a week to 15 days each year. Once the flowers open, they're plucked from the earth and spread out on a table, where it's more comfortable for people to pick out the stigmas.

Harvesting is a laborious endeavor, which increases the spice's value. It takes between 210,000 and 225,000 stigmas to make a single pound of saffron. Saffron is sold by the gram, which is approximately 180 flowers.[2] Once picked, the threads are then dried under the sun or in a low-temp heating apparatus. They lose 80 percent of their weight during drying, becoming brittle and thin. Dried stigmas are called *threads* or *filaments*. They're stored in tight containers immediately after drying, lest the air and light dilute the strength of flavor and color.

-----

[2] *The Essential Saffron Companion*, 39.

The saffron flower

A *style* connects the stigma to the interior of the flower. Often, when plucking the stigma, the style will come out with it. On saffron, the style is a light yellow or white color, and it's a handy way to tell what quality of saffron you have. The more style you see—the more substance is anything but the signature red of the saffron thread—the less potent the saffron, as the yellow style doesn't have the same aroma and coloring agent as the red stigma.

Like most other spices, saffron should be used as soon after production as possible. In general, it will keep for at least five years in a dry place in an airtight container, but after that may lose potency. Whereas most other spices become lighter as they age, saffron will grow darker, the dark red thread turning a brittle brown. It will lose its aroma and possibly even smell bad. While it's red and smells like saffron, it's good to use. I've heard of saffron staying good for ten years, but if that's true, it leads to a question: Why on earth would you keep good saffron around for ten long years without using it?

A LITTLE GOES A LONG WAY

Saffron is very expensive, so it's lucky that only a small amount is needed when using it in cooking. Saffron is commonly used in rice, curries, breads, and even baked goods. While the threads are dark red in color, saffron imbues food with a brilliant gold color, adding a beautiful brightness in addition to a beautiful flavor. A pinch added to plain rice during cooking will make the rice golden and add interest; using it in a curry deepens the spicy flavor and adds to curry's typical colorfulness.

At the Spice House, my grandfather included a penny in the jars of saffron he sold, along with an old measuring rule: the amount of threads that thickly coat a penny is right for four servings of a saffron dish, such as saffron rice. The rule supposedly came from England, and the coin was an English sixpence. Regardless of its origin, when pressed for an exact number by those who didn't want to measure out saffron on a coin, my grandfather would say it's about 33 threads of saffron—he considered 3 a sacred number, because he had three grandkids at the time.[3]

---

[3] This number also mattered when blending a seasoning, which required exactly 333 stirs.

Enough saffron for most recipes

THE SAFFRON WAR

If history is written by the victors, saffron is the real winner of the Saffron War. Because we humans have always, it seems, had a penchant for the dramatic, what's called the Saffron War was actually more of a prolonged spat between some extremely corrupt nobility and the people whose saffron they stole in the 15th century. This story starts with the Great Plague, which killed so many people that the laborers who survived found their smaller numbers meant they had more bargaining power against their nobles and oppressors. Places where the new population numbers upended the traditional power structures included the independent city of Basle (or Basel, in current-day Switzerland). The nobles around this area, fearing for their fragile hold over the serfs, decided to merge their town councils, seeking to reassert themselves through the channels of local law.

The plan didn't work out too well, this new bid for oversight over Basle's governance mostly serving to piss off both the other wealthy power players nearby and the poor serfs. Lashing out over their dwindling power, the nobles stole a saffron shipment passing through their territory. It was huge, too: *eight hundred* pounds. The story gets murky here and it's not clear if they planned to hold the saffron as ransom until their demands were met, or if they were simply grasping to assert their dominance in this pathetic display without a solid endgame. The nobles held the saffron hostage for 14 weeks, and it wasn't until Leopold of Austria got involved, by bringing in the Basle's bishop, that the Saffron War ended. The nobles returned it to the merchants, and the bishop, for some reason, was forced to pay the nobles for their expenses during the 14 weeks they were holding the saffron.

TYPES OF SAFFRON

Spanish coupé saffron: In coupé selections, the thread's yellow/white style has been cut, so only deep red threads remain. This is the strongest and most expensive of the Spanish saffrons; as Spain is considered the country with the best saffron in the world, Spain's top saffron is therefore the world's best saffron. Coupé saffron isn't always available due to high demand. It will be 100 percent red stigma.

Superior saffron: This is often labeled *90/10*, which means the saffron contains 90 percent stigma and 10 percent yellow style. It's therefore not as potent as pure coupé saffron, but still quite good for the lower price.

Lower-quality Spanish saffron: When you see saffron labeled as Spanish but without the coupé or superior designations, it might have the numbers *80/20* on the label, meaning 80 is true saffron filaments, while 20 percent is style and other saffron byproducts, like petal. I recommend against this lower-quality product, unless you're using large amounts and it gets too expensive to buy the better stuff.

La Mancha saffron: Like champagne, La Mancha saffron is a "protected designation of origin" (PDO) product, meaning only saffron from the La Mancha region of central Spain can carry the label *La Mancha saffron*. The name does not signal a specific grade, so it will also come with a percentage, like *100* or *90/10*.

Kashmir saffron: Grown in the Kashmir Valley of India, this saffron is typically on par with Spanish coupé saffron in that it is pure, without style or other byproducts. A side-by-side comparison between Kashmir and Coupé shows the Kashmir saffron to be slightly thicker, with a longer stigma.

Iranian saffron: Iranian saffron is among the world's highest quality saffron. Some speculate that the saffron flower originated in Iran, though we can't be sure. Unfortunately, Iranian saffron is not available in the United States because of the trade embargo against Iranian products. I've never tried Iranian saffron, though I've seen pictures of it tied up like a sheaf of wheat.

"Mexican," "American," or other saffron: Sometimes marigold petals or other yellow-red colored plants are sold as "saffron," either as a blatant rip-off to fool the gullible tourist or as a "cheaper alternative" that is no alternative at all. Be extremely wary of cheap saffron, as there is no such thing.

BASTARD SAFFRON

When fake saffron crops up for sale, it may be called *Mexican saffron* or *American saffron*, but these counterfeits all live under the umbrella term *bastard saffron*[4] (the description is intended to insult both the fake saffron and the person responsible for it). The spice's marvelous flavor and staggering cost made it extremely profitable, which led enterprising swindlers to adulterate or simply create fake saffron to make a pretty profit. My mother warned me that powdered saffron is inherently suspicious because there's no telling what's been done to it. Unlike saffron threads, which are easy to identify as the real thing if examined closely, powdered saffron may have other substances added to it—or it may just be plain turmeric.

While bastard saffron isn't much of a concern today (at least not if you're buying spices at reputable outfits), fake and adulterated saffron was a real problem during Europe's Middle Ages. In those days, saffron wasn't only valued as a tasty spice, but also considered a potent medicine. It was therefore doubly important that the hefty sum of money bought customers the real deal. Unsurprisingly, then, saffron was one of the earliest foodstuffs to be regulated in Europe.

Officials in medieval Nuremberg faced a problem. Their city had grown into the epicenter of the German Renaissance and a hub of trade. The previous few centuries had seen Nuremberg become the unofficial capital of the Holy Roman Empire, where its legislative body regularly met. It was granted an imperial title, meaning it had its own customs policy overseen by the Empire and was relatively free from the constraints of the royals who typically oversaw trade in their districts. By the 15th century, it had become one of the two main trading outposts on the route from Italy (where much product was imported from India and other Eastern countries) to Northern Europe. The phrase *Nürnberger Tand geht durch alle Land* ("Nuremberg trinkets go through all the land") exemplified the city's long arm of trade. Business was booming and prospects were rosy.

---

[4] The *bastard* prefix is a somewhat common way to indicate a false spice. There's *bastard cardamom*, for instance, and cassia is sometimes called *bastard cinnamon*, showing that not all bastards are bad.

But the thriving city was rife with crooks. Undoubtedly, plenty of swindling went on in the trading stalls in the market district of Nuremberg, but saffron presented a special case. It came from so far away that by the time it got to Nuremberg it had passed through countless middlemen, ferried across seas into Italy before making its winding way through the Alps.[5] Expensive to begin with, by the time the saffron passed through so many hands, the price was exorbitant. It's easy to see the opportunity saffron presented to the unsavory merchant or sly citizen looking to turn an easy profit. Mix something heavy and red into the saffron, like dried meat slivers, and you could double the weight, double the profit. Alternatively, you could present shredded flower petals that looked, at a glance, like saffron threads and turn nearly worthless blooms into a huge amount of money.[6] It must have become a big enough problem for Nuremberg officials to do something about it, for do something about it they did.

The Safranschau was instituted in 1358 and remains carved into the annals of history for how gruesome the regulation of saffron turned out to be. Under the Safranschau, a governing body inspected saffron for tampering or impurities. Other such Middle Age versions of regulatory agencies existed in Nuremberg, and sellers peddling tainted meat, for example, might be kicked out of their guild for a year if found out.[7] But punishment was more severe for tampering with saffron.

Jobst Findeker found this out when, in 1444, he was found guilty of saffron adulteration and burned at the stake. His "saffron" was burned with him, presumably to make a point to other potential fraudsters. Twelve years later, Elss Pfagnerin was buried alive as punishment, and her impure saffron was buried with her. Further examples of those who went against the might of the Safranschau have been lost to

---

[5] The saffron also came from all over: On any given day, "there were at least seven different varieties of imported saffron for sale in the city's market." (*Secrets of Saffron*, page 102.)

[6] Additives included mixing safflower, shredded marigold petals, or arnica into the pure saffron. Slivers of dried beef, grass, or corn silks were used to increase the weight. (*The Essential Saffron Companion*, page 33.)

[7] Brandy, drugs, syrups, hops, roses, tobacco, iron, meat, salt-fish, honey, and leather were all goods that were inspected to ensure anyone buying them was getting the real deal. (*Foods: Their Consumption and Analysis*, 13.)

history, though just the threat of being burned or buried alive would strike fear in the hearts of other Nurembergers looking to make a quick buck.

The Safranschau predates the famous German beer purity law, the Reinheitsgebot, by 158 years. The punishment for breaking the water, hops, and barley rules of the Reinheitsgebot were simply that the impure beer was confiscated. While the Reinheitsgebot has stood the test of time, the Safranschau, thankfully, has not. Ironically, it's in part due to Columbus and his peers' quest for spices that the city of Nuremberg fell out of power. Thanks to the New World and the recently discovered circumnavigation of Africa, the 16th century saw the once-mighty Holy Roman Empire decline, and Nuremberg's good fortunes went with it.

Spice swindling, however, remained well into the 20th century. W. M. Gibbs's authoritative *Spices and How to Know Them* (a much-referenced family favorite from 1909) opens with a long-winded plea for the spice merchant to sell wholesome goods. "Spice millers should not be counterfeiters!" Gibbs declares. "A miller or retail dealer of mixed or adulterated spices is as much a criminal as the man who has ingenuity enough to shape a coin from alloy and stamp it as a legal standard, or as one who counterfeits a bank note, for all are guilty of illegal acts to obtain wealth."[8]

While counterfeiters are no longer burned with their wares and modern-day nobles hold on to their power in ways more discreet than thieving from spice merchants, saffron is still faked today, a tradition that outlives much of the quackery it came

---

[8] Gibbs goes on enthusiastically in this vein for quite some time.

Annatto seeds, whole

of age with. I still hear of saffron fakery, and it usually involves American tourists believing, perhaps because of optimism or currency exchange rates, that they've found saffron for far cheaper than they've ever seen it in the US. Every story like this ends with the people realizing they've been duped.

ANNATTO

Annatto is used as a saffron substitute, as much as there can be any substitution for such a distinctive spice. All poor annatto can do is replicate saffron's glorious yellow hue—there's nothing else on Earth that can replicate saffron's flavor. Annatto is a seed native to Latin America, where it's used to color rice dishes and stews; the flavor is mildly tangy. Annatto seeds are turned into an oil by steeping in oil, causing the skins to dissolve—the skins are where the color is. For this reason, ground annatto should be considered with care.

MEANWHILE, IN ENGLAND

Old English names for flowers and plants that were passed off as saffron abound, including *dyer's thistle*, *gold tuft*, *saffron thistle*, and the aforementioned *bastard saffron*.[9] The Guild of Pepperers, an early predecessor to the grocers' guild, was founded in London in 1180 to regulate not just pepper, but also saffron, ginger, cinnamon, mace, and cloves. The Guild had more problems on its hands than just overseeing the purity and quality of the spices moving in droves through London. Wasting of saffron (which was, after all, seen as a valuable medicine as well as a spice) led the Guild to issue a stern proclamation prohibiting the "anointing with oil or the bathing in water of saffron."[10]

An abundance of saffron, enough that throwing it away in a bath didn't seem outright wasteful, may have come during the small window when England was dabbling

---

[9] *The Essential Saffron Companion*, page 32.

[10] This proclamation happened in 1316 (according to *The Essential Saffron Companion*, page 21). I tried a saffron bath, with a feeling of heavy guilt for the saffron I was wasting. For a fleeting moment, I felt the decadent luxuriousness those Brits must have felt. It faded quickly. The saffron clung to my skin uncomfortably; the bathwater slowly turned a dull yellow; and, eventually, several dollars's worth of delicious spice just went down the drain.

in saffron production itself. A mythical origin story posits that a man from Chypping Walden smuggled a few immensely valuable saffron corms from a distant country into England by hiding them in the hollowed-out head of a cane. It's true that saffron was jealously guarded by those in control of its production, but the story of the clever pilgrim and his cane is the type of tale that feels a little too neat to be true.[11]

Regardless of whether the story is apocryphal or not, saffron growing thrived in Chypping Walden for some 400 years, beginning in the 14th century. By 1514, saffron cultivation was going so well that King Henry VIII approved a charter to change the town's name to Saffron Walden. For a period during the town's heyday, it was a main supplier of saffron to the rest of Western Europe. In England at least, the saffron was used primarily as a dye, feeding the textile industry's appetite for the rich golden color it produced in wool and other fabrics, but it was an incredibly expensive practice. By the late 18th century, the demand for saffron must have dried up, as Saffron Walden's supply dwindled to nothingness. Today, Saffron Walden's coat of arms still bears the saffron flower, along with the legacy that reminds us spice sometimes flowed against the current of the spice road.

---

[11] It's also very similar to the story of the village of Mund in HautValais, Switzerland, which also once produced saffron, the practice of which supposedly began when a soldier returned from Spain hiding a few corms in his wig in the 17th century.

Vanilla

The tiny stigmas of the world's most expensive spice make a handy visual of the intense labor that goes into saffron's production. The world's second-most expensive spice, however, is a close competitor in terms of labor, though it may not be obviously so. The vanilla extract beloved by bakers is the result of patient, pains-taking growing, harvesting, and infusing. Making vanilla is an arduous, lengthy project. Whereas saffron must be quickly harvested over a few short days and dried over another few days, the process of creating true vanilla extract is measured in years. While the days of fake saffron look like they're (hopefully) firmly in the past, the present of vanilla is one where the knockoff, inferior version is more common than the real thing.

The vanilla plant is a member of the orchid family, and the only member to produce an edible fruit. Vanilla is actually the bean, or pod, of an orchid that climbs like a vine.[1] The pods are harvested unripe, while still yellow in color. They're then cured and dried, which turns them into the dark brown vanilla beans we're familiar with. To yield high-quality vanilla, the pods are first "sweated" in an airless container, which induces a fermentation process that creates vanilla crystals responsible for giving the pod its distinctive vanilla flavor. Then they're laid out in the sun for an hour or two each day for months, to dry out. Each night, they're packed back into boxes to cool. Done properly, this takes anywhere from two to three months. The drying and packing cycle allows an enzymatic reaction to take place within the beans, heightening the vanilla flavor. After this, they are aged for *another* four to nine months. At last, they are the brown, stringy, tough vanilla beans that can be sold commercially. But many customers, especially in the United States, prefer to use vanilla extract, which requires the beans to undergo a further process and for the extract to sit, like Scotch, maturing into its flavor.

---

[1] Vanilla has no essential oils, so it is often not categorized as a true spice by those who feel the need to define such things.

And like a good aged Scotch, vanilla's intoxicating, warm flavor is popular and beloved the world over. Its symbiotic relationship with baked goods is its most common and well-known use; the nearly alchemical process by which vanilla extract elevates cookies and cakes makes it indispensable. Vanilla imparts a distinctive flavor that's complex and sweet without being sugary, brightening bland doughs and deepening their flavor at the same time. Vanilla's use goes beyond traditional baked goods, too. It's a potent and underappreciated component of chocolate and other candies, ice creams (beyond just vanilla and French vanilla), and caramels. It's a secret ingredient in hot chocolate and adds zest to smoothies and protein shakes. Just like salt enhances the flavor of, well, pretty much everything, vanilla enhances the flavor of sweet foods.

A NEW WORLD SPICE

Vanilla's modern ubiquity is something of a miracle, and its story starts with the Totonac people in what is now Mexico. They first discovered that cropping the vanilla pod, which looks similar to a long green bean when ripe, then allowing it to dry and slightly ferment created a delicious flavor and aroma. The Aztecs, conquering the Totonac people, copied their early process of deriving the vanilla flavor and enjoyed this *tlilxochitl* greatly in their cocoa, the world's first *chocolatl*.

The Aztecs, in turn, introduced vanilla to the Spanish conquistadors, including Hernán Cortés. While others had brought vanilla to Europe before him, it had been used mainly as a perfuming agent; Cortés is credited with embracing vanilla as a flavoring. Cortés and the Spaniards delighted in this new hot chocolate beverage, and it was they who renamed the *tlilxochitl* bean as *vainilla*, a diminutive of *vaina*, Spanish for "sheath." The leaves and pods could be described as sword-shaped.[2]

Of course, *vaina* and *vainilla* stem from the Latin *vāgīnae*, meaning "sheath," "scabbard," or pod,"[3] and from whence we also get *vagina*. Perhaps they decided upon the name from the vanilla plant's flower, which looks, much like other orchids, somewhat similar to

---

[2] National Geographic's *Edible* puts the "sheath" name down to the bean's appearance.

[3] In 1955, the Vanilla Bean Association of America's *The Story of Pure Vanilla* pamphlet reads, "It was the Spaniards who named the bean Vanilla, meaning 'little pod,' or 'little scabbard.'"

female genitalia. Eventually, other European languages adapted the word *vainilla* with slight variations, including English, which dropped an *i* and landed on *vanilla*.

In Europe, vanilla was incorporated into medical practices alongside other spices and, also like many other spices, was believed to be an aphrodisiac (as well as a stimulant and an antidote to poison).[4] The French philosopher Denis Diderot wrote of vanilla's provocative qualities, warning that "the pleasant scent and heightened taste it gives to chocolate has made it very popular, but long experience having taught us that it is extremely heating, its use has become less frequent, and people who prefer to care for their health rather than please their senses abstain completely."[5] Vanilla was just too exciting for some people.

Vanilla isn't vanilla

Surprisingly for a spice quite possibly named for its resemblance to vaginas, the word *vanilla* has come to stand for the boring, the lame, the bland, and the sexually unadventurous. It's not fair. The origin may be the ubiquity of vanilla ice cream, overlooked in favor of other, more exotic flavors, like rocky road or tutti-frutti. Because vanilla ice cream is always there, it is the boring choice, as though constant availability is not a sign of the exact opposite: everyone, everywhere loves vanilla, while sexier options like peanut brittle and marshmallow are niche fads, loved briefly or by only a few. And so vanilla—beautiful, complex, wonderful vanilla—became slang for *jejune* and *anodyne*. My standard ice cream order at the small custard stand near my childhood home was a scoop of vanilla in a waffle cone, but every time I ordered it, I experienced the strange twinge of shame that came with liking something so . . . *ordinary*.

Then there's chocolate. Why is vanilla's foil and rival considered more interesting, more adventurous? If only chocolate lovers knew that their favorite flavor is only possible *because of* vanilla. The two flavors should not be pitted against each other at all! Chocolate also comes from the Aztecs, who roasted seeds from the cacao tree and ground it into a drink that was the progenitor of today's hot chocolate. They

---

[4] *The Book of Spices*, 435
[5] *The True History of Chocolate*, 223

used vanilla to sweeten the bitter liquid,[6] marrying the two flavors together in what would be a long and lasting relationship.

Today, vanilla is most crucial for its role in white chocolate, where it does the heavy lifting of flavor in a blend that is typically only cocoa butter, sugar, and milk powder.[7] Without vanilla, these ingredients would taste as bland as they sound. Vanilla is also used to enhance the flavor of milk chocolate, though to a lesser extent. In years past, when vanilla was cheap, it was sometimes used in heavier doses to smooth inconsistencies in large-batch chocolate, and to mask the poor flavor of low-quality cocoa beans.[8] But presently vanilla is too expensive to be used in this way.

THE MYSTERY OF VANILLA SEX

In his *Book of Spices*, the fastidiously unflashy Frederic Rosengarten Jr. describes the male and female parts of vanilla while never once winking at the reader or even telling them how the plant got its name: "It is necessary to pollinate the flowers by hand, since a fleshy lip, or rostellum, lies beneath the male and female organs. The worker lifts this rostellum with a sharp bamboo stick, so that the pollen grains from the anther (male organ) may be smeared with the left thumb upon the stigma (female organ)."[9] Come on, Fred, have a little fun in your vanilla chapter.

All this fleshy talk is necessary because the plant's version of sex (pollination) has preoccupied vanilla growers since they first tried to grow vanilla outside of its native Mexico. Appropriately for a plant essentially named *vagina*, much of the history of vanilla is the story of how it procreates, and how long it took humans to figure it out. More than 100 years after Cortés introduced vanilla to Europe, the French tried and failed to grow it themselves. So popular was vanilla in French cooking—in those days, their prodigious culinary energies were focused on pastry—that enterprising Frenchmen established a plantation on Bourbon Island (the modern-day island of Réunion), which was a French colony at the time.

---

[6] *Encyclopedia of American Indian Contributions to the World*, 290.
[7] *Chocolate*, 108.
[8] *Chocolate*, 108.
[9] *Book of Spices*, 430.

Transporting the plant from Mexico successfully, these men planted it in the rich island soil, where it took root marvelously. The orchid grew, however, without the key part of the whole operation: the plant's seedpods, a.k.a. the vanilla bean. Imagine the frustration of planting a beautiful garden where the plants bear no fruit. Other attempts, including on the Indonesian island of Java, were similarly unsuccessful. The only place vanilla would grow with pods was Mexico, the same place it had always grown. Thus, Mexico's Tetonac region produced all the world's vanilla until the mid-19th century, when the secret was finally cracked.

The secret is bees. The insect's role in our food chain has become well known of late, as their disappearance has catastrophic results. A Belgian botanist named Charles Morren finally figured out that vanilla, a kind of orchid, must be pollinated by a specific species of bee native to Mexico.[10] His discovery came in 1836 and he adapted the bees' activity into a method for hand-pollinating vanilla so they could finally be grown elsewhere. It was extremely tedious, however, as the flowers only open for a brief window lasting less than 24 hours.

Then, in 1841, 12-year-old Edmond Albrius—either a former slave or the son of a former slave (historical texts describe him both ways)—devised a method to hand-pollinate the vanilla flowers far more efficiently. Crafting a pointed end on a long, thin bamboo stick, Edmond stuck the sharp tip into the anther, then transferred the pollen into the open flower. Per Rosengarten: "With a pointed tip of a small bamboo stick, he picked up the adhesive pollen masses, and prying up the flaplike rostellum inside the flower, he pressed the male pollen mass into contact with the sticky female stigma."[11]

Albrius's method is still the basic method used today, and it's thanks to him that the Indian Ocean region became the world's largest producer of vanilla. The name of the island has changed, but thanks to the vanilla method devised there, vanilla from the region is still exported under the Bourbon label. Vanilla from both the islands of Bourbon and Madagascar were called originally Bourbon and, while the vanilla is

---

[10] Local hummingbirds may pollinate the vanilla as well, though the connection is not as well established yet.

[11] *The Book of Spices,* 428–429.

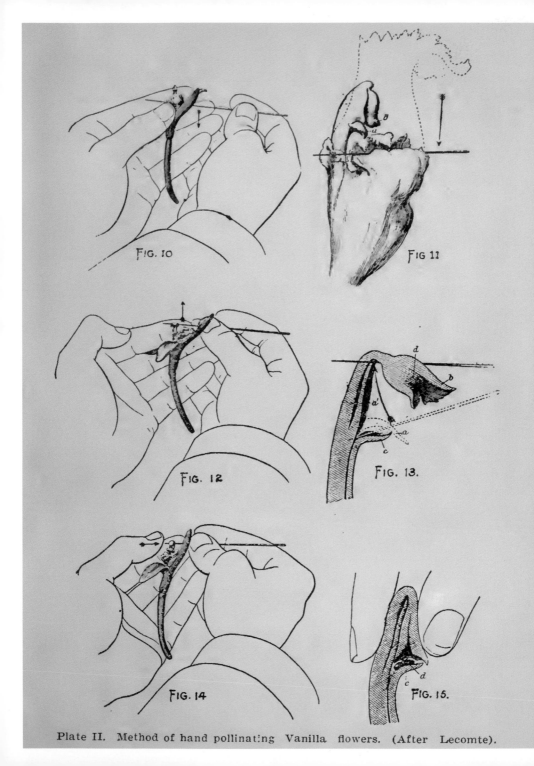

FIG. 10

FIG 11

FIG. 12

FIG. 13.

FIG. 14

FIG. 15.

Plate II. Method of hand pollinating Vanilla flowers. (After Lecomte).

now commonly referred to as Madagascar vanilla, its old name still comes up. It has nothing to do with the American whiskey,[12] and everything to do with the lengths the French went to grow their beloved flavor for themselves.

VANILLA EXTRACT

One last bit of vanilla and female anatomy, courtesy the Vanilla Bean Association of America: after describing the typical modern method of extract production—essentially percolation, with the chopped beans immersed in an alcohol solvent that's pushed through the beans, then brought back up and repeated many times—their 1955 trade pamphlet continues: "In order to extract vanilla from its natural cells, it is obviously necessary to bring the ground beans in contact with some liquid that will dissolve the aromatic constituents. This liquid is known as a solvent or *menstruum*. There are many possible solvents, but dilute ethyl alcohol is specified by the United States Department of Agriculture as the solvent for all flavoring extracts." Emphasis mine. *Menstruum*, according to Merriam-Webster, is "Medieval Latin, literally, menses, alteration of Latin *menstrua*." Menses, of course, being menstruation. Making it through the VBAA's stilted yet grandiose prose is no easy task, but it does reward careful attention.

But there's more to vanilla extract than its chemical menstruation. Under US law, extract must be at least 35% alcohol by volume, with further rules about the ratios of vanilla bean to liquid and the water weight in the beans, to make a standard pure extract. Thus, this unique spice experiences the strange duality of existing in two vastly different forms. Vanilla beans (the little black specs you see in real vanilla ice cream) can be added to sugar or powdered, but vanilla is predominantly used in its extract form. Lesser known is yet a third form: vanilla paste, which essentially combines the previous two, being made from vanilla beans, vanilla extract, and a binding agent, such as xanthan gum.

---

[12] Bourbon whiskey is thought to be derived from the French dynasty as well, though the connection isn't clear. A bourbon historian believes that it comes from where it was first primarily sold: Bourbon Street, New Orleans (and so named by French engineer Adrien de Pauger, in tribute to, who else, the Bourbon family.) (Smithsonian.com)

Vanilla pollination by hand

I can't be the only person to, as a young child, drink vanilla extract straight, believing it must taste as good as it smells. But the overwhelming taste of extract is just an alcoholic burn. The alcohol in vanilla extract can, theoretically, be any kind of alcohol. Mass-produced, commercially sold vanilla extracts use high-proof (typically 190 proof) alcohol that's so high in alcohol content there's no other flavor. (Whiskey, for comparison, is typically 90 proof; or roughly half alcohol and half other flavor components/water.)

It can be difficult to tell what sort of alcohol is used in vanilla extract, as it's not marked on the label and the only given is the high proof, which is the only way to reach the 35% by volume limit. Higher-quality vanilla probably uses corn alcohol, though, as alcohol from other grains runs the risk of bad reactions for people with celiac disease. The only other ingredients in pure vanilla extract are the vanilla itself, a small amount of sugar, and water. If you make vanilla extract at home, however, you can use whatever you have around, or choose your favorite drinking alcohol to make a tasty vanilla extract/liqueur.

Standard vanilla extract is *single strength*, though it's also available in more powerful *double-strength* formula. For once, the name is a straightforward explanation of function: Double-strength is twice as flavorful as single-strength. Specifically, double-strength extract uses 200 vanilla beans per gallon, while single-strength uses 100. Double-strength is sometimes called *twofold* or *extra rich* extract. While double-strength is more expensive than single, you can use half as much as called for, knowing that your extract is twice as potent. However, many people (myself included) opt to still use the same amount, seeking more of that delicious vanilla flavor.

Homemade Vanilla extract

Homemade Vanilla Extract

Use vodka. It doesn't contribute much flavor to the vanilla, whereas brandy, gin, and rum will color your extract with their own flavors (which is fine if that's what you want, but if you just want vanilla extract, vodka is the way to go). You'll want six beans per 1 cup (8 fluid ounces) of alcohol.

Using a new (read: sharp) razor blade, hold the bean down with one hand and carefully, slowly slice down the center of the bean. (A sharp knife will do, but a razor blade is much easier to handle.) Put the sliced beans and the alcohol in a jar, cutting the beans in half if necessary to fit. Shake well.

Tuck away in a cool, dark place where it can age in peace. Except when you come to shake it, which you should do every third day or a couple times per week. After eight weeks you'll have decent vanilla extract. Wait longer, and the flavor will only get better.

A Method to the Sweetness

Vanilla extract contains a lot of alcohol, but that alcohol burns off during baking. Using a small amount of extract in things that aren't baked, like whipped cream, is typically fine, since such a minor amount is used that the alcohol isn't noticeable. I recommend sweetening ½ cup of whipping cream with only ½ teaspoon vanilla extract plus 1½ teaspoons confectioners' (powdered) sugar and beating with a mixer, or by hand if you have an hour to spare.

In general, though, if you want to add the vanilla flavor to something that won't spend time in a hot oven, you'll need to use beans, powdered vanilla, or paste to avoid adding a lot of straight alcohol. Vanilla pods are somewhat like tea leaves: they can be reused several times, their flavor diminishing with each use. If the beans are used in liquids, they can be removed, dried, and saved for another use later. Beans can be infused into sauces or the milk base of ice cream/custard.

Another easy way to add vanilla to a recipe is with vanilla sugar. You will need to plan ahead, adding a vanilla bean to a jar of sugar and letting it sit for a few months. One bean is enough for 2 pounds of sugar; just split it in half lengthwise and chop into 1-inch pieces (or ¼-inch pieces, for stronger flavor). After two weeks, remove and rub sugar and chopped beans into a small basket sifter or strainer (with fine mesh or very small holes) and mix together vigorously, then store back in covered container. The vanilla flavor will permeate the sugar, which can then be added to recipes to achieve an alcohol-free, color-free, vanilla flavor. When using vanilla to flavor sugar, the sugar can be used and refilled several times with the same bean.

In baking recipes, 2 teaspoons vanilla sugar is equivalent to 1 teaspoon of single-strength vanilla extract. The shelf life of a bottle of vanilla extract is long; with 35% alcohol, it lasts for years (five, according to my grandparents). But that's only if you can keep a bottle around that long; I never have.

Types of Vanilla

Madagascar vanilla: Madagascar is the classic vanilla. It's rich and round. If you're buying vanilla from a reputable outlet that just lists the extract as "vanilla," it's probably Madagascar. Madagascar vanilla is my personal favorite and a go-to, all-purpose vanilla. If you're working with beans, the ones from Madagascar are the easiest to cut into, as they're neither dry (like the Mexican variety) or oozy (like the Tahitian). Madagascar beans are also typically the longest, at 8 inches or more. It's sometimes called Bourbon vanilla or Bourbon-Madagascar vanilla, named for the royal French family who ruled France when it colonized the island of Réunion (Madagascar's next-door neighbor; both islands produce vanilla).

Mexican vanilla (Papantla vanilla): Mexican vanilla is just as good as Madagascar vanilla, though the flavor is darker, fruitier, and smokier. These beans are dried longer than their Madagascar counterparts, resulting in a thinner bean that can be almost brittle. Contributing to their dryness, is the different method for "killing" the beans. All vanilla beans are picked from the vine as they turn from yellow to green. In Madagascar, they're plunged into hot water to stop them from ripening further; in Mexico, they're laid out in the hot midday sun. Therefore, Madagascar beans are bendier, while Mexican ones are drier and stringier. Sometimes the term "pruny" is used to describe the quality of Mexican

Vanilla paste, with visible seeds

beans, though I think that somewhat unfairly casts the Mexican product in an inferior light.

Mexican extract: While Mexican vanilla beans are of equal quality to Madagascan ones, it's likely they have a bad reputation because the vanilla extract made in Mexico is very different from the extract in the United States Mexico doesn't regulate extract as strictly as the United States does. Some Mexican extracts don't contain any alcohol at all, so it's not preserved. That's fine if you're using it relatively quickly, but means that it's like any other perishable food product and could go bad. Furthermore, vanilla extracts from Mexico often include tonka beans, which adds their own pleasant flavor, but also contains coumarin, a blood thinner.[13] So it's likely that cheap vanilla extract in Mexico is cheap for a reason: it's not up to the same quality as the US extracts. But that's the extract, not the bean. The beans from Mexico are great.

Tahitian vanilla: The overall vanilla crop from Tahiti is much smaller than the vanilla crop from Madagascar and Mexico, so Tahitian vanilla is only found at smaller spice and specialty stores. Tahitian vanilla is the Hermès Birkin handbag of vanillas: flashy, expensive, and rare, it's thought to be better because it's harder to find and significantly more expensive. Many people assume that the higher price

---

[13] This is an issue for people taking anticoagulant medication for heart conditions, who shouldn't be eating anything that contains more blood thinners in it.

means it's of better quality, but I don't think so. Again, it's just a *different* quality: sunny, floral, almost perfume-like, with a bright cherry sweetness. Plenty of people love Tahitian, but I think the main attraction is rarity, which implies quality and exoticism. Because the export is so low, you won't typically find extracts made from Tahitian vanilla beans. The beans themselves look quite different from the beans from Madagascar and Mexico: they're much thicker, as the Tahiti an curing process doesn't dry them as much as the other countries', so more water is retained. If you bend them around your finger, they'll ooze.

Indonesian vanilla: Historically, Indonesian beans were commodity beans: shorter (5 to 6 inches as opposed to the previous three's standard of 6 to 8 inches), and not as high a quality as the previous beans, but still decent. Big corporations that use vanilla in food and beverage products would buy these inferior (but still acceptable) beans because of the huge volume needed. Over the past decade, though, Indonesian vanilla's reputation has improved, with some bakers enjoying the sharper flavor that complements the sweetness.

A side-by-side comparison of vanilla beans is instructive. Madagascar, Mexican, and Tahitian vanilla beans look quite different: the Tahitian is very plump, the Madagascar is full-bodied, and the Mexican is thinner and dryer. (Indonesians are so short, they stick out like a sore thumb, so are not included here.) First, wrap each bean around your finger, and you'll see how the difference in water weight makes for a markedly different bean. Then, using a razor blade on a flat surface, cut each bean in half and smell. You'll be able to tell the differences in flavor this way, and maybe even determine your vanilla preference.

A GLOBAL CROP

Vanilla prices skyrocketed in late 2017, after a cyclone hit Madagascar that March, destroying much of the vanilla crop. But the industry as a whole has been in turmoil for much longer. The demand is so great that many vanilla farmers have started using a quick-cure process that brings vanilla to market faster, but the product is inferior. As my aunt explained, it's as if wine producers harvested grapes the moment they appeared, instead of waiting for them to mature, then produced the wine as fast as they could and sold it quickly. On top of that, global corporations are meeting consumers' demands for natural foods and flavorings (by all accounts a good thing), and have started shifting from using cheaply made artificial vanilla to the real deal, causing higher demand and further shortages. Instead of the fermenting, drying, and aging process that takes more than six months, shortcuts are taken, including vacuum-packing the pods, which results in less flavorful, weak vanilla.

Vanilla prices constantly ebb and flow, and big spikes are often due to weather-related problems like droughts or floods that hurt or outright destroy vanilla crops. The cyclone that hit Madagascar had such a devastating effect because Madagascar produces the majority of the world's supply: more than 80% is harvested on the island nation. Vanilla is also a delicate and rather finicky plant that's vulnerable to disease and blights.[14] But humans bear just as much responsibility for vanilla prices as Mother Nature, with market speculation and old-fashioned capitalist interests further inflating the price. It all means that, sadly, there's a high chance you'll be paying far more for vanilla that's of a worse quality than the vanilla you bought for less just a few years ago.

VANILLIN

A flavor wheel is a tool used by food scientists to identify and label the aromas and tastes of food products. The sometimes arcane adjectives in wine descriptions—earthy, big, steely—may be derived by this method and coffee tasters also use the color-coded wheel to convey the qualities of beans. Vanilla is incredibly complex, with dozens of flavors used to describe its rich aroma and to pinpoint the subtle differences between vanillas that grow in different climates. The flavor wheel is a helpful tool to use to describe how vanillin, the vanilla imitator, falls sort. It has fewer of the components that make vanilla what it is, leaving it somewhat like vanilla but lacking depth and nuance.

---

[14] The vanilla plant also has to be shaded just so, its vines arranged just right, and, of course, pollinated in the small window of time the flower opens. It really is an extremely temperamental, difficult spice.

Vanilla bean pod, with visible crystals

But vanillin *is* cheap, and plentiful. That's why the majority of vanilla-flavored products are actually flavored with vanillin: it's a single chemical compound that is the main flavor in vanilla, can be easily made in a lab, and approximates the flavor well enough. Vanillin is just one of the many elements that come together to make vanilla, and it's those other elements that science has yet to reproduce.

Vanillin was first created in 1874 from pine resin, but scientists have since figured out ways to create vanillin from a wide variety of cheap goods, including paper pulp, which comes from any recycled paper, wood, and paper products like napkins and toilet paper. Paper pulp is one of the most abundant and cheapest materials in the world. In 1969, Frederic Rosengarten Jr. decried that "a single chemical plant in Wisconsin is now capable of producing from wood pulp enough imitation vanilla flavor to supply the total United States requirements of this flavor."[15]

Vanilla demand has only grown in the last 50 years, so vanillin demand has, too. *Scientific American* estimates that less than 1 percent of the vanilla flavor in our food comes from true vanilla.[16] Today, the paper method for creating vanillin has fallen out of favor, but others have replaced it. With many food companies looking to slap an "all-natural" badge on their products, they face the challenge of using real vanilla or trying to convince regulatory bodies that vanillin produced from, say, clove oil is natural, despite its time spent in a lab. The desire for all-natural

---

[15] *The Book of Spices*, 95.
[16] "The Problem with Vanilla," *Scientific American*

products is so strong that some are turning to real vanilla to flavor their goods, driving up the demand and price for pure vanilla to ever greater heights.

SWEET TEETH

We have the sweet teeth of Queen Elizabeth I and Thomas Jefferson to thank for bringing vanilla to wider acclaim. Jefferson fell in love with it while ambassador to France, and in 1789 brought vanilla beans to Monticello (though, of course, they had already been in the Americas for centuries). 187 years before, Queen Elizabeth I and her legendary penchant for sweets brought vanilla into the kitchen for the first time in Europe. Though Cortés was an enthusiastic proponent of drinking vanilla in the early hot chocolate, it mostly existed in Europe as a medicine and perfuming agent. In 1602, Queen Elizabeth's pharmacist, Hugh Morgan, figured out that vanilla could be used to add a pleasant flavor to candies.

It may be strange to read that Elizabeth's pharmacist was tinkering with vanilla, but in the Middle Ages and through Elizabeth I's reign in the early modern period, the pharmacist and the cook were one and the same. To quote the historian Jack Turner: "Not all drugs were spices, but all spices were drugs."[17] For Europeans, up until just a few hundred years ago, spices were one of the very few connections they had to the outside world, and their origins were steeped in mystery so deeply they took on mythical properties. Spices played an essential role in balancing the four humors, the wildly fanciful conjunction of dry, wet, hot, and cold that Europeans sought to keep in harmony. Their place was in the apothecary's store of cures, not the kitchen.[18] So it is that Queen Elizabeth's pharmacist had access to vanilla when her cooks probably didn't. Luckily for her, and the vanilla-flavored foods that followed, her pharmacist was a man who recognized the power of vanilla not just to settle the stomach but to please the tongue.

---

[17] *Spice: The History of a Temptation*, 159.
[18] Vanilla was included in the US Pharmacopeia (the annual compendium of drug information) from 1860 to 1910, making us just a few generations removed from a time when vanilla was used medicinally.

Cinnamon & Cassia

Vanilla was a fairly late addition to the aphrodisiac club. For more than 2,000 years, spices have been considered libido enhancers, acting as a placebo for legions of men worried about their performance. Across ancient Roman, Greek, and Egyptian cultures, through the Dark Ages of Europe, people turned to spices to give them a boost. Spices were scarce and steeped in mysticism, making them a perfect vessel for populations to pour their hopes and desires into, both medical and sexual. Just like 21st-century men ask their doctor for Viagra, so our ancestors turned to healers for a prescription of spices. With the right assortment and application, they could cure practically anything, from ailments of the liver to a lovesick heart.

Spices were understood to have near-magical powers because of their potent flavors and aromas, of course, but also because they came from faraway places that the average medieval citizen could scarcely begin to fathom. With virtually no knowledge of the outside world, spices were the one great link to other parts of the globe, but those places may as well have been the realms of the gods. It was commonly understood that exotic wares flowed along a fragrant river from paradise into the mortal world. When stories were told about the actual homes of spices like cinnamon, their origins were even more fanciful. Some merchants even played up the heavenly heritage of their goods, as in the spice known as *grains of paradise.*

Herodotus of Halicarnassus wrote in the fifth century BC that cinnamon grew only in the homeland of the god Dionysus, the hard-partying, hard-drinking socialite of the Greek pantheon. Among the ancient Greeks, stories circulated that birds were instrumental in harvesting cinnamon. In the telling, on the distant islands where the cinnamon grew, natives offered birds massive pieces of meat to feast on, which the birds carried back to their nests. The weight of birds and meat combined to overburden the canopies, knocking the cinnamon down to where the people below could harvest it.[1] Aristotle believed that a certain bird used the cinnamon bark to build its nests, which people shot lead arrows into, similarly causing the nests to be sunk with too much weight.[2] Another tale claims that the cinnamon trees grew in the middle of a large lake guarded by griffin vultures. These vultures protected the cinnamon, attacking those who tried to harvest the spice for themselves.[3] Perhaps this traditional avian-cinnamon connection is why the phoenix is rebirthed from the fire of a cinnamon pyre.[4]

A BARK BY ANY OTHER NAME WOULD TASTE AS SWEET

There are several types of cinnamon, and there are several explanations for how they differ. The easiest is to use the volatile oil levels as an indicator of flavor strength. Volatile, or aromatic, oils are often used as shorthand for the potency of spices, and cinnamons range from 1–2% on the low end up to around 7%.

Saigon cinnamon (a.k.a. Vietnamese cinnamon) is on the high end, 6–7%, so is the strongest of the cinnamons. It's extremely flavorful, as I would tell customers: "Great if you really want a strong cinnamon kick in whatever you're baking." Chinese cinnamon, at 3–4%, is strong and rich, but without Saigon's Big Red kick. Korintje, hovering around 3%, is the cinnamon middle ground. Ceylon cinnamon exists in the low 1–2% range, offering a delicate, lightly aromatic flavor.

But actually, only Ceylon cinnamon is *cinnamon*; Saigon, Korintje, and Chinese are actually *cassia*. Cinnamon and cassia are different species in the same genus of trees, but only Ceylon cinnamon is "real" cinnamon as it comes from the *Cinnamomum verum* species: Latin for "true cinnamon." Remember that onions and garlic are also sibling species in the same family, but they are their own culinary entities. The distinction between cassia and Ceylon "cinnamon" is real, though nowhere near as drastic. If it weren't for the historical fluke that all cassia was known as cinnamon,

---

[1] *The Lore of Spices*, 122.

[2] *The Lore of Spices*, 124.

[3] *The Home Garden Book of Herbs and Spices*, 144.

[4] Not everyone was so easily seduced by these stories. The spice historian Jack Turner quotes a 13th-century Franciscan monk's comment regarding cinnamon tales: "Thus men feign, to make things dear and of great price." (*Spice: The History of a Temptation*, 50).

Freshly harvested cinnamon bark

people today would be walking into spice stores asking for some sticks of or ground cassia.

We've been using the cassia varieties for so long that they've become our standard. The flavor the majority of Americans consider to be cinnamon—that found in coffee cakes and buns, added to Mexican hot chocolate, and sprinkled on toast—is cassia.[5] For at least the past 50 years, and probably even longer, cassia has been the predominant "cinnamon" product in this country, imported in greater amounts than "true" cinnamon and preferred for its stronger flavor. Because Ceylon cinnamon has the lowest percentage of volatile oils compared to the varieties of cassia, the flavor is not as strong, though it is still potent, with a complex flavor.

If you have cinnamon on your spice rack, there's a very high chance it is technically cassia. So prevalent is cassia marked as "cinnamon" that Merriam-Webster recently updated its Saigon Cinnamon definition: "the dried, aromatic bark of a Vietnamese tree (*Cinnamomum loureirii*) that yields a sweet and spicy cassia **sold as cinnamon**; also: the powdered spice produced from Saigon cinnamon bark" (emphasis mine). Americans have decided that cassia simply *is* cinnamon, and their dictionaries reflect this usage. Even the American Food, Drug and Cosmetic Act doesn't try to distinguish between the two.[6]

---

[5] *The Book of Spices,* 186.

[6] The FDA's definition begins "Cinnamon (Cassia)" and goes on to define the different types described above: "The dried bark of *Cinnamomum zeylanicum* Sees (Ceylon cinnamon), *Cinnamomum cassia* Blume (Chinese cinnamon), or *Cinnamomum loureirii* Nees (Saigon cinnamon). It is brown to reddish-brown in color."

Historically, people were more attuned to the difference between cinnamon and cassia; the overlap is a relatively modern phenomenon. Both cassia and cinnamon crop up in the Bible, indicating that those writers were at least cognizant of two different ingredients being put in their holy ointments, though they didn't explicate a preference for one over the other. This leads to an ongoing debate, as no one can agree which is better.

Galen, the 2nd century Greek physician, believed cassia was the higher quality spice, noting that twice as much poor-quality cinnamon was required to match it. For much of the Middle Ages, however, that thinking was reversed, with cassia considered a "poor relation" to cinnamon. [7] But the preference swung back to cinnamon by the 15th century, when John Russel wrote, in his *Boke of Nurture*, that "Synamome" was "for lordes" but "canelle" (cassia) was for "commyn people."[8]

In 1909, W.M. Gibbs attempted to settle the cassia/cinnamon question in his authoritative *Spices and How to Know Them*: "The most inferior ground cassia," he writes, "bears such a close resemblance to the best cassia and to the true cinnamon that it may be substituted for it or used as an adulterant without being easily detected."[9] Gibbs wrote with the aim of helping spice merchants identify whether their products might have been tampered with, but this note highlights that "the best cassia" kept close company to "true cinnamon," such that "inferior ground cassia" might be substituted for either superior cassia *or* cinnamon. He suggests that all cassia is not inferior whole cloth, but has grades of quality, and the top grade is similar to top grade cinnamon.

Writer Henry Ridley continued this line of thinking in 1912, questioning whether cassia is actually inferior, and postulating that it was the preparation and selection, not the product itself, that was to blame for its poorer quality: "Good cassia has the flavour of cinnamon and is as sweet and aromatic, though it is often described as less fine and delicate in flavour. It is probably that by more careful preparation and

---

[7] "It is disconcerting though hardly surprising to find the medieval consumer more attuned to the difference." *Spice: The History of a Temptation*, Xxiii.

[8] *The Book of Spices*, 190.

[9] *Spices and how to Know Them*, 100.

selection, after the methods in use in the cultivation of cinnamon by the Ceylon planters, a form of cassia might be turned out which would be nearly or quite as good as true cinnamon."[10]

In a 1984 pamphlet about spices for food industry professionals, I found a succinctly distilled explanation that's no explanation at all: cinnamon is considered better than cassia by those in the know. It admits that "these two spices resemble each other very closely, and are therefore considered together. They are used for identical purposes in food flavouring." But then it continues: "Experts consider cinnamon flavour to be far superior to that of cassia. The former is more expensive, especially the Sri Lanka cinnamon."[11] It fails to consider the conundrum of correlation and causation. Perhaps cinnamon is more expensive because of its superiority, though perhaps it is simply *presumed* to be better *because* it is more expensive.

More than a century since Gibbs argued for equality, what we call cinnamon is mostly cassia, and no one really cares. Lingering elitism around "true" cinnamon certainly exists, but ask the average home baker what their favorite type of cinnamon is, and they'll tell you the preferred kind without ever mentioning that it is technically cassia. Following the lead of spice merchants, their customers, lexicographers, and cinnamon lovers everywhere, I'll continue to use the word *cinnamon* to describe not only "true" cinnamon, but also the several varieties of cassia.

PUT YOUR CINNAMON WHERE YOUR MOUTH IS

Volatile oils are still a sound explanation of cinnamon options and their relative potency. Gibbs notes that "cinnamon and cassia oils are of the same chemical compositions; their value being estimated by the amount of cinnamyl aldehyde they contain."[12] But you won't ever know which you prefer by reading about them. You must try them for yourself. Maybe you really do appreciate the subtle delicacy of

---

[10] *Spices*, 229.
[11] *Spices and Herbs for the Food Industry* 47.
[12] *Spices and how to Know Them*, 103.

Ceylon cinnamon. Maybe you love the punchy Vietnamese, or appreciate the sweet mellowness of Korintje.

The best way to understand the difference between the cinnamons—or, to be accurate, between the cassias and Ceylon cinnamon—is to try them yourself. When I was in middle school, my mother came to give a demonstration to my class. She laboriously baked mini pop tarts, each with a different cinnamon, then had the class try one of each. The differences are immediately apparent with the side-by-side tasting, and my class's wide array of preferences is reflected in the general population.

TYPES OF CINNAMON

Ceylon cinnamon: Light, delicate, with a hint of citrus. Because of its gentle flavor, Ceylon is best used in dishes that don't have other strong flavors that would overpower it. Cinnamon ice cream and custard highlight Ceylon's soft flavor.

China cinnamon: The most common cinnamon, often the basis on which people judge the flavors of others. It's sweet, mild, and the standard for baking. It blends well with other flavors, holding its own without masking them. When a recipe calls for simply "cinnamon," this variety is the perfect choice.

Indonesian Korintje: Sharp and strong. It can have a slightly bitter edge, and doesn't have the depth of other cinnamons. It's cheaper, though, so is most at home in commercial bakeries and food production factories. Some Korintje cinnamon is better than others; it's graded, so if you buy a "grade A" Korintje you're still getting a quality cinnamon. The lower grades are used in large-scale food production.

Saigon cinnamon (Vietnamese cinnamon): Much stronger than the others, with a sweet, spicy heat. The volatile oils range from 5–7%, higher than any other cinnamon. Use this when you want a punch of cinnamon, like in cinnamon rolls.

I like the softer flavors, so I tend to stick with Chinese or Korintje. But if I can only find the Vietnamese on my ever-disorganized spice shelf, I'll use that too. I don't pick favorites or prioritize one for a certain dish, except in my hot chocolate: When

Cinnamon curls: Ceylon on left, Indonesian on right.

I want to add a cinnamon flavor to my go-to warm-up beverage, I always favor a mild cinnamon, or just a cinnamon stick. The stick (actually cassia) imparts just a hint of cinnamon flavor, and sucking the stick when it's softened with chocolate is a delightful way to end the drink.

Some people blend two or more cinnamons together to achieve their desired ratio of sweetness to spiciness, which I endorse wholeheartedly. You should absolutely test different kinds and mixtures until you reach something you love.

WHOLE CINNAMON

Cinnamon is the inner bark of a tree, harvested by felling the tree and removing the outer layer to reach the inner, fragrant layer. The outer layer is milder, and the inner is very rich. The bark is peeled from the trees and rolled into long, slender *quills*. These may be ground into familiar cinnamon powder or sold in sticks of various length. These attractive sticks of rolled bark can serve many functions.

At my grandparents' shop, we kept a basket of cinnamon sticks at the counter as an offering to children who came in. It was quaint and most kids loved the opportunity to suck on a piece of tree bark like a lollipop. Sucking cinnamon sticks is an excellent way to stop biting nails: When you want to gnaw on your nails, take a bite of a cinnamon stick instead; same crunch, better taste. My aunt has people write their signature on large sticks instead of paper. Her impressively large cinnamon bark is similar to the ones Pliny the Elder is said to have displayed on a fancy gold plate, much in the same way that Christian churches display relics.[13]

CASSIA BUDS

Cassia buds are the dried, unopened flowers of cassia trees. They're harvested before they bloom and are laid out to dry in the sun. They taste like typical cassia, or perhaps a bit more earthy, and are especially good for making cassia tea: just add a tablespoonful (or more) to hot water and steep like normal tea. They're sometimes added to pickling spices and used in marinades.

Perhaps because of cinnamon's traditional pairing with apples, my grandparents paired cassia buds with the apple brandy Calvados. Among several dusty, empty alcohol bottles in the shop were many of Calvados, without dates but appearing to be decades old, just one of the mysteries I came upon while living with my grandma during grad school (grandpa had died some years before). I found the answer recently, opening *The Herbalist* to a page my grandfather had bookmarked with a typically loving note from my grandma. The page was about the Spice House handing out whole spice samples at the 1988 Herb Society of America convention (which must have taken place in Milwaukee), along with sips of their Calvados/cassia bud concoction.[14] They must've been the most popular stall.

CINNAMON BLENDS

While visiting Boston in October a few years ago, I ordered a pumpkin beer and was asked by the bartender if I wanted "a rim on that." I agreed, with no clear idea what he meant, and watched him roll the rim of the pint glass in a plate of cinnamon sugar. The sweet cinnamon paired excellently with the mellow pumpkin, and I

---

[13] *Spice: The History of a Temptation*, 231.

[14] Unrelatedly but charmingly, at the bottom of one page it reads "To obtain a 1988 list send $1 (or a saffron recipe) to the original SPICE HOUSE." My grandparents sometimes bartered, exchanging spices for goods or services, and apparently recipes, too.

Cinnamon, ground (L to R): Korintje, China Tung Hing, Vietnamese, and Ceylon

unwittingly became a fan of the pumpkin spice craze gripping the nation.[15] I became so enamored with this seasonal Boston tradition that I've incorporated it into my pumpkin beer drinking habits back in the Midwest. Last October, I smuggled a jar of cinnamon sugar into a street festival, where I ended up pouring the blend onto the lip of the bottle of beer. It was an undeniably odd thing to do, but my drink was delicious.

Beyond cinnamon, *pumpkin pie spice* contains allspice, nutmeg, mace, ginger, and cloves. This combination of sweet baking spice blends proliferates because they bring a cinnamon sweetness, ginger kick, and an elusive depth of flavor. *Apple pie spice* leans more heavily on the cinnamon, highlighting the apple-cinnamon combo that ruled muffins and breakfast cereals before pumpkin spice became king. I know it best as a combination of cinnamon, powdered cassia buds, nutmeg, and mace.

Even basic *cinnamon sugar* often contains ingredients beyond just cinnamon and sugar: cardamom, vanilla beans, and other sweet spices like nutmeg and clove are included in small ratios to add flavor complexity. Cinnamon sugar is a lovely thing. I typically use China cinnamon, a mild variety, in a ratio of 1 cup sugar to ¼ cup

---

[15] Part of me wonders if the pumpkin boom is fueled by consumers discovering they love cinnamon and warm baking spices, and the pumpkin part of the equation has little to do with it, but I could be biased.

cinnamon. I like my blend to be heavy on the cinnamon side but you may find you want half as much for your own or, conversely, you could select a stronger, punchier cinnamon like Vietnamese.

Once you get a batch started, never let it run out; keep feeding it, like an insatiable sourdough starter, adding more cinnamon and sugar but also leftover spices you may find yourself with, especially a previously used vanilla bean, and other baking spices, like nutmeg and allspice. If you're feeling adventurous, add a small amount of dried lavender or cardamom. Don't worry if you add too much of a new spice and don't care for the flavor, you can simply add more sugar and cinnamon, returning the sugar to its normal levels but perhaps with a flavor deeper and somewhat more interesting than before.

AN OBSESSION WITH CINNAMON

Cinnamon was one of the first and most important spices used by our ancestors. Its anthropological history begins with the Egyptians, who went to great lengths to import cinnamon some 2,000 years before Christ was born. Along with other spices, it's partly thanks to cinnamon that mummies are so well preserved. A rub of ground spices dried the bodies of pharaohs right up. Other religions and cultures continued the tradition, including Judaism: his followers only discovered that the body of Jesus Chris was missing when they returned to properly treat his corpse with spice.

The Romans and Greeks also used cinnamon as a medicine and perfume. Emperor Nero supposedly burned a year's worth of cinnamon to show his grief at his wife's funeral: that much cinnamon was astronomically expensive, so burning it was a grand display of his love for her.

Along with pepper, nutmeg, and clove, cinnamon was a major motivation for 15th- and 16th-century explorers seeking new trade routes. A desire to find the source of cinnamon initiated the first European contact with Ceylon (modern-day Sri Lanka) and the Spice Islands, which, of course, indirectly led them to the New World. The two major players in the brief overview of spice-driven European colonization are the Portuguese and the Dutch. Portugal colonized Ceylon in the early years of the 16th century, seizing the land in 1505 to ruthlessly enforce and manage cinnamon production. In the mid-17th century, the Dutch pushed the Portuguese out and controlled the island even *more* ruthlessly, attaining a strict monopoly over cinnamon and attempting to do so for other spices.

It's an ugly example of the colonization that went hand-in-hand with the spice trade. The Portuguese invaders were bad and the Dutch were worse, executing landowners found to be harboring cinnamon plants not registered with Dutch officials, as well as anyone trying to smuggle cinnamon out of Ceylon. Their monopoly was total and they would go to any length to maintain it. Once, Dutch officials learned of an outside source of cinnamon in Kochi, India (then called Cochin). Through a combination of bribery and threats, the Dutch coerced the local Cochin government to destroy all the cinnamon, leaving the Dutch as the sole distributers for many years.[16]

Once the Dutch controlled the cinnamon, they were able to keep prices artificially high. To do so, it seems, spice must *not* flow. In June of 1760, officials in Amsterdam burned an enormous amount of cinnamon—one account valued it at 16 million French livres[17]—and the sweet, pungent smoke was said to have covered all of Holland.

---

[16] *The Lore of Spices*, 127.
[17] *The Lore of Spices*, 129.

Nutmeg & Mace

Cinnamon wasn't the only spice the Dutch ruthlessly colonized, controlled, and subsequently burned to keep the prices high and profitable. Nutmeg was grown on only a few islands in modern-day Indonesia so, once the source of the spice went from one steeped in fable to a tangible location reachable via sea, European maritime powers wasted little time making their way to it. The Portuguese, with their formidable naval forces at full strength in the beginning of the 16th century, were the first to wrest control of nutmeg from the islands' inhabitants and establish a colony. But this conquest of nutmeg went the same as with cinnamon before it: eventually the Dutch wrested control from the Portuguese and, fearful another nation with a strong naval presence (like Spain or England) would take from the Dutch what the Dutch had taken from the Portuguese, they imposed an even more draconian system.

The Dutch would stop at nothing to ensure nutmeg remained solely in their possession. They restricted its growth to the Banda Islands and Ambonia (Ambon Island). They efficiently chopped down nutmeg trees growing elsewhere and, just to be absolutely sure of their monopoly, covered the nutmegs in lime or citric acid to render them sterile, meaning people couldn't buy a nutmeg from the market and plant it to grow their own trees. However, effort to limit nutmeg production to two islands, and to more easily control the growth and distribution, was undermined by local pigeons. The birds didn't care for the Dutch rule and their laws, and ate the nutmeg fruits just as they always had, enjoying the fleshy meat that surrounds the nutmeg and spreading the seeds to nearby islands before the Dutch had a chance to harvest and sterilize them. Despite the Dutch's best efforts, the pigeons spread the nutmegs exactly as nature intended.

When the production was too successful, the Dutch would burn nutmeg and mace to keep the spices artificially scarce and prices high. In 1735, Amsterdam officials burned 1.25 *million* pounds of nutmeg, as the surplus crop meant prices would plummet.[1] According to historian Jack Turner, "one witness saw a bonfire of nutmeg so great that the oil flowed out and wet the spectators' feet. An onlooker was hanged for taking a handful of nutmegs from the flames."[2]

There was always more nutmeg than mace, leading an Amsterdam official to pose a seemingly reasonable fix: Why not grow more mace trees, and back off on nutmeg planting?[3]

ONE PLANT, TWO SPICES

The Dutch official did not understand that nutmeg and mace come from the same plant. Nutmeg is the seed of the fruit from the tropical *Myristica fragrans* tree, which is native to some of the islands in Indonesia and the Philippines. In both appearance and structure, the nutmeg fruit is like a plum, with the nutmeg at the center of bright yellow fruit flesh. A whole nutmeg looks like a small wooden egg, around which grows a striking seed covering, or aril, which we call mace. When it's fresh, the mace is a deep red; when dried it becomes yellow-brown, with tinges of darker brown, deep gold, and red. Whole mace retains its shape, like a plaster molding that remains when the inside mold is melted away.

Every 100 pounds of nutmeg produces 3 ½ to 4 pounds of mace.[4] Once the mace is separated from the nutmeg, these spices are distinct, as they do have slightly different chemical makeup, though each is spicy and sweet. They are similar enough that if you've run out of one, the other can be substituted in a pinch. Mace is softer and fruitier than nutmeg, and for this reason I like it a bit more than I do its brother. (Thought that may be because I'm partial to the attractive mace blade.)

Americans frequently think of nutmeg as a sweet spice used in baking, but that does a disservice to its versatility. Nutmeg and mace should not be forgotten about when making savory dishes. Nutmeg, used sparingly, adds an element of depth and interest to baked fish, sauces, and vegetable dishes (especially with carrot and cauliflower).

---

[1] *Spice: The History of a Temptation*, 291.
[2] *Spice: The History of a Temptation*, 291.
[3] *The Book of Spices*, 297; *The Lore of Spices*, 96.
[4] "What You Should Know About Nutmeg & Mace," American Spice Trade Association.

Its sharp edge complements rich, fatty flavors like cream sauces, cheesy sauces, and pizza, where it's becoming common in a white sauce pie. Many mac and cheese recipes call for a pinch of nutmeg. Scottish haggis pudding requires nutmeg, and in Italy it's commonly paired with spinach. Alexandre Dumas' recipe for scrambled eggs calls for salt, pepper, and nutmeg.[5] It's an extremely strong spice, and one, like cloves, that I am careful not to overdo, lest it overwhelm the dish. My great-grandma Eva's measurement for nutmeg was a "fingernail full," demonstrating the necessary restraint.

I typically use nutmeg in conjunction with other strong spices, like black pepper, and have found it to be a surprisingly good addition to soups and stews. Of course, it's an important garnish for rum-based cocktails and a key component in holiday eggnog, too. It's probably most often used in pumpkin pie. Without nutmeg and cinnamon, the pie would just be pumpkin and crust: the spices add the subtle essence that come to mind when we dream of pumpkin pie.

Nutmeg can be bought ground or whole and then grated at home. Personally, when I'm adding nutmeg to a soup or something similar, I opt for the pre-ground stuff; you can always add a bit more if its favor seems to be fading. However, nutmeg loses potency in its ground form faster than most other spices, so it's a happy coincidence that it's so easy to grate. All you need is a fine grater or Microplane and a little elbow grease to get the freshest nutmeg. This is also called for when adding it atop homemade eggnog. In cases where nutmeg is used as a garnish, grinding it fresh will always be better, lest you sully your cocktail with the sawdust equivalent that old nutmeg becomes. One nutmeg, fully grated, yields approximately one tablespoon.

Mace is a key ingredient in doughnuts and pound cake. It's also good used very sparingly on fruit desserts. It's almost always used in powdered form, though whole mace is sometimes called for to add to casseroles and stews like a cinnamon stick, then removed before eating. Mace blade can be useful when making clear jellies, when ground mace would color it.

---

[5] *Dictionary of Cuisine*, 111. In fact, Dumas seems to have been a great lover of nutmeg, as it appears in many recipes in his *Dictionary*, usually along with salt and pepper.

Mace blades

TYPES OF NUTMEG & MACE

Nutmeg is grown in two places: The East Indies (Indonesia) and the West Indies (Grenada). It originated in the East Indies, and this type is a bit longer and thinner (making it somewhat easier to grate by hand). But the real difference between the two is their fat content. West Indies nutmeg is much more buttery. If you break it in half, you can take your fingernail and scrape it; you'll see it's not like wood at all, but soft, and the flesh yields easily. The East Indian nutmeg is harder, with a slightly milder flavor than West Indian, and a lighter color. All said, there's not a stark difference between the two types when it comes to cooking with them.

Nutmeg is further broken down by grade and quality, though by the time you're purchasing it, you're unlikely to be made privy to the distinctions. East Indian nutmeg comes in an "ABCD" grade, which is different sizes of nutmegs mixed together, and another classification called "Shrivels," which means wrinkly nutmegs.[6] Then there's the lowest grade, "BWP," a wacky acronym meaning "broken, wormy, and punky."[7] These dismal nutmegs are used for nutmeg extractions only. West Indian nutmegs are typically shipped to the United States under the "SUNS," or "sound, unassorted nutmegs" grade.[8]

---

[6] "What You Should Know About Nutmeg & Mace," American Spice Trade Association.

[7] Which would make a good title for my memoir.

[8] "What You Should Know About Nutmeg & Mace," American Spice Trade Association.

Mace, naturally, comes from the same places as nutmeg, and similarly follows the subtle differences between West and East Indian varieties. East Indian mace is a darker orange color when it dries, while West Indian is more yellow. A side-by-side comparison shows the subtle difference in flavor between the two. One is not better than the other.

Not that kind of mace

I would occasionally encounter a customer looking for liquid mace, the pepper-spray-adjacent self-protection liquid sprayed into people's faces to temporarily disarm them. The spray and the spice are two different things; liquid mace isn't made from the spice. Pepper spray, on the other hand, *is* made with capsicum compounds from hot chili peppers, the same ones that give them their bite.

Before the Dutch

Thousands of years before Europeans battled for control of a handful of islands providing the world's most sought-after spices, nutmeg and mace were in high demand. Unlike with cinnamon, though, just how far back nutmeg goes is an open question. Pliny the Elder, the Roman naturalist and philosopher, wrote of a tree with two kinds of spices (or, depending on the source you read, a tree with a fragrant nut and two kinds of perfume). Some believe this to be a clear reference to nutmeg and mace, coming as they do from the same fruit. But the Romans' understanding of the spices they attained through a mysterious patchwork of merchants and caravans was far from accurate in most cases. By the time information arrived alongside the spices, it was so distorted, and the stories surrounding spice harvesting so steeped in mystery, that Pliny writing of a tree that bore two spices might have been little more than fantasy (or a fanciful tale concocted by merchants). One thing was certain: everyone knew nutmeg thrived when it was surrounded by the sea, a reference to the small islands it grew on.

Nutmeg makes an undisputed appearance in Constantinople in the 6th century, however, and eventually spread through Europe so thoroughly that by the 12th it had reached Scandinavia.[9] Two prolific writers, a monk/chronicler and an abbess/composer/naturalist/mystic, give us early examples of nutmeg's uses. The mystic polymath, Saint Hildegard, includes in her revelations a book about healing; written around 1147. In it, she highlights the medical uses of nutmeg, including the fanciful story that carrying a nutmeg on your person on New Year's Day will protect you from falls in the coming year (you could fall as hard as possible and not suffer any broken bones). Nutmeg also protected against stroke, hemorrhoids, scarlet fever, and boils in the spleen.[10] Though Hildegard's medical philosophies were influenced by the prevailing medical theories of the day, which included balancing the four humors, her work is noteworthy because she actually did hands-on healing, including using herbs from her monastery garden, and recorded in Latin when very little folk medicine was being written down (she was one of the very few women who wrote in Latin at all).

A few years later, a monk and poet wrote about the 1191 coronation of Emperor Henry VI.[11] Petrus de Ebulo set down the event of the emperor's holy body walking through Rome, the streets of which were first fumigated with nutmeg and other spices.[12]

Nutmeg had more traditional uses than making a city street smell special and avoiding broken bones. One demonstrates that the fear of being snubbed at a high school dance is in fact a rich tradition, though it's difficult to imagine any contemporary 16-year-old trying out an old remedy: If you kept a nutmeg in your left armpit, the wisdom went, you would spend your night in high demand for dancing. But, according to the author of a black magic book that includes this advice, it only works on a Friday night.[13]

These historical examples of nutmeg use highlight early mystical and medicinal understandings of spices, which were mostly used medically and religiously before

---

[9] *The Book of Spices,* 296–7.

[10] *The Lore of Spices*, page 98.

[11] *Spices*, 99.

[12] Besides recording this early use of nutmeg, D'Ebulo also provided the first widely distributed guidebook to thermal baths (also written in poem).

[13] *The Lore of Spices*, 98.

they became staples in the kitchen. The Salerno School, a late-medieval school of medicine, indeed the first such place of study in medieval Europe, had a warning on nutmeg. Its *Regimen sanitatis salernitanum*, or the *Salernitan Guide to Health*, "held that one nutmeg is good, two bad, and three deadly."[14]

Drugs and Alcohol

Perhaps three nutmegs was considered deadly in medieval Europe because of nutmeg's toxic properties when taken in high doses. This is the infamous "nutmeg high," a state I've never been in as I take care to never overdo it with the nutmeg. It's a spice wonderful in creamy vegetables and in my baked goods but, on its own, nutmeg is so sharp and bitter I could never imagine voluntarily smoking, snorting, eating, or otherwise trying to ingest the stuff in its pure form. Some people, apparently, do. (You can Google it, but why would you?)

The essential oils of nutmeg and mace contain *myristicin*, a highly toxic substance. Being around spices growing up, I heard some stories about supposed nutmeg highs, and they never ended happily. Most seemed to involve truly painful episodes, making one wonder why anyone would want to try this particular method, rather than other, more pleasant ones that are readily available.

In 1969's *The Book of Spices*, Frederic Rosengarten Jr. warns of nutmeg's toxic effects, combining old-school drug fearmongering with delightful '60s terminology:

> The essential oils of nutmeg and mace contain about 4 percent of a highly toxic substance, myristicin, which, taken at excessive amounts, can cause a fatty degeneration of the liver cells. For this reason, the oils are used in very small amounts, with great caution. Large doses of nutmeg spice are said to have a powerful narcotic effect and to be stupor-inducing. In an attempt to escape from reality at "nutmeg parties," beatniks and hippies sometimes eat two or three tablespoonfuls of powdered nutmeg as a hallucinogenic drug for "kicks." Its narcotic use is said to be frequent among prison inmates. Following these nutmeg "jags," serious hangovers, headaches,

---

[14] *Spices: The History of a Temptation*, 166.

nausea, dizziness, and other toxic side effects have been reported by the nutmeg-eaters.[15]

In his 1970 book *Herbs, Spices and Flavorings*, Tom Stobart emphasizes nutmeg's potency when mixed with alcohol, writing that "punches and drinks to be taken at night usually contain nutmeg, which has slightly soporific qualities. In fact, nutmeg in large quantities is poisonous, and when put into alcoholic drinks it greatly increases their effect."[16] Stobart unwittingly reiterates an ancient belief in spices' abilities to influence the effects of alcohol, whether acting to amplify its potency or stifle it.[17] Having had many mulled wines and eggnogs taken at night containing nutmeg, I don't believe that nutmeg has any noticeable effect on the soporific qualities of alcohol taken all by itself. It is possible that, as nutmeg makes some drinks tastier, it leads the drinker to consume more alcohol, thereby inducing the soporific effect.

MULLING IT OVER

The craft beer boom has brought spices back to the forefront of brewing in recent years, but spice and beer have been well-acquainted with each other for a long time. While cinnamon and cloves have long been commonplace in wine, in medieval times, nutmeg became a popular way to extend the shelf life of ale, which went bad much faster back then than it does today. Chaucer references "nutmeg for to put in ale/All whether it be fresh or stale," indicating that, while nutmeg may have originally been added to ale as a preservative, drinkers developed a taste for it regardless of whether the ale was "fresh or stale."

Like beer, spices in wine were a necessity that, over time, we developed a taste for, so that dumping spices in wine over the stove in wintertime is done out of desire, not need. Spiced wine started in ancient Rome, when prevailing wisdom held that spices kept wine from going bad, or at least extended its shelf life. With bottle and

---

[15] *The Book of Spices*, 301.

[16] *Herbs, Spices and Flavorings*, 174.

[17] Aristotle claimed cinnamon in wine was less intoxicating than plain. (*Spice: The History of a Temptation*, 71).

cork technology emerging in the 16ᵗʰ century, however, the need for spices diminished. But spices were never totally kept out of wine. Mulled wine or cider is still the best drink to warm yourself in deep winter. *It's a Wonderful Life*'s angel, Clarence, shares his preferred recipe: "heavy on the cinnamon, easy on the cloves." He's right. Mulling spices also typically contain nutmeg or mace and cardamom seeds, and, optionally, ginger and allspice. In my family, we add an inch or so of vanilla bean.

Mulling spices are typically added to red wine only, a delicious and economical way of saving a bottle of red about to turn. Add a healthy glug of brandy and some fresh orange slices if you have them, heat together with the mulling spices over the stove, and you'll have a wonderfully warming beverage. Ideally, the mulling spices go in a muslin bag for easy removal, but if you don't have one, that's okay. At a holiday party thrown with more enthusiasm than planning, I simply poured the pot of mulled wine through a strainer to remove the floating bits of spice, directly into a mug. It was messy, but effective. For an alcohol-free aroma, dump some mulling spice in a pot of water and leave it to simmer on the stove during afternoons spent indoors, which steeps the house in an aromatic, intoxicating smell of winter warmth.

ANGOSTURA BITTERS

Manhattan cocktails wouldn't be Manhattans without Angostura bitters. This popular addition to cocktails started as a medicine in the 1830s, and its path from medicine to ingredient traces how spices morphed from cure-alls to flavor agents. A German doctor named Johann Siegert originated the infusion in the Venezuelan town of Angostura,[18] and his mixture is thought to have contained mace and nutmeg, as well as cinnamon, cloves, orange peel, lemon peel, prunes, prune stones, quinine, and rum.[19] Today the recipe is jealously guarded by the House of Angostura company. The spices and fruits add a crucial flavor to many cocktails. Angostura bitters can also improve the flavors of fruit dishes and fruit ice creams. An old remedy for hiccups involves sprinkling sugar and Angostura bitters on a wedge of lemon and sucking.

[18] Angostura does not contain angostura bark, but is named for the town where it was invented.
[19] *Herbs, Spices and Flavorings*, pages 45–46.

Mulling spices: Cinnamon, Cloves, Allspice & cracked Nutmeg

The Nutmeg State

Why is Connecticut known as "The Nutmeg State"? Nutmeg was never grown there—like most spices, it can only be grown in a tropical place, which Connecticut is not. Most of the various explanations contain one common story: At some point, shrewd Yankee peddlers carved "nutmegs" out of local wood and sold them as the real thing.[20] That this happened at the same time the Dutch had total control of the nutmeg trade makes a certain amount of sense.

Early America was served by traveling salespeople, as my grandfather writes: "When Wauwatosa first started, before any small general stores came into existence, it was a wonderful happening when a covered wagon selling pots & pans & specialty rare things like spices & nutmegs came through our area. Nutmegs were a nickel and the German ladies loved them especially for grating over desserts, custards, eggnogs, especially for sweet spicy Christmas holiday drinks."[21]

Knowing how expensive and scarce nutmeg was, it must have been easy for unscrupulous salesmen to figure out that carving a "whole nutmeg" out of wood would fetch a high price. One account even tells of an ingenious huckster dipping his wooden creations in lime and selling them back to the Dutch.[22]

---

[20] *The Book of Spices,* 298; *Spices: What they are and where they come from,* 11.
[21] He continues: "Also a little might be grated into soups and very tasty in apple stuffed pork chops with fresh new Wisconsin apples in the fall."
[22] *The Home Garden Book of Herbs and Spices,* 162.

A FRENCHMAN CHANGES THE GAME

With an appropriately spicy name, Pierre Poivre[23] is partly responsible for breaking the Dutch's stronghold over the Spice Islands and bringing nutmegs into wider, cheaper availability—perhaps ending crafty peddlers' fake nutmeg schemes once and for all. His ambitions were greater than the American "nutmeg" seller, though. With the Dutch in total control of much of the lucrative spice trade, Poivre saw an opportunity. He would go to the source of the spices himself, steal seedings, break the Dutch monopoly, and bring some of that sweet spice money into his country (while enriching himself, of course). France, which was also a colonial power, had tropical islands on which to grow the spices. All they lacked was the seeds.

It did not turn out to be as simple as covertly sailing up to one of the small islands under control of the watchful Dutch. Poivre failed to steal seedlings several times, though he avoided arrest or other consequences. Still, it seemed his dream would die with him. But then he penned his memoir, telling the tale and the ambitions that had been thwarted as much by the apathetic French government as bad luck and poor ships. His memoirs rekindled interest in the project and the effort was made again. Poivre didn't actually go on the expedition that successfully stole nutmeg trees but, nevertheless, in 1770, his deputies attained nutmeg seedlings from a less diligently guarded island. Their success is due to helpful islanders, who directed the crew to the source of the nutmeg trees and helped them smuggle young plants on board. After years of Dutch inquisition, the islanders were eager for revenge.

---

[23] *Poivre* is French for Pepper, making him the likely subject of Peter Pepper/Piper rhymes.

Nutmeg: whole, split, and ground

Cloves

Once the French sailors had nutmeg seedlings safely in the holds of their ships, they pushed their luck by hanging around the Spice Islands in hopes of also attaining clove seedlings. Once again, it was thanks to the locals on the island that they found success. Oppression foments unrest, and the Europeans' brutal treatment of native populations spelled the undoing of their incredibly lucrative monopolies time and again.

The French, like the Dutch and the Portuguese, had seized control of several countries, oppressing their peoples in order to further commerce, exotic spices among them. Cloves were transplanted to the small island of Mauritius, where enough clove plants were successfully grown to be spread to other French-controlled territories with similar climates. In Madagascar, Pemba, and Zanzibar, the plants quickly took to the environments and began to thrive.

After the French broke the Dutch monopoly, the ugliest chapter in the history of spices neared its close. European powers, though, did continue to occupy and oppress for other reasons, and their capitalist greed left a legacy that continues today. It's the reign of the Dutch that is most well-remembered, for their brutality and for the lengths they went to ensure their control. Sadly, this nasty epoch is mostly skated over in discussions of spice history, and the Dutch East India Company is lionized as part of the Age of Sail rather than questioned as an oppressive economic force.

A FLORAL SPICE

Cloves are the dried, unopened bud of a flower: look closely and you'll see the stem (which looks like a small carpentry nail), four petals, and a softer ball on top (containing more unopened petals). They're the flowers of an evergreen tree that can produce buds for up to 80 years. The bigger the flower bud, the sweeter and milder the flavor. The smaller the clove, the spicier it is (like hot chilis: the smaller the pepper, the hotter the flavor). The head is softer and sweeter than the stem, and the petals are even softer and sweeter than the head. Because clove is such a strong flavor to begin with, the softer touch from just the head and petals is sometimes preferred when grinding cloves at home (manually breaking off the nail before preparing).

It's possible that cloves are the strongest spice there is. A tiny amount of clove contains an amazing volume of flavor. I will eyeball measurements or purposefully add additional amounts of spices like cinnamon to recipes, but I carefully measure out ground clove amounts and rarely, if ever, go beyond what a recipe recommends. It's very easy for cloves to dominate gentler flavors.

Cloves are so potent because of the eugenol chemical that gives the clove its distinctive and brassy flavor, which is present in concentrations over 80% in clove oil.[1] This same compound has a numbing effect, which I discovered to my chagrin when, as a 16-year-old in the throes of a tragically clichéd teenage rebellion (in my case against spices, which was the same thing as rebelling against my family), I suffered the indignity of a clove derivative stuffed into the dry sockets of my mouth after getting my wisdom teeth removed. I had endured dry socket for days, and it seemed the height of injustice for my suffering to be compounded with the oral surgeon adding yet more spices to my life. But clove has long been used for its numbing properties, a tradition incorporated into modern dentistry.

Like nutmeg, Americans generally group cloves in the baking spices category, along with cinnamon and cardamom. Pumpkin pie needs cloves, sure. But clove is also essential in Chinese five-spice blends, adding its heady flavor to Chinese marinades and meats. Clove plays a part in barbecue seasonings and curries, and can be one of the many "secret ingredients" of chili that chefs like to share far and wide. Clove is one of the most interesting of the spices, as it combines both heat and freshness in a unique way, bringing both a cooling numbness and a warmth of flavor. There are spices that are cooling (cardamom, for example), and spices that are warm (cinnamon and ginger), but only cloves combine the two elements in the same spice.

---

[1] Eugenol is present in smaller amounts in the essential oils of cinnamon, nutmeg, basil, and bay leaf.

Whole cloves

Types of Cloves

Today, cloves are still grown on their native Moluccas (or Maluku Islands, in modern-day Indonesia), though they've also spread far beyond the French territories where they were first transplanted. Brazil, India, Sri Lanka, and Jamaica also grow and export cloves alongside Madagascar, and Zanzibar. Whole cloves bought for cooking in the United States are typically the best of the crops, with smaller, skinnier cloves pressed for oils or ground into powder.

Moluccas/Spice Islands: These cloves are usually the biggest and sweetest. They are somewhat darker than Ceylon cloves.

Ceylon: These come from Sri Lanka, retaining the island's previous name of Ceylon. The best Ceylon cloves will be plump. Lighter brown than cloves form the Spice Islands, they are a little less pungent, though still high quality and potent.

Madagascar: Madagascar cloves are smaller and very spicy. Much of the world's clove supply comes from Madagascar.

Indonesia: While Indonesia produces a large volume of cloves, much of the product stays in the country in the form of clove cigarettes, called "kreteks," which are two parts tobacco to one part cloves.[2]

---

[2] Clove cigarettes were effectively banned in the United States by the 2009 Family Smoking Prevention and Tobacco Control Act. The ban was challenged by Indonesia, and the World Trade Organization ruled against the US law in 2012, though it stills stands as of this writing.

Brazil: Brazilian cloves, along with much of the rest of the world's clove products, aren't as high quality as those from Madagascar, Sri Lanka, and Moluccas. These types are used commercially and by large corporations that buy mass amounts for food flavorings. Brazilian cloves are not as potent as those previously mentioned.

STUDDING HAM

Whole cloves are difficult to grind yourself, and I usually only make use of them in when studding an impressive cut of meat for holiday dishes. I've encountered two explanations for clove-studded Easter ham. One is that the cloves represent the nails used during Jesus' crucifixion. The other is that, before modern refrigeration, hams were cured in winter and cloves are an excellent preserving agent. Then, come springtime and Easter Sunday, a ham with cloves would be served. I'm inclined to believe the latter explanation, though the direct connection between cloves and the word *nail* gives the former explanation some credence.

THE POMANDER BALL

The making of a pomander ball is a holiday tradition typically done in November or December, when it's cold outside and warm inside, ideal for sitting hunched over a table, sticking cloves into an orange while sipping hot mulled wine or cider. This activity is an appropriate reminder that *clove* comes to English from the word for "nail" in French.[3] I should add that cloves actually make very poor nails, as they are not sharp, and it takes a great deal of patience to puncture the tough skin of an orange with cloves. When making your pomander ball, use a thumbtack to make the initial hole, then insert the cloves. Your pomander experience will be more enjoyable this way.

The word *pomander* also comes from French (specifically Old French): the *pome d'embre* or "apple of amber" was used to shore up immunity against the plague. All sorts of

---

[3] In many languages, in fact, the word for clove is the word for nail or derived from or related to the word for nail: Spanish *clavo* (nail), Russian *gvozdika* (nail), Italian *chiodo di garo-fano* (nail of flower or carnation), and Latin *claus* (nail). The oldest reference that is certain to be referring to clove comes from the Chinese Han period, 206 BC–220 AD, and refers to cloves as *tin-haing*, or "nail spice" (*Spice: The History of a Temptation*, 179).

spices were supposed to help avoid catching the plague, or, once a person was infected, to cure it. Plague masks, which made the wearer look like a long-billed bird, were worn to purify the air one breathed: The beaks of the mask would be filled with spices, herbs, and other sweet-smelling substances like ambergris,[4] camphor, and tree resins. By breathing in the aromatic potpourri, the plague fumes were kept at bay, or so the

logic went. The original pomander was different from its modern descendent: "a lump of amber or ambergris aromatized with a mixture of spices so as 'to be worne against foule stinkyng aire.'"[5]

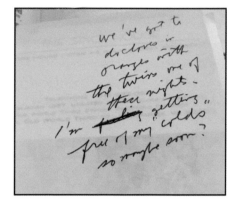

During the 14th-century outbreak of the Black Death, a pomander generally consisted of a soft, resinous substance— wax was the most common—bound together, studded, or sprinkled with spices, and enclosed within a portable

metal or ceramic container worn around the neck or attached to a belt or wrist. Simple variants of the same were made from a hollowed-out piece of fruit. One popular 17th-century remedy was "a good Sivill Orenge stuck with cloves."[6]

Pictured is a note in my grandfather's writing, from perhaps 20 years ago. He frequently left notes for my grandma and either used them as bookmarks for whatever spice book he was reading at the time, or stuck them in the books as a way to keepsake them. In this one, he writes, "We've got to do cloves in oranges with the twins one of these nights." (My sister and I are "the twins.") Note that "pomanders" here are simply called "cloves in oranges."

---

[4] Ambergris is waxy substance found floating or on seashores, and is believed to originate in the intestines of sperm whales. It's used in perfumery and is sometimes included in lists of spices, according to *The Oxford Companion to Food* (744) "if only for want of any other category into which to put them."

[5] *Spice: The History of a Temptation*, 179.

[6] *Spice: The History of a Temptation*, 179.

Smoking bishop

> *"A Merry Christmas, Bob!" said Scrooge with an earnestness that could not be mistaken, as he clapped him on the back. "A merrier Christmas, Bob, my good fellow, than I have given you for many a year! I'll raise your salary, and endeavour to assist your struggling family, and we will discuss your affairs this very afternoon over a bowl of smoking bishop, Bob!"*

What is the smoking bishop referred to by Charles Dickens in *A Christmas Carol*? This warm drink, along with a promise to pay Bob Cratchit a better wage, represent Ebenezer Scrooge's thawing heart at the end of the play. The Smoking Bishop was a popular mulled wine at the time of the writing, in 1843; one year later, the Irish novelist Charles Lever mentions it in his *Arthur O'Leary, his wanderings and ponderings in many lands*, during the course of which the befuddled Arthur wakes up one morning, when he fails to remember anything of the night prior: "I could merely recollect the spicy bishop."

In 1845, Eliza Acton's *Modern Cookery, in all its Branches* included a recipe for the drink. The "excellent French receipt," as Acton calls it, requires a "wineglass and a half" of water, three ounces of fine sugar, and a quarter of an ounce of spice, including cinnamon, "ginger slightly bruised,"[7] and cloves. These ingredients are mixed together over heat until formed into a "thick syrup, which must not on any account be allowed to burn." To this, one pint of port wine is added, brought to a boil, then served immediately. "The addition of a strip or two of orange-rind cut extremely thin," notes Acton, "gives to this beverage the flavour of bishop."[8] In France light claret takes the place of port wine in making it, and the better kinds of *vin du pays* are very palatable thus prepared."[9]

---

[7] "Slightly bruised" ginger probably means Acton calls for small pieces of whole dried ginger, which in the 19th century was much tougher and more fibrous than today's. Hitting the whole ginger with a mallet would break down the fibers, helping to release the ginger flavor.

[8] Others cite the name as a reference to the traditional mitre-shaped punchbowl used for serving. Similar drinks have other ecclesiastical names including Smoking Beadle for ginger wine with raisin and Smoking Cardinal if made with Champagne. *Food and Cooking in Victorian England*, 154.

[9] Acton also advises that, "Sherry, or very fine raisin or ginger wine, prepared as above, and stirred hot to the yolks of four fresh eggs, will be found excellent."

In 1980, Charles Dickens's great-grandson, Cedric Dickens, published the book *Drinking with Dickens*. In it, he gives a different recipe for the Smoking Bishop, which combines the drink with a sort of pomander. The instructions begin with baking six Seville oranges in an oven until they are pale brown. Then, each orange is pricked with five whole cloves, which are then put into a warmed earthenware bowl, along with sugar and wine, and left in a warm place for a full 24 hours. After, the oranges are squeezed into the wine, which is then poured through a sieve. The port is added and it's all heated up together, becoming the Smoking Bishop. "Not only is its taste exquisite," Cedric Dickens writes, "but equally its medicinal qualities are great. You can feel it doing good. Temperatures go up, from the top of the head (bald heads turn red) right down to the toes."[10]

Cocktail historian David Wondrich gives an updated recipe in a 2010 article published in *Esquire* magazine. His drink, simply called "The Bishop," calls for a single orange studded with 16 to 18 cloves, baked until browned, cut into quarters, and added to a mixture of one bottle of ruby port and one cup of water, simmered with sugar, ginger, nutmeg, allspice, and 4 ounces cognac "for a little more bite."[11]

My recipe for the Smoking Bishop calls for brandy (or cognac if desired, though cognac is just a type of brandy), brown sugar instead of white sugar, a bit of orange juice, and orange rind—with, of course, cloves studded in oranges, other spices, and a small bit of freshly roasted cumin to enhance the "smoke" in the Smoking Bishop.[12]

---

[10] *Drinking with Dickens*, 54.

[11] "Whiskey for the Winter," *Esquire*.

[12] The full recipe is in the back of the book.

Juniper

Spices and other aromatics played a pivotal role in attempts to ward off the plague and other diseases. The long-beaked "plague masks" were so designed to allow plenty of space to stuff spices, herbs, and aromatics that the plague doctor would breathe in.[1] These strong aromas, the prevailing knowledge taught, served to both replace the Black Death vapors and perhaps even neutralize them, as using spices for medicine was still practiced. Potently aromatic, juniper berries were often called for in these fragrant efforts.

Juniper berries are actually the cones of a shrub that grows wild in North America, Europe, and Asia. If you come across juniper in the wild, the shrub's branches make an excellent addition to wood cooking fires, adding their earthy aroma to foods being grilled or smoked. Like the berries' usefulness in the beaked masks, the pleasant-smelling needles and twigs were used to treat bad air elsewhere; juniper and its berries were supposedly used to "sweeten" the unpleasant air in sickrooms, and in Switzerland, were added to the stoves that heated schoolrooms when it was too cold to open the windows for fresh air.[2] In his *Dictionary of Cuisine*, Alexandre Dumas wrote that "many fine properties are attributed to juniper. It preserves the brain, strengthens the sight, cleans the lungs, banishes wind, and facilitates digestion. It is also," he went on archly, "frequently employed in medicine."[3] Juniper's medicinal use can be traced back as far as ancient Egypt, with medical papyri recommending the berries to treat tapeworm.[4] Dioscorides believed the crushed berries, put directly where they were needed, acted as contraception.

---

[1] The French doctor who designed the masks, Charles de Lorme, lived to be 94, living, breathing proof of the efficacy of his invention.

[2] *The Complete Book of Herbs and Spices*, 153.

[3] *Dictionary of Cuisine*, 144.

[4] *The Book of Gin*, 9.

Dumas may have been influenced by Nicholas Culpeper, the English apothecary who wrote extensively of plants and their use in healthfulness. Of the juniper plant, he wrote: "to give a description of a bush so commonly known is needless," but listed a great many aliments the berries were capable of treating, including "in the first, being a most admirable counter-poison, and as great a resistor of the pestilence, as any growing: they are excellent good against the biting of venomous beasts, they provoke urine exceedingly . . . There is scarce a better remedy for wind in any part of the body, or the cholic, than the chymical oil drawn from the berries . . . [The berries] are admirably good for a cough, shortness of breath, and consumption, pains in the belly, ruptures, cramps, and convulsions. They give safe and speedy delivery to women with child, and they strengthen the brain exceedingly."[5]

SPICE OF THE WOODS

Today, dried juniper berries are an oft-forgotten spice that is usually only pressed into service when cooking meat, especially gamey meats like venison. Juniper berries have their own woody flavor, resinous and fresh, adding a complementary piquancy that pairs well with wild meat and masks some of the gaminess. Juniper berries are also good in marinades for pork, chicken, and beef. In Europe, they're commonly added to pâtés, and Germans sometimes add them to sauerkraut.

My grandmother told me of another use for juniper berries. According to a customer at her store, if you know you're going to drink a lot, chew three juniper berries beforehand. It won't stop you from getting drunk, according to the source, but it will stop you from getting a hangover. There's more: If you didn't chew the juniper berries and wind up with a hangover the next morning, crush juniper berries and brew them like a tea in hot water. The woman assured my grandmother of the efficacy of this method, and that her family had used both prevention and aid many times over the years. (At the time, though, she was buying the juniper berries for sauerkraut.)

Used whole, they're often added as an aromatic, as they give off their tangy, somewhat peppery aroma to whatever's nearby. Whole juniper berries can be used like

---

[5] *The English Physitian, Or, An Astrologico-Physical Discourse of The Vulgar Herbs Of This Nation.*

whole peppercorns in marinades and pickling brines. They're found, for example, in the marinade of the festive preserved beef served at Christmas in some European countries. Elizabeth David, the prolific cookery writer who dedicated much of her long career to appreciating and restoring traditional British dishes, has a recipe for preserved beef that includes juniper berries, black peppercorns, allspice, and salt.[6] The beef is soaked in a brine composed of spices and brown sugar, and aged for three weeks to three months.[7]

GIN AND BEAR IT

Juniper berries are best known for giving gin its distinctive piney flavor. Indeed, the principal flavor comes from juniper berries alone, though other aromatics are usually added. While gin regulations in the United States only require gin to be produced by distillation or redistillation and to be at least 80 proof, regulations in the European Union make clear the importance of juniper in gin. EU regulations define gin as "a juniper-flavoured spirit drink" first and foremost, and require that the flavoring agents used in production of gin taste "predominantly of juniper."[8]

The etymology of the word *gin* can be traced directly to juniper, too: it is a shortening and alteration from *geneva*, which is the "modification of obsolete Dutch *genever* (now *jenever*), literally, juniper, from Middle Dutch, from Old French *geneivre*, ultimately from Latin *juniperus*."[9]

Juniper berries were used to flavor drinks before gin emerged on the scene in the late 16th and early 17th centuries. Slavs drank *borovicka*, a juniper brandy, starting around the 14th century, and Finns used the berries instead of hops to flavor their *sahti* beer in the 16th century, possibly even earlier.[10] *Brinjevec* is still used, mostly

---

[6] *Spices, Salt and Aromatics in the English Kitchen.*

[7] *The Oxford Companion to Food*, 743.

[8] No. 20, Regulation No 110/2008 of the European Parliament and of the Council, Annex II, *Spirit Drinks*, "Gin" and "Distilled Gin."

[9] *Merriam-Webster.com.*

[10] *The Book of Gin*, 8.

in a medicinal way, in some areas of Eastern Europe; this tart alcohol is made from fermenting and distilling juniper berries directly.[11]

---

[11] *The Book of Gin*, 11.

SPICED LIQUEUR

Spices and herbs and alcohol have always been good friends. Few liqueurs, however, are defined by a single ingredient, as gin is by juniper. Predominant single flavors are commonly found only in flavored liquors, which have a significantly higher sugar content than liqueurs. In those, flavor is infused or simply mixed in after the distilling process. While some products use whole spices or quality extracts, most are artificially flavored and may use sugar syrup, too. Common bases are vodka and white rum, though any liquor can be used in theory: it's easy to find cinnamon-flavored vodka, rum, whiskey, brandy, and tequila.

Spiced liqueurs often tout the sheer number of ingredients included, while often being vague about particulars. Bénédictine is known to contain 27 herbs and spices, though only 21 are confirmed. Galliano claims to have some 30 ingredients while Jägermeister specifies 56; both have detailed fewer than 10 specific ones. Strega contains approximately 70 herbal ingredients, one of which is saffron, giving the liqueur a bright yellow color. Chartreuse is the winner, at 130, though most are plants and plant extracts rather than the spices and herbs discussed here (and they claim only two monks know the identity of all the plant ingredients).

Of more specific flavor profiles, there are the likes of allasch (caraway, with almonds and angelica), fernet (saffron, cardamom, chamomile, and myrrh), and kummel (caraway, cumin, and fennel). Canton is a ginger liqueur with honey, though even they previously boasted of using six different varieties of ginger (the new recipe is focused on crystallized baby ginger). If a product is labeled simply as "spiced" without any details, you're likely to encounter some combination of star anise, cinnamon, cardamom, cloves, and/or vanilla, especially in a spiced rum.

Juniper berries and tips

BATHTUB GIN

Ironically, the Prohibition turned a great many American citizens into booze-making lawbreakers, including my grandmother's mother, who made beer,[12] and grandfather's father, who made bathtub gin. The recipe, unfortunately, is lost to time, but there is a story that's been passed down: Al Capone's men would come to Milwaukee for Great-Grandpa William's gin, bringing it back to Chicago for Capone's personal bar. I haven't been able to find any evidence of this, though given the illegality of making gin and the secrecy of Capone's operation, there's little information available on his favorite bathtub gin.

If it *is* true, maybe Capone drank the gin plain, but most homemade gin wasn't as smooth as the liquor we're used to today. Gin is relatively easy to make at home, as it doesn't require aging in oak barrels, which was essential to the average bootleg-ger during the Prohibition who couldn't bother with the time and expense whiskey required. The flipside of its accessibility is that homemade gin generally tasted foul, and in order to drink the stuff down it was necessary to mask its unpleasantness with strong-flavored ingredients. Luckily, the nature of gin makes it relatively easy to add an ingredient or two to the spirit to mask its unpleasantness,[13] which is how

---

[12] Great-Grandma Eva was transporting a batch of beer down the snowy street at Christmastime on a Radio Flyer wagon, covered with a blanket, her two children on top, when a policeman approached. She thought she was done for, but he had noticed her struggling to lift the heavy wagon over a curb and offered to pull it up the street for her. Then he went on his way.

[13] *The Art of Distilling Whiskey and Other Spirits*, 74.

a great many cocktails were born that are still enjoyed to this day. Were it not for Prohibition, gin may have never gotten the boost. Today, the United States is the world's largest, most enthusiastic gin market.[14]

It's easy to make your own gin at home. At its most basic, you're soaking juniper berries in vodka; the juniper imparts the vodka with its signature pine flavor, *et voilà*. In reality, there is much more that goes into gin making. Other spices and citrus are usually included, and if you make your own gin at home you can add in your favorites. Aniseed, caraway, whole nutmeg, cinnamon sticks, cassia chunks, fennel seeds, cardamom (whole pods or seeds), cumin seeds, allspice, coriander, star anise—basically any whole spice can be used. Dried herbs may be used, too. After the vodka has aged with its juniper berry and spices mixture, citrus is usually added. By the end, you have a piney, aromatic gin.

Instructions

You don't need a bathtub or a distiller to make gin at home. While proper commercial gin makers craft their liquor by extracting flavors through distillation, you can instead steep the botanicals. The gin won't be clear, like the store-bought kind, but other than that it can be just as good.

1. Boil water to sterilize glass jars. Pour the boiling water into the jars and their lids, then rinse. I suggest using several jars and experimenting with different spices and botanicals in each.
2. Put the spices in the bottom of the jar. Use 2 tablespoons juniper berries and just a few of each of the whole spices you want to use.
3. Cover the spices with vodka, leaving an inch or so space at the top. Seal with lids.
4. Tuck the steeping vodka in a dark and cool place where it will feel safe and protected for 24 hours.
5. Add orange and lemon peel, but only the peel, no pith. The pith is bitter and you don't want that flavor coming through. Cover with lid.

---

[14] Ibid., 77.

6. Tuck the jars away once more, infusing for another 24 hours, but no longer.
7. Run through a sieve to strain out the spices, then pour through a cheesecloth or coffee filter to get the small particles. Let it sit for two days.
8. *Alternatively, if the flavor isn't appearing as you'd like, sieve, strain, and add more spices, then let sit another 24 hours. Repeat the straining process.
9. Let the jars sit, without spices, for 2–3 days.
10. Once more, pour through a cheesecloth or coffee filter.
11. Enjoy a gin and tonic or Prohibition gin cocktail.

Ginger

Every day when I went to work at my grandparents' shop, the front door would greet me: "Please remember: a pinch of ginger every day to keep the heart warm." This was painted in an appropriately red color on the glass of the door, a reference to *One Thousand and One Nights* (also called *Arabian Nights*), a favorite of my grandfather's and a text rife with spices. While most ancient cultures used spices in bizarre and ineffective ways, ginger is perhaps the only spice whose modern medical understanding matches rather well with one if its ancient ones.

Dioscorides, a physician hailing from ancient Greece, recommended it for its beneficial effects on the stomach and digestion. He also said it was an antidote to poison; like all the recommendations of those long-dead healers, his should be taken with a large grain of salt, even if he *was* correct about ginger settling nausea. Medicinal ginger goes back further, at least to the time of Confucius, who discusses it, along with other thoughts on food, in his *Analects*. He "was never without ginger when he ate," and "would always have ginger served on the table."[1]

Ginger ale is probably the most well-known beverage made with a spice, so commonplace it's easy to forget to appreciate the spice that gives it its warmth and flavor. Ginger ale is a good drink to settle an upset stomach, and while lots of spices have nutrients and associated health fads surrounding them, ginger is one spice I can say with confidence really does do what it's reported to do, and quickly. When nausea strikes, reach for the ginger ale or, even better, candied ginger bits.[2]

Thousands of years after Dioscorides, the spice reached England, where its use was recorded in Old English texts.[3] When King Edward I sailed to Norway to secure a marriage for his son, in 1290, his ship carried offerings of solid British goods (beer, beans, nuts, and flour) and rarer supplies included to show off King Edward's

---

[1] *The Analects* (William Edward Soothill), 484.

[2] I always carry candied ginger on car trips for motion sickness.

[3] *The Book of Spices*, 246.

wealth, reach, and power. These included ginger, gingerbread, pepper, zedoary,[4] figs, rice, and raisins.[5] Gingerbread dates back to medieval times, though the gingerbread of yore is described as more of a "stodgy paste"[6] rather than the bread we're familiar with today.

GINGERBREAD OF KINGS, QUEENS, AND THE PEOPLE

I've only ever made gingerbread in December, as a Christmas tradition and an excuse to buy and eat the candy that's supposed to decorate a gingerbread house. The gingerbread houses of my childhood were thick with frosting glue and Necco shingles, which look like a real joke compared to those of Jacques Duché, a Parisian merchant who, in the year 1400, built a walk-in gingerbread house, inlaid with precious stones and spices (themselves precious).[7] Today, his craft has a become a tradition in San Francisco, where the city's Fairmont Hotel annually constructs a spectacular, life-sized gingerbread house within the hotel lobby. It requires 10,250 gingerbread "bricks," 3,300 pounds of icing, and 1,650 pounds of candy.[8]

But gingerbread wasn't just for building impressive structures in the past: Queen Elizabeth satisfied her well-known sweet tooth with "fancy" gingerbread.[9] Cheaper "common" gingerbread was also available for the masses.[10] Adoration for gingerbread was endearingly expressed in Shakespeare's *Love's Labour's Lost*: "An' I had but one penny in the world, thou shouldst have it to buy ginger-bread." A few decades later, Tsar Alexis received more than 100 loaves of gingerbread upon announcement of the birth of Peter (later: The Great). Some loaves supposedly weighed as

---

[4] Zedoary is a spice that's part of the ginger family, tasting reminiscent of ginger but much more bitter. It was once popular as a spice in Europe, but fell out of favor in the Western world hundreds of years ago. It's still used in India, Indonesia, Thailand, and other South-Asian countries.

[5] *Spice: The History of a Temptation*, 132.

[6] *Spice: The History of a Temptation*, 113.

[7] *Spice: The History of a Temptation*, 131.

[8] "Building a Life-Sized Gingerbread House Takes Over 10,000 Cookie Bricks," *Atlas Obscura*.

[9] "A Glossary of Spices," 8, *The Book of Spices*, 247.

[10] *The Book of Spices*, 247.

much as 200 pounds and were shaped into Russian symbols like an imperial eagle or Moscow's coat of arms.[11]

ALL'S WELL AT SEA

The Renaissance was a period of great productivity in the arts, science, and literature, leading to many discoveries, including the cause of scurvy, that pesky seafaring disease. A lack of vitamin C on the high seas led to spongy gums, loose teeth, and eventually death, but it wasn't until the early 1740s that the connection between scurvy and diet was noticed. If only the British knew what Chinese sailors knew as early as the 5th century AD; Chinese ships carried live ginger plants on board because eating the ginger kept scurvy at bay,[12] though they couldn't yet pin the benefit on ginger's vitamin C content.

In 1747, a naval surgeon named James Lind conducted an experiment (the scientific method was back in vogue) and deduced that sailors given citrus fruits recovered from scurvy and were able to get back to work.[13] The British sailors became known as "Limeys" because they were fed limes (cheaper than lemons), a term still used today.[14] Around the same time, the Dutch noticed that sauerkraut, which also contains vitamin C, was an effective—and, more importantly, easily preserved—food to fight scurvy. Captain James Cook tried to get his British officers to eat it, but had great difficulty convincing them to ingest fermented cabbage.[15]

The Brits never added ginger to sailing vessels, but they did appreciate it at home. A trend swept through British pubs in the late 1800s: an ale was tapped, ginger

---

[11] "What You Should Know About Ginger," 2.

[12] *The Oxford Companion to Food*, 707.

[13] He published his work in *A Treatise on the Scurvy*, in 1753. This breakthrough is believed to be a key reason the British were able to stop Napoleon's fleet from breaking through the naval blockade: the Royal Navy were able to stay at sea much longer, without any dying of scurvy. (Andrew George, "How the British defeated Napoleon with citrus fruit").

[14] *The Oxford Companion to Food*, 707.

[15] *The Oxford Companion to Food*, 707.

Ginger, powdered

sprinkled on top, and a red-hot poker plunged into the beer with a flourish.[16] This theatrical treatment is thought to have caramelized the sugars in the beer, giving it a nice, full mouthfeel. And the ginger? It's always been a "hot" spice, so perhaps it just made good sense to the 19th-century barkeep to add it to an ale that would receive the hot-poker method.

PEELING THE GINGER ROOT

I do not peel fresh ginger. I cut away the skin with my heavy, sharp chef's knife. I just want everyone to know that this is an option. I have hurt myself in the kitchen more with a peeler than a knife or any other utensil; peelers are difficult to use, especially on a wobbly, knobby item like a hunk of ginger root. It's hard to hold the root in one hand and peel with the other without also peeling off some of the hand holding the ginger.[17] A key way to *not* hurt yourself preparing food in the kitchen is to create a flat surface on whatever food you're slicing and dicing. You can create a flat (or at least flat-ish) surface on a side of the ginger with a knife, then lay the cut side down to balance the root while carefully cutting away the skin.

---

[16] *The Book of Spices,* 247; *Spice: The History of a Temptation,* 113.

[17] I once peeled a whole chunk of my finger off while peeling an apple. I had to throw away the whole bowl of sliced apples because I couldn't find the chunk of flesh. Peeling apples is a fool's game.

In all its various forms, galangal looks very similar to its cousin, ginger. While both are rhizomes in the same family (as are cardamom and turmeric), galangal has a related but distinct aroma and taste, more citrusy than the sweeter ginger. Rhizomes look like roots and are often misidentified, as with *ginger root*. A rhizome is a stem that acts like a root, creeping along the ground and often partially submerging itself underground. Rhizomes are different from roots because they still act as stems, sending off both roots and shoots. Galangal is sometimes called *wild ginger* and *Thai ginger*, and is also spelled *galingale*. It's called for in some curries, especially from Southeast Asia. Premade Thai and Indonesian curry powders often have galangal in them.

TYPES OF GINGER

No one knows where ginger originated; it's never been found growing in the wild, though other members of the ginger family grow across much of southeast Asia.[18] Most ginger consumed in the United States comes from India and China, though it's increasingly planted domestically and available at many farmers' markets. Both countries have experience cultivating and curing ginger going back thousands of years, which is a good thing, as ginger is a spice that takes real expertise to get right. It's not easy to farm and is difficult to dry without molding, since the raw rhizome, when first harvested, is very wet. In the past, ginger was treated with chemicals to hamper molding; today, with better curing techniques (and countries that have made such chemicals illegal) it is possible to get very good dried ginger that hasn't been doused with chemicals. Take note, however, if you ever buy cheap ginger and smell a hint of mold.

Knobby and resembling several thick thumbs, freshly harvested ginger rhizomes are called *hands*. Once the ginger is harvested and cured, it becomes dried ginger, also called ginger "root"; this is what's turned into ginger powder. After it's ground, it will slowly lose its potency, though it takes a few years for it to seep away to the point where the flavor is dull. Whole dried ginger lasts indefinitely; you can keep some around for aesthetic reasons and then grind it yourself when needed. It can also be rehydrated

---

[18] *Spices*, 392.

to form a state that's pretty close to fresh ginger (close enough to be substituted in a pinch, anyway). To rehydrate dried ginger, soak it in water for about an hour.

Indian ginger: Much of the world's ginger comes from India. It is typically aromatic, with a darker, earthier flavor than Chinese.

Chinese ginger: Chinese ginger has a brighter flavor than Indian, with notes of lemon sharpness. The *number one* grade is light and less fibrous; it will often bear the grade on its label, and should be more expensive than *number two*. The highest grade of Chinese ginger is some of the best ginger in the world. Chinese ginger may be used in Indian food, and Indian ginger works well in Chinese food, but Chinese ginger is better for baking due to its brighter, less earthy flavor.

Jamaican ginger: Jamaican ginger doesn't make much of a dent in the US market today, but Jamaica was once the main exporter and the product was considered very good. Today, it's more expensive than other kinds, but that is because it's a much smaller crop than those from India and China, and the expense is not necessarily a sign of superior quality.[19]

Australian ginger: Most of the candied ginger in the US comes from Australia. Old-fashioned iterations of candied ginger were much different, being extremely fibrous and tough by today's expectations. Ginger growers in Australia began harvesting their ginger at a much younger stage and cultivated less fibrous gingers, contributing to the soft, tender candied ginger that is now standard. Australia cornered the market on this type of candied ginger, which was and remains popular.

CANDIED GINGER

To make candied ginger, fresh ginger is boiled and sugared, or cooked in a sugary syrup, with the sugar acting as a preservative. Old-fashioned candied ginger didn't use the young and tender ginger, so the candy was very fibrous and chewy, forcing the eater to suck on it rather than chew. You can still find this kind of candied ginger outside the US

Candied ginger comes in different sizes, though all are good for eating plain. Some people prefer the smaller pieces for the higher sugar-to-ginger ratio, while others

---

[19] Many other countries grow ginger, including several in Africa, but they rarely produce enough ginger (or ginger of high enough quality) to export to the rest of the world.

Ginger, candied

want the larger sizes for the opposite reason. Smaller is better for cooking, as it mixes well into cookie doughs, gives trail mix a spicy element, and adds a delightfully pungent/sweet surprise in oatmeal and granola.

A SECRET INGREDIENT

Ginger is potent in all its forms. Fresh, pickled, candied, dried, or powdered, it packs a huge amount of flavor, so much so that it can be overwhelming at times. Every time I have a ginger-forward meal, I'm reminded why ginger was traditionally thought of as a "warming" spice. It brings a sweet heat when used in baking; cookies and pies with a strong ginger component make for a simultaneously sweet and spicy treat, and the same goes for ginger ice cream, which is hot in flavor while being cold on the tongue. It's excellent with other fatty dairy dishes, too, especially creams; add powdered ginger to whipped cream for a showcase of this marvelous pairing.

Ginger brings the same heat and intense flavor to savory dishes, like curries and Chinese noodle and vegetable recipes. It enlivens whatever it comes into contact with and leads every part of the dish to be their best selves. Ginger is included in Chinese five spice and pumpkin pie spice blends because its diversity is astounding: In fish dishes, it can take the fishy edge off. On fruit like plums, it adds a bright, almost citrus aspect.

Ginger is a true friend in baking and in cooking. It can stand alone in flavor, as it does in gingerbreads. But it is a remarkable spice to use in conjunction with other spices. The power in ginger lies with its ability to brighten a dish and complement other flavors, acting as one of those underappreciated ingredients that works an alchemical magic to meld a dish's flavors together.

Cardamom

ike ginger, cardamom is a spice that works best in conjunction with other spices. Both do a lot of heavy lifting in flavor profiles but bow their heads when praise is doled out; each acts as a base from which more spices and flavors can spring forth. Also like ginger, cardamom can live happily in close proximity to cinnamon; cinnamon smooths out the brasher elements. Most people today are probably familiar with chai,[1] the spicy black tea beverage recently incorporated into the mainstream US diet thanks in part to national coffee chains. In India, the word *chai* simply means *tea*, of any kind, but here it's come to be shorthand for a certain flavor profile more than a specific blend or method. The flavor is heavily dependent on cardamom, as well as cinnamon, black pepper, vanilla, and a bit of clove and/or nutmeg.

Before I'd ever ordered a large chai from a corner conglomerate coffee shop, my grandparents introduced me to a cardamom-milk "tea" that we made by mixing cream, sugar, and a healthy amount of cardamom in one of the large metal bowls they used to create spice blends. After stirring it together in the driveway of my grandparents' quiet suburban home, we let it sit out all night, uncovered, as the milky concoction would only be complete when it was imbued with the light of the full moon; my grandfather was especially partial to making it under a blue moon.[2] If moonlight could be bottled and sprinkled into food and added to tea, no doubt it would stand on the shelf next to the cardamom.

When I asked my grandma why this blend received such special treatment, she said it had something to do with an Indian tea. Digging through the spice shop's internet archives, I came upon a project that was "to be thought out and blended soon by Eva, Caity, and Lucas": *Taj Mahal Spices*, containing "vanilla bean sugar with saffron,

---

[1] The proper name is *masala chai*, meaning "mixed-spice tea." Many American coffee shops call it a *chai latte*, alluding to the steamed milk, as in a café latte.

[2] A blue moon is the second full moon in a calendar month, a rare occasion that begat the phrase "once in a blue moon" to indicate something done or occurring rarely.

cardamom, and moonlight blended in, made with heavy cream and ground-up almonds." My grandfather's note continues in an appealing stream-of-consciousness style, especially for a retail website: "The night of the harvest full moon might be best to do the first batch? Based on very old ideas about the moon actually giving a certain lovely quality; yes, perhaps even a flavor, to a milk dessert."

AROUND THE WORLD

Even the dry *Spices and Herbs for the Food Industry* drops its functional prose to write that "Cardamom is one of the most important and valuable spices of the world and is often called the queen of spices."[3] *The Burns Philp Book of Spices* says, "In India, [cardamom] is called the queen of spices, second only to pepper, the king, in economic importance."[4] The aroma is certainly fit for royalty: powerful, sweet, almost citrusy, cooling and warming at once, with a sparkling brightness that brings good cheer to savory and sweet dishes. It can be brash if misused, smothering if overused, but in the right quantities, and in concert with spicy friends, cardamom uplifts whatever it's added to.

While it may certainly appear to the average American that cardamom has been demoted since then, many outside the US still hold cardamom in high regard. Beyond our version of chai, Americans may be familiar with cardamom as a flavor in frankfurters and other German sausages, or perhaps in authentic Danish pastries. In Scandinavian countries, cardamom is used in baked goods like we use cinnamon. While we enjoy cinnamon rolls, Scandinavians enjoys cardamom rolls. Its flavor permeates breads, sweet rolls, buns, doughnuts, cakes, and cookies. Sweden, Denmark, Norway, Finland, and Iceland all use cardamom heavily in their baking but it's not just for sweets: cardamom is also added to hamburgers and meatloaf. Sweden loves cardamom the most: their per capita consumption is 60 percent greater than in the US[5]

However, cardamom only comes from two places: India and Guatemala. Cardamom is native to India, which was the world's only exporter until the 1930s. Then it was

---

[3] *Spices and Herbs for the Food Industry,* 47.

[4] *The Burns Philp Book of Spices,* 38.

[5] *Agronomy and Economy of Black Pepper and Cardamom,* 290.

introduced to Guatemala, where the conditions were so favorable that it overtook India in production and export by the 1980s.[6] Part of Guatemala's surge is because the spice is not part of Guatemala's cuisine, so virtually none of their cardamom is kept in-country. India experiences the reverse, with a very high demand for cardamom keeping much of the product from ever leaving.

In India, cardamom contributes its heady but sparkling flavor to curries, kormas, and other sauces and dishes, as well as sweets like puddings and rice porridges, and it's sometimes added to cheese. Indians frequently nibble on cardamom seeds between meals to freshen their breath. Indian cardamom is higher quality and more expensive, with a more potent, rounded flavor than Guatemala's, though cardamom from Guatemala can be satisfactory.

Types of Cardamom

Cardamom is the dried seedpod of a plant that's related to the ginger family.[7] Cardamom can be one of the more confusing spices, since it comes in so many different forms: whole pods, whole seeds, and ground (only the seeds are ground, not the pods). There are three colors to choose from as well: black, green, and white.

Green cardamom pods: The green pods are a tapered oval shape, and don't smell like much of anything. Crack one open with your fingers and you'll find the light brown seeds and the distinctive cardamom aroma. When a recipe calls for green cardamom, you can crack the pod open and deposit it into the dish, fishing out the empty shell later, like you would with a bay leaf. Sometimes a recipe will call on you to grind the whole pod, but I find there's almost always a sharp, stingy bit left over from the pod, so I opt to either remove the seeds from the pod or leave the pod whole and find it later. (If you don't find it, that's okay too; it'll be obvious when it's in your mouth, and you can spit it out or just eat it, since it's soft and pliable and can be swallowed, unlike pokey bay leaves.)

---

[6] *Agronomy and Economy of Black Pepper and Cardamom*, 296.

[7] Spices are full of strange relations, like cinnamon being cousin to bay leaf.

White cardamom pods: White cardamom pods are just green pods that have been bleached. Many Scandinavian countries use the white pods as their standard cardamom, and a Scandinavian customer once told me that they're far superior to the green ones. What's so great about the pod being whitened? First, bleaching mellows the flavor, which is normally strong and pungent. Second, only the best green pods get selected for the bleaching process in the first place. The resultant white pods are fatter and rounder than the tapered green ones, and contain plumper, darker seeds.[8]

Black cardamom pods: Black cardamom is actually brown, not black, and it's not the same as green (and white) cardamom, but a relative in the same plant family. Black cardamom tastes very different, with a bolder, smoky, almost peppery flavor. It can be used as a baking spice and lends itself to savory dishes like stews, rice, and meat rubs. Black cardamom is a necessary ingredient in garam masala, though it's a spice best added when you want a singular, interesting flavor profile. I like it in homemade pho for its warming quality.

Ground cardamom: Ground cardamom loses its potency fast, so it's smart to use it up relatively quickly, being especially sure to keep it tucked away in a dry, dark space between uses. Grinding or roasting seeds fresh adds more labor to meal prep, but if you have the time, it's worth it. Ground cardamom is necessary for baking, when you don't want big chunks of seed in the dough. Ground cardamom is also used in Middle Eastern and Indian dishes, especially curries and teas. I like my chai with a strong spicy kick, and it's impossible to get the degree of flavor without cardamom. Starting curry by roasting whole cardamom seeds fills the kitchen with an intoxicating hint of the flavor to come.

CARDAMOM BLENDS

In the Mideast and across parts of Africa, cardamom is used in a variety of dishes and added to food much more liberally, similarly to how Americans add black pepper.

---

[8] How did the bleaching process originate? My mother hypothesizes that it was a way to keep them from propagating, like how the Dutch put nutmegs in lime and citric acid. Some people say bleaching makes the pods easier to open, but in my experience, it doesn't make any difference. Besides, that's what the bottom of a glass spice jar is for: crushing cardamom pods.

Cardamom plays a crucial role in several seasonings used in these areas, including many versions of *ras el hanout*, which translates to "top of the shop," meaning the finest-quality and most expensive spices blended together. This blend is a staple of Moroccan cooking but is found in many countries. Like many spice blends popular across large regions, the recipes vary from town to town, household to household. It can include anywhere from a dozen to over twenty spices, often some combination of cardamom, black pepper, salt, dried capsicum peppers, ginger, nutmeg, mace, cloves, lavender, cinnamon, white pepper, turmeric, paprika, saffron, and fennel. Ras el hanout is commonly used on roasted meats and vegetables, rice dishes, soups, and couscous. It can be mixed with oil to make a marinade, or mixed with yogurt for a dipping sauce.

Baharat, the Arabic word for *spices*, is a similar blend that features cardamom, as well as coriander, cumin, ground black pepper, hot dried capsicum peppers, cloves, and cinnamon. When combined, Baharat is a mildly hot but slightly sweet concoction that works as an all-purpose seasoning. Its bright red color gives dishes a pleasant orange hue. A pinch brings flavor and color to stews, sauces, rice, lentils, vegetables, and meats.

Hawaij, a savory spice blend used in Yemen, generally consists of cardamom, turmeric, cumin, coriander, cloves, and ground black pepper. It's excellent in soups and as a marinade rubbed onto meats before roasting. The name is also applied to an aromatic blend of cardamom, cinnamon, ginger, aniseed, and fennel, which is added to coffee. If you enjoy spiced chai, you may want to try a spoonful or two of sweet Hawaij in your morning brew.

When it comes to other variations of Arabic coffee, cardamom is a necessary spice, and some recipes call for as much, or more, ground cardamom as ground coffee. Arabic coffee beans are very lightly roasted, making the coffee flavor more aromatic and more caffeinated (the longer beans are roasted, the more caffeine is burned away). Other spices may be added in smaller amounts, including saffron, clove, ginger, rosewater, or orange blossom water, depending on personal preference. So popular is this drink that Saudi Arabia is the world's number one consumer of cardamom.[9]

---

[9] *Agronomy and Economy of Black Pepper and Cardamom*, 298.

Seeds, Part 1
Fennel, Aniseed, Star Anise, Caraway & Coriander

Like cardamom, many spices are the seeds of plants. Spices in general often represent unique strategies in plant evolution: some plants, like cinnamon, developed hot spiciness to deter herbivores that would otherwise chew on their bark or consume their roots. At the same time plants were developing inedible or unpleasant exteriors, they were also developing ways to propagate and spread. That's why fruits, holding seeds, often taste so good; if an animal comes across a strawberry, eats it, and poops it out later, the seeds have successfully spread. This is the lesson the Dutch learned when they tried to restrain nutmeg production to just a few small islands; pigeons carried the fruit, with the nutmeg safely inside, away from the Dutch-controlled land, and nature spread the seeds as it always had.

THE LICORICE SPICES

Star anise, aniseed,[1] and fennel are spice seeds that share a licorice-like flavor. Though they're bonded together by this unmistakable aroma, each of these spices come from different plants that are botanically unrelated. Their distinctive, pungent flavor is one you either strongly like or strongly dislike; there seems to be little common ground when it comes to the sharp sting of licorice.

Perhaps because the aroma is so powerful that it feels medicinal, licorice and licorice-like spices have a long history of being used to cure ailments. Romans, after their famous food binges, would stuff in a final aniseed cake to aid digestion.[2] This ancient digestif, according to Pliny, also improved the breath—another plus if you've just

---

[1] *Anise* and *aniseed* refer to the same plant: *Pimpinella anisum*. I used *aniseed* throughout to distinguish it from *star anise*, a similar but unrelated spice. More confusing still: the Greek root, *anison*, is a reference to dill, which is only distantly related.

[2] *The Book of Spices*, 113; *The Lore of Spices*, 144.

Fennel, whole & ground

consumed a feast. That legacy continues on in, of all things, dog food. Both anises, fennel, and licorice are common additives to the pulverized meat we feed our pets, the producers claiming they have digestive benefits and a flavor that dogs enjoy. In a similar vein, the "hare" on greyhound racing tracks is typically covered with aniseed oil/scent (and lure manufactures sometimes apply it to attract fish).

While each smell of licorice, and at first blush seem very similar, closer examination reveals differences between the three, especially fennel. To understand the difference for yourself, line up a sample of each. Smell star anise last, because it's so strong it'll blow your nose out. Start with fennel seeds, then aniseed, and finally, ground star anise. You'll smell fennel's brash, earthy flavor that cries out to be added to sausage; the sweet, pushy aniseed that wants to be put in baked goods; and the simply insane, overbearing star anise, which should be used in moderation at all times, lest it overwhelm the flavors of the dish.

FENNEL

Fennel is part of the parsley family. While the seed is dried and used as a spice, the plant's foliage and bulb are used fresh in cooking. The bulb is similar to celery: when fresh, the fennel flavor, somewhat licoricey, is sharp, but when cooked it mellows out and goes well with seafood and in vegetable medleys. The feathery fronds are added to salads or chopped and used to garnish a dish.

Though more mild in licorice flavor than aniseed and star anise, fennel seed is still a strong spice that should be used discreetly. Alexandre Dumas hedged: "The odor, at first agreeable, becomes disagreeable when fennel is used too freely, as it is, for example, by the Neapolitans, who put it into everything."[3] Ground fennel is good in anything meaty: meat-based soups and stews, pork dishes, steak sauces. Whole fennel seeds are generally used in sausage making. Its robust flavor calls for an equally robust base; adding it to delicate flavors is ill-advised.

Puritans used to chew fennel in church, which gave it the nickname "the meetin' seed."[4] But people were meetin' 'round this seed long before the Puritans indulged themselves. It was used in ancient China, India, Greece, and Egypt. In Greece, it's called *marathon* and is a symbol of a Greek victory over Persia in 490 BC, which was also celebrated by an unconscionably long run. Pliny, who never met a plant he didn't write about, thought fennel was good for eyesight. This belief was strong enough to last hundreds of years, carrying through much of medieval Europe. In the mid-13th century, Pedro Juliao, who would become Pope John XXI, wrote of "eye water" composed of fennel, endive, and rue and meant to improve inflamed or tired eyes.[5]

Still others believed that smearing a cow's udders with fennel paste would prevent the milk from being bewitched.[6] A more common and widely practiced use was hanging fennel over doorways to protect the rooms within from bad spirits. Fennel root contributed to sack wine, a type of fortified wine popular in Shakespeare's time: Falstaff says, "If I had a thousand sons, the first humane principle I would teach them should be, to forswear thin potations and to addict themselves to sack."

Many Americans know fennel seed as an after-dinner snack and digestive at Indian restaurants. This mixture of seed and candy is called *mukhwas*[7], and can contain fennel, aniseed, or both, often with bits of sugar, peppermint oil, or a candy coating. Fennel seed works great as a breath freshener and, unlike gum and mints, is a sugar-free way to improve bad breath. Fennel seed is actually quite enjoyable to chew plain, initial notes of loud licorice growing milder and sweeter the more you chew.

---

[3] *Dictionary of Cuisine*, 119.

[4] *The Book of Spices*, 233.

[5] *The Book of Gin*, 15.

[6] *The Book of Spices*, 233.

[7] The name is a portmanteau of *mukh* and *vas*, meaning *mouth* and *smell*, respectively.

Aniseed, whole and ground

ANISEED

Alexandre Dumas also had negative thoughts on aniseed: "Abundant . . . especially in Rome," he wrote, "where it is the despair of the foreigner who cannot escape its flavor or its aroma." Dumas, a Frenchman, doesn't write if he himself is this desperate foreigner, though his dismay implies personal irritation. And as with fennel, Pliny appreciated anise where Dumas did not: "It serves well for seasoning all meats and the kitchen cannot get along without it.[8]" While aniseed was well-known to ancient Romans, it must have also been rather popular in England: In 1305, King Edward I listed it among the goods taxed to raise enough money for repairs to London Bridge.[9]

Aniseed comes whole or ground. In either form, it can be used for both sweet and savory dishes, most commonly in meat products (like sausage), tomato dishes (especially sauces), and baked goods. It brings a strong flavor that's best paired with other bold foods, which is why aniseed is so at home with fatty meats, robust tomatoes, and in hearty breads, like German pumpernickel.[10]

---

[8] "A Glossary of Spices," 2.

[9] *The Book of Spices,* 113; *The Lore of Spices*, 144.

[10] Dumas writes of the distinctively dark bread that "the name is derived from the exclamation of a horseman who, after tasting it, gave the rest to his horse, whose name was Nick, saying "Bon pour Nick!' (Good for Nick), which, with the German accent, became *Pompernick*." It should be noted that this charming explanation is definitely not true. Pumpernickel comes from the German *pumpern*, to break wind, and *Nickel*, goblin, from its "reputed indigestibility," according to Merriam-Webster.

Many drinks made across Europe and the Middle East use aniseed as a flavoring agent. These include *aquavit* in Scandinavia, *ouzo* in Greece, *pastis* in France, *rakı* in Turkey,[11] *sambuca* in Italy, *mastika* across the Balkans, *absinthe* across much of Europe, and *arak* in Iran, Iraq, Lebanon, Jordan, Palestine, Israel, and Syria.[12] Interestingly, the European Union regulates aniseed-flavored spirit drinks, requiring proper technique of distillation, alcoholic strength, and flavor, but the flavor for drinks traditionally made with aniseed can also legally come from star anise or fennel.[13]

STAR ANISE

On a purely aesthetic level, star anise might be the most beautiful spice. Each seed is housed in a petal-like wing, with each fruit having five wings reaching out like the points of a star, giving the spice its name (though it is also called *badiam*). Aniseed and star anise are very similar flavors, though aniseed is slightly more vegetal and grassy, while star anise has a slightly stronger, more abrasive aroma in a side-by-side comparison. The oils of each (*anethole*) can be used interchangeably.[14] Star anise is important in Chinese cooking, where it's a staple in meat and poultry dishes, used most frequently with pork and duck. For a soup with a warm bite, especially a healing broth or pho, use two points off the star anise, or a very small pinch of the ground. Star anise can be added to coffee for an admittedly strange but interesting cup, and many people brew tea with it, in order to get those digestive benefits touted by the ancient Romans.

Star anise comes from a small tree thought to be indigenous to China, though it has never been found growing wild.[15] The brown fruits are picked and dried before

---

[11] Note that dotless *i. Raki*, with the dot, is a pomace brandy from Crete.

[12] Both not in India and Southeast Asia. There, *arrack* is an alcohol made from coconut flowers. *Arak* is just Arabic for *distillate*.

[13] No. 25, Regulation No. 110/2008 of the European Parliament and of the Council, Annex II, *Spirit Drinks*, "Aniseed-flavoured spirit drinks."

[14] The anethole compound is responsible for the *ouzo effect*, which causes alcoholic beverages to become cloudy. It's also a precursor to designer drug PMA and was originally fingered as responsible for the supposed psychoactive effects of absinthe.

[15] *The Oxford Companion to Food*, 751.

Star Anise, whole & ground

they're fully ripe.[16] There was a ban on the importation of spices from mainland China to the United States that was lifted in 1971, after which the spice made its way to the States for the first time.[17] This likely explains the relative absence of star anise in American baked goods, while Europeans use it frequently in breads, cookies, cakes, and candies. German Christmas cakes make use of the licorice flavor in sweet doughs, and whole seeds are used in Italian biscotti. Like aniseed, star anise is used ground in sausage, and tomato dishes.

---

[16] *Herbs, Spices, and Flavorings*, 247.
[17] *The Book of Spices*, 115.

CHINESE FIVE-SPICE

Chinese five-spice is a potent combination of spices that bring a savory and sweet element to dishes. Notoriously, the five spices are not necessarily the same across recipes, and some Chinese five-spice blends use more than five spices. The Chinese five-spice typically found in the US contains cinnamon, ginger, star anise, aniseed, and cloves. Other spices included can be fennel, ground Sichuan peppercorns, and cardamom. Star anise and ginger are necessary; both provide indomitable flavors that Chinese five-spice wouldn't be the same without.

Use it in any hearty dish, especially meat-based ones, though it's also good mixed into breadcrumbs for breaded and fried tofu. It adds a Chinese flair to marinated meats and meat products destined for the grill in summer. It can be used in baking, too: If you want to add panache to a recipe that calls for cinnamon or nutmeg, try replacing some or all with Chinese five-spice. It brings a similar warmth but with additional complexity. It also pairs well with chocolate, as chocolate's strong flavor can handle Chinese five-spice's equally powerful one.

CARAWAY

Caraway seed is nowhere near as strong as fennel, aniseed, and star anise, but its flavor is reminiscent of licorice. It is actually the whole fruit of the caraway plant, not just the seeds. (Caraway leaf is sometimes used as an herb, offering a much milder flavor than the seeds, akin to parsley, with a subtle hint of dill.) Caraway seed is most well-known in Western Europe, being used in the US mostly for German and Austrian recipes, including cakes, breads, cheese, sauerkraut, sausage, fresh cabbage, pork, and goulash. It's probably most common in rye breads, giving it the seedy, nutty flavor you want from a good rye. It's sometimes used for its clean licorice-y taste in mouthwashes.

Caraway is noted as one of the most ancient spices. It was found in Stone Age Swiss lake dwellings; Roman and Egyptians used it as a condiment and in medicines; and Dioscorides, the 1st-century Greek physician, recommended it in a tonic for pale girls.[18] Be aware: caraway is sometimes confused with cumin, as old translations combined or confused the two (much like hot new spices from capsicum chilis were called "pepper" or some variation thereof). If you're using an old recipe for curry that calls for caraway, they almost definitely mean cumin.

Caraway is the centerpiece of many old superstitions, my favorite being that placing caraway under a baby's crib will protect it against witchcraft.[19] It was supposedly introduced to Britain by Prince Albert, who was born in Germany and became a big proponent of the spice during his marriage to Queen Victoria.[20] However, other texts indicate it was popular in England a few years before Albert arrived: King Richard II's head cooks mention caraway in their ancient English cookery *Form of Cury*, circa 1390.[21] At any rate, by the time Shakespeare wrote *Henry IV* in the late 16th century, it was well-known enough to be familiar to playgoers:

> SHALLOW. Nay, you shall see my orchard where, in an Arbour, we will eat a
> last year's pippin of mine own Grafting, with a dish of caraways, and so forth . . .

---

[18] *The Book of Spices* 159.
[19] *The Complete Book of Herbs and Spices*, 85.
[20] *The Complete Book of Herbs and Spices*, 85.
[21] *The Book of Spices*, 159.

Caraway seed was the star of the mostly forgotten seed cake, now considered old-fashioned in Britain.[22] Victorian Era cookbooks often included separate recipes for *seed cake* and *caraway cake*, though caraway was the seed in all of them.[23] When made at all these days, it seems to be more in the service of old-world novelty. With health diets emphasizing seeds, though, the time could be ripe for seed cake to come back into vogue.

CORIANDER

Coriander seed is, like star anise and caraway, a whole fruit and not just a seed, one most commonly used to spice up rye breads. But the Mari, an ancient Syrian civilization from late in the third millennium BC, recorded using coriander (alongside cumin) to flavor beer.[24] Farther north, Belgian Weiss beers wouldn't be themselves without coriander, as the seeds complement the clean, hoppy taste. It's also a key component in bitters. It's mentioned in the Ebers Papyrus, a record of Egyptian herbal medicine from around 1550 BC. It was also recommended medicinally by Hippocrates in ancient Greece, though the Roman statesman Cato does mention it as a food seasoning.[25]

---

[22] *The Oxford Companion to Food*, 712.

[23] *The Cook and Housekeeper's Complete and Universal Dictionary* also included a recipe for caraway soap, touted caraway as a cure for "hysterics," and mentioned it as a good bait to use in rat traps.

[24] *Spice: The History of a Temptation*, 58.

[25] *The Book of Spices*, 211.

Coriander, whole

Like cardamom, it is generally toasted and finds a good home in curries. Coriander is excellent with beets and other earthy vegetables, and is sometimes called for with roast pork and ham. When the whole seeds are added to a curry, they will impart much better flavor if they're roasted first. Roasted coriander seeds are also a key ingredient in garam marsala, are added to some pickling spice blends, and can be enjoyed on their own as a snack.

Coriander seeds and coriander herb come from the same plant. In the United States, the coriander herb is called *cilantro*. Americans adapted the Spanish name because of the herb's prevalence in Mexican cuisine, and things have been confusing ever since. Coriander seed, though, has quite a different taste from the coriander/cilantro herb.

Herbs
A Digression

I wrote in the introduction that I call everything on my spice rack a *spice*. When I'm cooking, I don't distinguish between spices and herbs and salts; they all get shaken onto food with gusto, and they all do their part to make my food taste better. Under this framework, herbs are spices, so I'm going to spend some time with them.

Broadly speaking, there are *some* aspects that shepherd herbs into their own distinct group. Many (though not all) spices grow in the tropics and have a history of traveling around the globe, while herbs, generally speaking, are what grows locally, all over the globe. Botanically, many (though not all) herbs come from plants that do not have woody tissues such as trunks and branches. Bay leaf comes from a tree related to cinnamon, but the part of the plant we use is the leaf—so is it a spice or an herb? It can be categorized either way, because the lines between herbs and spices are as porous as the ground they're grown in. There's another factor that links most herbs: they do not make the same impact across the pages of history as their flashier counterparts, like cinnamon, clove, nutmeg, and pepper.

For this reason, herbs are often sadly overlooked or altogether ignored in discussions about spice. In his authoritative *Spices and How to Know Them*, W. M. Gibbs writes that herbs "are found in both hemispheres, and little, therefore, need be said about them." He follows this dismissal with a tiny section on herbs, stuffed at the end of his book like a shameful epilogue. Poor herbs. These humble leafy plants can't possibly compete against histories as splendid as those of classic spices, but they have their own rich heritage, stretching back to the ancient Greeks and Romans.

My aunt echoed Gibbs when, one day over an outdoor lunch, we discussed the topic and she said, "If it were my book, I don't think I'd talk about herbs at all." She went on to say that "herbs grow anywhere—herbs grow in the sidewalk cracks in

Chicago." She scanned the sidewalk around us, as if expecting to find a tenacious herb coming up nearby, something we could pick and add to our plates.

And okay, yes, I did find a bed of herbs growing unattended in an abandoned lot near my home in Chicago. There amongst the weeds and grass was a tuft of very distinctive rosemary. Closer inspection showed sage and chives were also growing nearby. Was there once an herb garden there, unattended but still proliferating? Did the herbs spread from a nearby garden or window box? I had no compunction about taking the herbs home with me, even growing wild as they were. Put that in the "pro" column in herbs' favor: I'd never find cinnamon growing down the block.

Had I been wandering the Greek countryside, though, stumbling on herbs would have provided a much tastier product. Long has the Mediterranean enjoyed the reputation of producing the world's best herbs, for it's there that herbs have been growing since antiquity. Americans are familiar with the wreaths of bay leaves on the heads of Greek and Roman heroes. Mediterranean herbs boast heritages similar to wine grapes indigenous to France; the upstart grapes and herbs in the western hemisphere lack the rich history, embedded in the very soil, that comes from thousands of years of cultivation.[1] Sure, you can buy "sparkling wine" in California, but you can only buy *champagne* from France. Luckily for spices, there's not quite the elitism that comes with wines, though herbs imported from the Mediterranean are generally seen as superior to herbs grown in California and elsewhere.

---

[1] Though, like some upstart California wines, herbs grown in the state are becoming better all the time, and some have surpassed the traditionally superior old-world varieties.

French Basil

USING HERBS WELL AND OFTEN

In my family, it's not uncommon to overhear strong opinions on which dishes require fresh herbs and when dried is preferred. The beauty of dried herbs is having their flavor always at hand, ready when you need to brighten a dish, their essence distilled into easily accessible shakers. In some cases, drying concentrates the flavors of herbs, making them a stronger ingredient than when fresh; these dried herbs are a critical component of many spice blends, melding the other spices and flavors together. I reach for dried rosemary and sage for chicken, dried cilantro for pastas, and dried thyme all the . . . time. In many cases, herbs lend a depth of flavor and a hint of something effusive, especially in soups and stews.

However, *The Herbalist* wanted to make it extremely clear to its readers that herbs should be used carefully. "The art of using these wondrous aromas and flavors lies almost entirely in one word—SUBTLETY" reads the all-caps introduction to using herbs in cooking. It goes on to shout, "THERE SHOULD BE ONLY A SUGGESTION OF FLAVORING HERBS."[2]

But what would pizza Margherita be without the flavor of basil? It certainly calls out for more than a "subtle hint." And there must be a big hit of rosemary to stand out in a balsamic-olive oil bread dip. Even sage, which *The Herbalist* compares to garlic's powerful aroma that "takes over completely unless used with discretion," is a big component of my sage butternut squash tarts. I *want* sage, rosemary, and basil to be the strongest aromas in these dishes.

A NOTE ON STORING HERBS

Most dried herbs start out potent and green. In some cases (like cilantro, rosemary, oregano, thyme, and basil) the dried herbs are *stronger* than the fresh, depending on the original product and drying methods. Herb producers have gotten very good at retaining flavor during the drying process, and drying acts to concentrate that flavor. To aid in flavor retention, herbs should be stored in an airtight container away from heat: be mindful of sun streaming through windows, the oven, and heating

---

[2] *The Herbalist* (Apothecary's Garden), 178.

vents/radiators in the kitchen. Think of your herbs like a leaf on a tree: if it falls off its branch in the middle of summer, it will bake in the sun, lose its green color, and coil into a lifeless thing. Your dried herbs face the same danger from light and heat. They should be tucked away lovingly, and in return they will retain their potency and vibrancy. If they are exposed to light and heat, they will slowly lose pungency.

Herbs don't go bad; they go pale and lifeless. When properly cared for, they'll last for several months, usually up to a year, though at that point you risk herbs that are less potent. In this case, you can use extra to make up for some of the lost flavor. In general, reduce the amount of herbs by one third if you're substituting dried for fresh. That is, if a recipe calls for 1 tablespoon of fresh thyme, use two-thirds of a tablespoon of dried thyme.

Basil

Crisp, sweet, and complementing a variety of flavors, basil is rightfully one of America's most popular herbs. There are as many as 40 varieties of basil, though only a few are dried and sold by American spice shops.

Italian and French cooking often call for basil, and it pairs especially well with tomatoes in all their forms, from sauces to salads to tomato soups and even tomato-based drinks like Bloody Marys. It's pleasant alongside eggplant and turnips as well. Added toward the end of cooking, basil can add a pep to heavier dishes like meatloaf and meat-heavy stews.

French basil is the old-world variety, with an exquisite, subtle flavor that can have a whiff of aniseed.

California basil is an example of New World crops improving upon the Old World's, a relatively recent phenomenon. While French is still preferred when dishes call for a hint of basil flavor, California is used when a powerful basil punch is desired. It tends to be darker green than its French counterpart, due to California's different drying methods.

Lemon Basil, also known as *Thai basil*, has a nice tang. It's not typically dried, though you may dry fresh lemon basil at home in an oven. Lemon basil can be added to salads and pairs well with fish.

California Basil

Purple Basil is, as the name suggests, purple. It is often used for its color, which adds an attractive element to salads. In flavor, it is similar to California basil.

Basil is an ancient herb, prominent in Ancient Greek cooking and medicine. Many of the legends surrounding it have to do with dragons and lizards. One theory of the *basil* name even supposes that it's shortened from *basiliscus*, or basilisk, meaning "little king."[3] The basilisk in some basil lore is a reptile (dragon, lizard, or otherwise) that can kill with a glance.

Many medieval Europe superstitions, however, speak of basil's connection to scorpions. One holds that scorpions would breed and thrive under basil pots. Another asserts that scorpions would be drawn to wherever basil was used; if some basil leaves were shredded and left under a pot, scorpions would soon arrive in droves.[4] Yet another claims basil is straight-up responsible for creating scorpions.[5] Of all the basil stored and sold at my family's spice stores, none have come with, or created, scorpions, though perhaps that's because we love basil, and the Ancient Greeks had a contentious relationship with basil. The Greek writer Chrysippus said it "exists only to drive men insane."[6]

---

[3] *The Book of Spices*, 122.
[4] *The Book of Spices*, 123.
[5] *The Lore of Spices*, 74.
[6] "What You Should Know About Basil," 1.

Bay Leaves

Bay leaves lend their pervasive but sweet flavor to everything they're added to. Many are familiar with adding a bay leaf to soups and stews, but they're also a good addition to stocks, fish and crab boils, sauces that simmer for a long time, casseroles, and Crock-Pot meals. They impart a subtle earthiness that's easy to forget about, but greatly missed when absent. You can (and should!) also add bay leaves to dry rubs. At home, we add them to our barbecue rib rub, and my dad's pot roast calls for bay leaf in the semidry rub.[7]

Bay leaves, also known as laurel leaves, are among the world's oldest herbs. It's easy to imagine these stately leaves enjoyed by toga-robed ancient Greeks and Romans, because we're familiar with the wreaths of bay leaf that were used to crown victors and heroes at Olympic games. Ancient Greek scholars were also crowned with bay leaf wreaths upon matriculation, and the title of *baccalaureate* comes from the words for "laurel berries."[8] Greek mythology contains a lengthy story of the laurel's origin: The sun god, Apollo, wouldn't take a hint from the nymph Daphne, but she just wasn't into him. Apollo pursued her so relentlessly that the gods did her a big favor and turned her into a bay laurel.

Bay leaves are used whole for good reason. The edges remain sharp and pointy even if they're in a hot liquid for a long time; while the outer ridges can get soft, they can still break down into smaller pieces with jagged edges. The worry isn't so much that you'll choke on them as it is that they'll scratch up your throat since they don't

---

[7] This recipe is in the recipe section at the end of the book.
[8] *The Lore of Spices*, 40.

Bay leaves

dissolve. So stick with the whole leaf, and don't break it up like you would other dried herbs. Most recipes call for you to fish them out before serving the dish, but I've heard from people who leave them in and reward the person who is served the leaf (with a wish or the right to pick the next movie, the ice cream flavor for dessert, etc.). If you find yourself with a sharp piece of bay leaf lodged in your throat, bread is the most gentle way to ease it along.

CHERVIL

Chervil is a sensitive herb, with a delicate, mild aroma that can be easy to miss. Therefore, it is usually added to a dish only toward the end of cooking, lest its subtle flavor get lost. It's sweet and aromatic, close to parsley in flavor but with lighter notes and a slight peppery, even aniseed-like, undertone. It's sometimes called *French parsley*, perhaps because is used more frequently in French cooking than any other country's cuisine. It pairs well with carrots, sweet corn, and spinach; lends sweetness to butter and butter sauces; and brightens seafood recipes and soups.

Pliny recommended it as a cure for hiccoughs. Other than this ancient anecdote, chervil has little lore or myth associated with it.

CILANTRO

Is there a more divisive herb than cilantro? This innocuous-looking bright green plant inspires hatred unknown to other herbs. Today, Facebook pages are dedicated to abusing it and, in 2002, Julia Child told interviewer Larry King that cilantro, along with arugula, are the only foods she despised. "They have kind of a dead taste to me," she said. "I would pick it out if I saw it and throw it on the floor."

Did Julia Child, like many others, have a genetic excuse for hating cilantro? Some cilantrophobes claim that they have the "cilantro gene" that makes it taste like soap to them, but the studies that have been done on this subject paint a more complex picture. One found a genetic correlation in people who dislike cilantro and a certain odor-detecting gene, which led the researchers to theorize that those people don't like cilantro because their genes increase the herb's soapy smell. However, people who like cilantro also have that gene, which may mean they simply don't mind the

Cilantro

soap factor.[9] A second study found three more genes that could influence how we smell and taste cilantro, and whether it's pleasant or not. Two genes influence how we taste bitter foods, and one detects pungent foods like wasabi.[10] Both these studies draw a connection between genes and whether we find cilantro pleasant or foul.

But even if you do hate it, that can change. For years, I picked cilantro out of my food, though, unlike Julia Child, I never threw it to the floor. I learned to tolerate it in my twenties and now I enjoy it. That's not the result of growing up in the spice business, but spending a year as a cook at a restaurant. One of my daily duties was to finely chop fresh cilantro, spread it on wax paper, and let it dry under a heat lamp. My petitions to use the already-dried stuff were ignored, despite my insistence that I was wasting time chopping and drying fresh stuff, thereby making it quite similar to the dried product. My nose wrinkled the first few weeks on the cilantro-cutting job, but eventually, I began to not notice it at all. With repeated exposure, it is possible to grow to tolerate cilantro. And while my case was more extreme—I would not suggest anyone chop cilantro only to throw it away (or to the floor)—you can add cilantro when you use other herbs, a little at a time, to build up a tolerance, and maybe even a liking for it.

Those who will never be swayed can take heart in learning that the Greeks named the herb *koris*, after the word for bedbug, which was meant to indicate the unpleasant smell, which is even more pronounced in the unripe fruit.[11] However, as the

---

[9] "A genetic variant near olfactory receptor genes influences cilantro preference," *ArXiv*.

[10] "Genetic Analysis of Chemosensory Traits in Human Twins," *Chemical Senses*.

[11] *The Lore of Spices*, 152.

fruit ripens and eventually dries out, the nasty odor fades.[12] The dried fruit become the *coriander seed* spice, because the plant's scientific name is *Coriandrum sativum*. Most of the world knows the whole plant, including the cilantro herb, as *coriander*. In tropical Asia, the herb is often called *Chinese parsley*. That name, however, is also applied to the unrelated plant *Heliotropium curassavicum*, which is more commonly called *salt heliotrope*.

Despite the small but passionate group of cilantro haters, it's popular the world over, and is used heavily in Mexican, Chinese, Egyptian, and Indian cuisine. It's a necessary flavor in salsa and spring rolls, and adds a fresh, clean pungency to roast meat, seafood, and lentil and bean dishes. Dried cilantro is milder than fresh cilantro.

DILL

This herb is often unnecessarily labeled as *dill weed* to distinguish it from *dill seed*, which is a spice that few people have ever even heard of.[13] Dill is an essential spring flavor, a herald of the fresh delights to come from gardens and farmers market. The herb is also well-known to dill pickle lovers, often the main flavor in the brine that gives these pickles their distinctive taste. Like chervil, it's a delicate flavor that can get easily lost if cooked, and should therefore be added near the end of cooking. It brings an earthy but fresh flavor to salads, potatoes, cabbage, carrots, zucchini, and meats, especially fish. Salmon and dill is a simple, but exceptional, pairing. It also blends wonderfully with sharp cheeses like feta, cutting the fatty acidity with its bright, fresh flavor. It's good in cheese and onion pie, and has gained popularity in Swedish *dillchips*, where it is combined with chives to season potato chips.

Dill was once believed to be both good for the digestive system and good for keeping witches away.[14] Because dill had magical properties, it could be used by witches but also used against them—a "hair of the dog that bit you" philosophy.

---

[12] *The Book of Spices,* 210.

[13] It's mainly used in cold dishes in the Middle East, including pickles.

[14] "A Glossary of Spices," 7.

Dill

FENUGREEK

Fenugreek, like the coriander/cilantro plant, yields both the green leaf that's dried into the fenugreek herb and the seed that's used whole and ground. The leaf is used in curries and flatbreads, mostly in India, the Middle East, and Northern Africa. The savory, somewhat nutty taste adds nice depth to sauces and soups, and it pairs well with potatoes.

The dried seed can be toasted and added to curries. It's also found in the Jewish confection *halva*, and can be used as a pickling spice. Papyri found in Egyptian tombs record fenugreek seed's use as a medicine. In Ancient Egypt, it was used to prevent and reduce fevers,[15] and (along with other spices) was used in embalming practices.[16] It was also once used as a skin and hair tonic, especially for horses, whose coats would get shiny and glossy when they were treated to a snack of fenugreek seeds (plus it aids their respiratory system).[17]

LAVENDER

Lavender is related to rosemary and has a similarly sweet, piney flavor. Dried lavender buds are added to the *herbs de provence* blend to bring a whiff of floral intrigue, and lavender sugar can be made by mixing dried lavender buds so their flavor permeates the sugar, giving it a flowery, almost rosemary-like aroma. Toss a teaspoon in your tea or a handful in a warm bath.

---

[15] *Spices: What they are and where they come from*, 9.
[16] *The Book of Spices*, 240.
[17] *The Complete Book of Herbs and Spices*, 126.

MARJORAM

Marjoram is similar to oregano: a sweet, fruity herb that pairs well with tomatoes and is often added to sausage and pasta sprinkles. Eggs and cheesy dishes benefit from a blush of marjoram, as do cream sauces and sour cream dips. It goes especially well with bright green, grassy flavors like peas and string beans.

Marjoram is sometimes called *wild oregano* (while oregano is sometimes called *wild marjoram*), demonstrating the thin line that separates the two. Often, they're used interchangeably in older recipes, and a great amount of confusion can come from their melded identities. It should be added toward the end of cooking, to not dampen its complex but subtle flavor.

MINT

Spearmint is the older mint; peppermint, though ubiquitous in packaged mouth fresheners, is a relative newcomer among herbs, coming into use only at the very end of the 17th century. The oil made from peppermint is what makes toothpaste and chewing gum minty and refreshing. That same freshness makes for an invigorating cup of tea, and peppermint is mostly used in candies and chocolates, a flavor it complements well.

Spearmint is the more common herb for cooking, and it's this variety that makes mint jelly, the table condiment reserved for holiday roasts. If a recipe just calls for "mint," you usually want to use spearmint. It's ideal for pretty much any meat: pork, lamb, duck, chicken, and veal can all be improved with a dash of spearmint. It should always be added to pea soup. Spearmint paired with fruit makes for a delectable summer flavor. It adds a breath of freshness to tangy yogurt sauces and lifts up lentil and bean dishes. Fresh mint is wonderful in mint juleps and any drinks with a base of fruit flavor, especially cranberry and orange; you can use a tea infuser with dried mint to replace fresh mint in drinks.

Mint is named for Minthe, a nymph turned into a mint plant by Persephone (Greek gods constantly turned people into plants; see also: Narcissus). Persephone was jealous of her husband Hades's affection for the nymph, and unfairly turned her rage against Minthe instead of Hades, transforming the nymph into a lowly plant.

Ancient Greeks and Romans enjoyed spearmint for use in perfumes and baths as well as a flavoring. Mint was first used to clean teeth in 6th-century Europe.

OREGANO

Dozens of subspecies of oregano exist, but commercially produced oregano is fairly standardized. Analyzing its flavor compounds (carvacrol and, to a lesser extent, thymol)[18] has allowed producers to grow a consistent product. Oregano is beloved the world over for its bright, citrusy flavor. Seafoods, broccoli, mushrooms, lentils, and Italian sauces all pair excellently with oregano, as do Turkish dishes like lamb and kebabs. Chimichurri, an Argentinian staple that Americans are becoming more familiar with, uses dried oregano, among other herbs (typically cilantro and parsley).

Greeks called oregano "the joy of the mountain."[19] Americans originally called it "the pizza spice." Oregano is well-known now, but it wasn't widely used or even available until after World War II, when American GIs in Italy became obsessed with pizza. Upon their return, they introduced both pizza and oregano to the rest of the country. Before 1940, imports were so small they weren't considered worth recording.[20] In the 25 years after 1940, American oregano use increased 6,000 percent.[21]

---

[18] "Oregano: Botany, Chemistry, and Cultivation."
[19] "A Glossary of Spices," 11.
[20] *Spices: What they are and where they come from.*
[21] *The Book of Spices,* 265.

Oregano, Turkish & Mexican

Mediterranean oregano should be used for Mediterranean dishes and is the kind brought to America with pizza from Italy, though the label covers varieties from Greece and Turkey, too. In general, oregano sold in the US as *Turkish* or *Greek* will be a sweeter, more citrusy oregano. This is the standard variety called for when an ingredient list simply says *oregano*.

Mexican oregano is ideal for Mexican cooking and should be used in chili con carne, chili powders, and moles. It's more pungent than Mediterranean, with a hint of pepper.

PARSLEY

"Parsley is the obligatory condiment of every sauce," wrote Alexandre Dumas.[22] Indeed, it does come up in many sauces and as a ubiquitous garnishing herb. "Take parsley away from the cook and you leave him in a situation where it is next to impossible for him to practice his art," said Bosc, someone who is apparently a cook, in Dumas's *Dictionary of Cuisine*.[23] He's not wrong. Parsley is indispensable for livening up dishes, from potatoes and white rice to green vegetables to chicken and fish. Its near-constant pleasantness is probably why parsley is the go-to garnishing herb: it brightens anything it touches, while adding a deep green color.

One popular medieval English myth seems designed to tell the frustrated gardener it's not his fault if his parsley won't grow. It explained that parsley took incredibly

---

[22] *Dictionary of Cuisine*, 185.
[23] *Dictionary of Cuisine*, 185.

Parsley

Rosemary

long to germinate because it had to go to the devil and back not once, not twice, but *seven times* before it would sprout.[24] It's also possible that the trouble was closer to home: another legend has it that parsley only grows if a woman is the master of the household.[25]

ROSEMARY

Dried rosemary comes whole, cracked, and powdered, but I prefer to purchase it whole. I crack it myself, between my fingers, before adding it to a dish to release some extra flavor. The astringent, potent flavor goes well with many meat dishes, especially baked chicken, lamb, and turkey. Mix it with some garlic in olive oil and balsamic vinegar as a quick dip for crusty bread. Rosemary brings a deeply interesting flavor to grapefruit and oranges, and a rosemary dressing is delightful over salads featuring those fruits. Rosemary potatoes, fried or baked in the oven, are common (as they should be), and it complements other starchy vegetables as well as cauliflower and mushrooms. When using ground rosemary, remember that a small amount goes a long way. Its flavor is condensed in this form, and very strong. Ground rosemary is useful in dishes where you might not want the dried needles, as in silky sauces.

"There's rosemary, that's for remembrance," notes Ophelia in *Hamlet*, and the idea remains common to this day: In the spring of 2017, British students started buying rosemary extract in huge quantities, convinced it improved memory and would

---

[24] *The Book of Spices,* 331; *The Complete Book of Herbs and Spices,* 200; *The Lore of Spices,* 82.
[25] *The Complete Book of Herbs and Spices,* 200.

help on tests.[26] This association between rosemary and remembering seems to have come about in the Middle Ages, when it was the unofficial herb of weddings, present as a helpful reminder to the newly wedded couple to be faithful to each other.

My grandparents sold a wedding gift box, which contained jars of spices presented on a pillow of dried rosemary. The large box held seven cups of the herb, which was supposed to be sprinkled on the floor and danced upon by the bride and groom. My grandfather learned this tradition from his adoptive

Rosemary dancing

father, a descendant of Italian immigrants from the southern Salentine region. My grandfather explained: "the dance floor is strewn with fresh rosemary; the bride and groom dance the first dance; just the two of them alone; looking into each other's eyes with the rosemary acting out its effect of earnestness. Later, the rosemary is collected and saved in a special vessel."

SAGE

Sausage without sage is a tragedy. Growing up in Wisconsin with so much German heritage around, the dishes I most associate with sage are sausage and poultry stuffing, which is a bit sausage-like. Sage is most friendly with onion, and the two of them together create a savory blend of flavors to accompany poultry, especially duck, though perhaps sage is best known as a key ingredient of saltimbocca. Charles Lamb's "A Dissertation upon Roast Pig" calls for sage in pig stuffing.[27]

Sage goes well with root vegetables and squashes, and is the perfect pairing for roasted butternut squash, either as dried sage added with the oil, salt, and pepper before roasting, or as whole fresh leaves fried in a bit of oil and added after the squash is finished. Sage is less popular in this country than it once was, culinarily

---

[26] "Rosemary sales double during exam season after study suggests it boosts brain power," *The Telegraph.*
[27] *The Book of Spices,* 382.

Sage, dried & rubbed

speaking; apparently, it was the emergence of oregano that dethroned sage from its position atop the herb hierarchy.[28] It also makes a refreshing tea, on its own or mixed with other herbs and tea leaves.

While sage has lost appeal in the kitchen, it's more than made up for it in a use that's new to most, but dates back centuries. The past few years have seen growing interest in the practice of sage smudging, or burning dried sage leaves to cleanse or "purify" air. This appropriation of a Native American cultural tradition has been adopted into various New Age rituals. Burning herbs unconsciously harkens back to ancient traditions of burning herbs and spices to connect with divine beings.

Ancient Egyptians burned myrrh, balsam, and frankincense to "banish evil spirits and appease the gods."[29] Similar traditions were practiced in Ancient Greece and Rome, where spices and herbs were burned so their fragrance might rise upward and meet the gods, who were themselves made of pleasing air. Later, during the Black Death that swept Europe, plague masks were filled with spices and herbs, among other sweet-smelling substances, to supposedly neutralize the bad air on which the plague traveled.

Sage is particularly appropriate for these purposes, as it's steeped in lore about magical properties. Ancient herbalists recommended sage for memory and bodily healing.

[28] *The Book of Spices,* 382.
[29] *The Book of Spices,* 8.

Its name is likely derived from the Latin *salvere*, which means "to heal" or "to save."[30] It came into English in the 14th century, around the same time as another meaning of sage, that of a wise person, derived from the Latin word *sapere*: to taste, to have good taste, and to be wise.[31] The Salerno School in Sicily, the Western world's earliest school of medicine, coined the phrase *Cur moriatur homo, cui salvia crescit in horto?* which translates to "How can anyone die who grows sage in his garden?" Pliny, Dioscorides, and Theophrastus wrote on sage's therapeutic values.[32]

In the Middle Ages, sage was a remedy for a wide range of troubles, from serious disease like cholera and epilepsy to irritations like constipation and colds. An old English rhyme says, "He that would live for aye, must eat sage in May" (to live forever, you have to eat sage in springtime).[33] Sage exemplifies the gender divide in medieval folklore. Like parsley, one tradition had it that sage would thrive in a home where its proprietors also thrived, but especially "if the wife rules the home."[34] Across medieval Europe, practical wisdom said that planting and gardening done by women would improve the plants' effectiveness. The delicacy of herbs associated them with the feminine sphere, while strong spices were considered masculine.

SAVORY

Savory tastes somewhat similar to thyme and is often used to flavor soups and meat along with it. Like thyme, there are several varieties of savory, with the two majors being summer savory and winter savory. Summer savory earned its name from the

---

[30] And *common sage* has the full Latin name *Salvia officinalis*. The medieval epithet *officinalis* denotes substances and organisms used in medicine and herbalism; it means "belonging to the storeroom of a monastery." Other so-named plants include rosemary, asparagus, jasmine, ginger, and many plants referencing specific uses like eyebright, lungwort, and soapwort.

[31] Merriam-Webster.

[32] *The Lore of Spices*, 86.

[33] *The Complete Book of Herbs and Spices*, 219.

[34] "A Glossary of Spices," 15. A woman who wants to rule the home would do well to sew mustard seeds into her wedding dress, as this old German myth tells that a woman who does this can be certain to "wear the pants" in the family. (*The Lore of Spices*, 27).

Tarragon

savory plant whose product was at its peak flavor in the early summertime. Winter savory, on the other hand, is a hardier version that provides its goods in the winter. Summer savory is sweeter, while winter has a stronger, somewhat more bitter and piney flavor. Use of "savory" without the prefix usually refers to the summer variety. Either savory goes well with beans, peas, eggs, vegetables, sausage, and pork, and lends itself well to herb blends.

Tarragon

A staple of classic French cooking, tarragon seems to be one of those "love it or hate it" herbs, though it's not as divisive as cilantro. Its flavor is completely unique, and I didn't like it as a child, though nowadays I enjoy it in a butter sauce over pork chops or chicken. It's a key ingredient in the French Béarnaise sauce, and often appears in Hollandaise and Béchamel, two of the five French "mother sauces." Tarragon is popular in mayonnaise-based recipes (sometimes replacing dill in tartar sauce) and creamy soups, and it pairs well with tomatoes and lobster. Alexandre Dumas managed to find no less than 26 recipes for egg dishes for his *Dictionary of Cuisine*, including Eggs Tarragon, where chopped tarragon is added to an omelet mixture along with salt, pepper, and cream.[35] He adds that vinegar is not good unless it has tarragon mixed in.

Ibn-al-Baytar, an Arabian botanist and pharmacist in Spain, wrote of tarragon as a breath sweetener, a drug to induce sleepiness, and a good herb for vegetables.[36] He

---

[35] *Dictionary of Cuisine*, 113.
[36] *The Book of Spices*, 404.

was certainly right about the last part: Tarragon is especially good with green earthy vegetables, including artichokes and asparagus.

French tarragon is the standard tarragon; recipes calling for tarragon are hoping for the French variety, as it has a better flavor than Russian tarragon.

Russian tarragon can be good, but is not as standard a product as French. It is, however, a hardier plant in American herb gardens than the French kind, so for that reason has a place in households that like to grow their own herbs.

The *tarragon* name has associations with the word *dragon*, though how the connection came into being is unclear. Pliny said that protection from snakes and dragons could be achieved by carrying a twig of the tarragon plant, which came to be called *dracunculus*, the "little dragon."[37] Another source claims the word *tarragon* is a corruption of the French word *estragon*, also meaning "little dragon," which comes from the Arabic *takhun*.[38] It's supposed to have acquired the name because it was believed to cure venomous reptile bites; others say it refers to the serpentine roots of the tarragon plant.[39] However the connection started, the word is similar in many languages: Latin calls it *Artemisia dracunculus*; it's called *esutroragon* in Japanese, *estragon* in Russian, and simply *dragon* in Dutch and Swedish.

THYME

There are few dishes that cannot be improved by a dash of thyme. Its fragrant, pleasant aroma is strong without being overpowering, and a little bit added whenever herbs are called for brightens the dish.[40] Along with salt and pepper, I sprinkle thyme on potatoes (sweet, red, or russet), onto meat roasts, in oil for dipping bread, and into virtually any soup or stew. It's also a crucial part of the *za'atar* blend, and goes well in many Middle Eastern dishes. I like it in lentils along with cumin.

------

[37] *The Lore of Spices*, 76.

[38] *The Book of Spices,* 403.

[39] *The Book of Spices,* 403.

[40] "Escoffier always recommended one part wild thyme in his herb blends." *Spices, Seasonings and Herbs*, 186.

Thyme

The pungent thyme is just as strong dried as it is fresh. One sprig of fresh thyme is equivalent to half a teaspoon of dried. Dried thyme is especially nice to avoid the laborious effort that goes into trimming fresh thyme. Unlike many other herbs, its strong earthy flavor can survive time in a hot pot, so it can be added earlier in cooking without losing its flavor.

There are many varieties; though we have a standard thyme here in the US, there are estimated to be over 100 varieties that grow wild in the Mediterranean. Supposedly one "mother of thyme" was the progenitor of all the varieties. Mediterranean is the standard thyme, while French is slightly sweeter. Lemon thyme is a variety bred to have a stronger citrus flavor.

Thyme lore abounds from both Ancient Rome and Greece. In Greece, thyme was a connection to the gods: *thyme* comes from the Greek verb meaning "to sacrifice" or "to make a burnt offering."[41] In Rome, it was thought to enhance courage, so soldiers would bathe in thyme water.[42] Pliny believed it helped "melancholy" people, and wrote that anyone suffering melancholy should stuff their "crying pillows" with thyme.[43] On the other hand, a recipe from 1663 instructs thyme and beer be added to soup to "cure shyness."[44]

---

[41] *Spice: The History of a Temptation*, 233.

[42] I tried it. It felt nice but I didn't notice an uptick in courage. Just an uptick in hunger.

[43] "A Glossary of Spices," p. 17. As someone who sometimes gets melancholy, if herbs cured depression I'd be a case study for the effects of near-constant exposure. Alas, it doesn't work. (Though perhaps the point is to get a better cry out. I must investigate these "crying pillows" in more detail.)

[44] *The Complete Book of Herbs and Spices*, 251.

In the 18th century, William Shenstone wrote about "the tufted Basil, pun-provoking Thyme," and the punning tradition remains as strong as ever. I heard a lot of them working at the Spice House, mostly of the "I've run out of thyme!" variety. I myself have a large old spice rack that reads "Never Enough Thyme." I don't remember how I got it, but I assume I found it at my grandma's house.

HERB BLENDS

BOUQUET GARNI

The classic bouquet garni is fresh herbs tied together in a neat bundle. When using dried herbs, they're sometimes put in a muslin bag so, like the fresh bundle, they can impart their flavor during cooking but be removed before serving. There is no standard composition of the bouquet garni, though one authority has it as thyme, bay leaf, and parsley.[45] It can also include rosemary, oregano, basil, marjoram, sage, tarragon, savory, and dill weed. These herbs will give flavor to soups, stews, and anything made in a slow cooker. Dried, they're good to rub on meat that will be roasted. In 1656, Pierre de Lune put bouquet garni into print for the first time; his recipe included chives, thyme, cloves, chervil, and parsley tied with a strip of bacon.[46]

FINES HERBES

A French mainstay typically consisting of parsley, French chervil, French tarragon, and chives, depending on the person doing the combining. Fines herbes can also involve thyme, rosemary, or marjoram if you're feeling peppy. These are typically fresh and chopped, though dried combinations are oftentimes just as good.

HERBES DE PROVENCE

The most interesting of the French herb combinations, Herbes de Provence adds dried lavender flower and fennel seeds to make for a more aromatic blend. There's also some combination of basil, thyme, rosemary, tarragon, and chervil, savory, oregano, marjoram, and dill added to the base.

---

[45] *The Oxford Companion to Food*, 91.

[46] Pierre de Lune's *Le Cuisinier,* in *Oxford Companion to Food.*

Seeds, Part 2
Mustard, Cumin, Poppy & Sesame

All spices and herbs have lore and legends associated with them.[1] Some are beautiful and some are bizarre; some are lewd while others are holy. Such is the case with biblical references to spices. They're often referenced in the Hebrew and Christian Bibles for metaphor and their aura of magic, demonstrating both their familiarity and importance throughout millennia.

The Song of Songs uses spices to evoke sensuality, comparing the object of affection to "an orchard of pomegranates with all choicest fruits, henna with nard,[2] nard and saffron, calamus and cinnamon, with all trees of frankincense, myrrh, and aloes, with all chief spices." The Old Testament mentions juniper berries as a sign of fruitfulness. Cassia is mentioned frequently, most importantly as part of a holy anointing oil ("all your garments are scented with myrrh and aloeswood and cassia," Psalms 45:8), but also as a perfume ("500 units of cassia, measured by the standard shekel of the holy place, along with of olive oil," Exodus 30:24) and a general commercial good ("Ve'dan and Ja'van from U'zal gave wrought iron, cassia, and cane in exchange for your goods," Ezekiel 27:19).

Spices may be symbolic, or they may serve as calls to remembrance. Hot cross buns are so called because the cross cut on top represents the cross of Jesus's crucifixion, while the interior is filled with spices, standing in for the spices anointed on Jesus's body.

Mustard, yellow & brown seeds

---

[1] With the possible exception of chervil, an herb somehow overlooked by our story-loving, herb-growing ancestors.

[2] _Nard_ is an aromatic plant oil, also called _muskroot_.

MUSTARD

Jesus used the tiny mustard seed as a parable for small beginnings growing into a firmly rooted, life-giving entity:

> *The kingdom of heaven is like to a grain of mustard seed, which a man took, and sowed in his field: Which indeed is the least of all seeds: but when it is grown, it is the greatest among herbs, and becometh a tree, so that the birds of the air come and lodge in the branches thereof.*[3]

But mustard was more often associated with witchcraft, both in service of evil deeds and in their prevention. In Shakespeare's *Macbeth*, the witches mention *eye of newt* as the first ingredient in their famous "double, double, toil and trouble" spell, but the reference is not to salamanders: it's to an archaic name for the mustard seed, used by herbalists. Mustard seeds have a tradition of being used to confuse and disorient, hence their contribution to the potion to befuddle poor Macbeth.

But people can use mustard *against* evil, too. Vampires are compulsive counters and will pause their vile plans to obsessively tally any group of items thrown their way.[4] Mustard seeds are small enough that a handful buys time to plan your escape or wait out the threat until sunrise (or so the working theory went in Shakespeare's time).

ABUNDANT BUT INVISIBLE

Mustard is one of the world's oldest spices, and also one of the most popular. Though the yellow condiment is ubiquitous at picnics and hot dog stands, the tasty little seed is seriously underrated. Mustard appears in a broad array of dishes, as both spice and condiment. It adds heat and zing to everything from a holiday ham to a quick weekday sandwich. It's used in Chinese hot sauces and French Béchamel, in fancy cheeses and children's mac & cheese; in homemade salad dressings and on stadium hot dogs. It's highbrow and lowbrow, common and fancy, simple and complex.

---

[3] King James Version, Matthew 13:31–32.

[4] It's no accident that *Sesame Street*'s Count von Count is a vampire. The lore is further explored in *In Search of Dracula*, by Radu Florescu.

Where's the line between a spice and a condiment? For much of the last few thousand years, *spices* and *condiments* were conflated and used interchangeably; it wasn't until spices ventured beyond the pharmacies and doctors' prescriptions into the kitchen that they became condiments at all. The word comes from the practice of using spices to dry a corpse for burial, which was "to season" it, *condire*, which became *condimentum*, meaning seasoning.[5] In his exhaustive *Oxford Companion to Food*, Alan Davidson addresses the classification, first taking umbrage at the authors who write whole books on spice without attempting to define it, before seeming to settle on a distinction laid out by Herbert Stanley Redgrove in his 1933 book *Spices and Condiments*:

> *Herbs* are the herbaceous parts of aromatic plants; *spices* are their dried other parts—rhizome, root, bark, flower, fruit, seed; and *condiments* are spices or other flavourings added to food at the table. Thus mustard greens would be a herb, and mustard seeds a spice, while mustard in a mustard pot, at table, would be a condiment. This would be a convenient set of definitions, and has the merit of being as close to common usage as any rational definitions could be expected to come.[6]

The spices and herbs, with their broad definitions, make sense, though the example of mustard is flawed: Is stone-ground mustard, applied to a roast in the kitchen, a spice, while the same mustard spread on a sandwich at the table becomes a condiment?

Regardless of whether mustard is added in the kitchen or at the table, it has long been used to improve the taste of food. Medieval peasants frequently used mustard in the winter months, when many subsisted on diets of bland dried meat.[7] Take the sage advice of French novelist Anatole France, a Frenchman who lived in France:[8] "A tale without love is like beef without mustard: an insipid dish."[9]

---

[5] *Spice: The History of a Temptation*, 158.
[6] *The Oxford Companion to Food*, 744.
[7] *The Book of Spices*, 286.
[8] France received the Nobel Prize in Literature in 1921 for his contribution to literature and his "true Gallic temperament."
[9] "I am a great eater of beef, and I believe that does harm my wit."—William Shakespeare.

Mustard was enjoyed on food in China almost 4,000 years before Pythagoras, the Greek mathematician known for his geometric theorem, recommended spreading it on stings and scorpion bites.[10] When Alexander the Great began his conquest of Persia in 334, the last king of the Persian empire, Darius III, sent over a bag of sesame seeds, each seed representing a soldier in his vast army. Responding in kind, Alexander sent Darius a bag of mustard seeds, to represent that he, too, had a great many soldiers at his command, but that *his* soldiers also had the panache of the spicy mustard seed.[11]

TYPES OF MUSTARD

Whole mustard: Seeds come in yellow, brown, and black. Sometimes the yellow seeds are called white, and sometimes the black ones are actually brown. Kept whole, mustard seeds are typically used as a pickling spice or in boiled dishes with shrimps or vegetable (like cabbage and sauerkraut). Yellow mustard seeds have the mildest flavor, while brown and black are hotter and hotter still.

Ground mustard: Mustard is unusual among its fellow spices in that, in its dried form, it has virtually no aroma. You must add water to it and let it sit for about 10 minutes to draw out the tangy, hot flavor. Mustard reaches peak hotness around that 10 minute mark, after which the flavor begins to fade.

Powdered mustard: The seeds are ground to make a powder (sometimes called *mustard flour,* as the process is similar to flour production: seeds are milled and the husk removed). This dry powder is used to make a smooth mustard condiment and in cooking.

Prepared mustard: Like peppercorns, the mustard seed is at its most flavorful just after it's been cracked, and the intense heat level will taper off quickly as it oxidizes. That's why prepared mustard you buy from a grocery store is made with vinegar and is less hot than the kind you make at home. The vinegar holds the flavor longer, but also makes the flavor less potent. Adding water to dry mustard activates its enzymes; if you do this in your kitchen you'll get a hot, pungent mustard paste.

---

[10] *Good Cook's Book of Mustard*, 8.
[11] *The Book of Spices,* 285.

Hot water will hurt the enzymes, so cold water should be used when hydrating mustard. Freshly prepared mustard is also somewhat bitter, especially if you eat it right away, but letting it age for a few days mellows it out, reducing the bitterness (and also the heat level).

Prepared yellow mustard: Yellow is the most mild and widely used prepared mustard. It's not hot, but still has the sharp mustard taste. Yellow mustard powder is used to make the final product smooth and spreadable; a dash of turmeric brightens the yellow color. This is usually what's called for in salad dressings, as its thick texture helps bind oils and vinegars together, in addition to imparting flavor.

Prepared brown mustard: Brown mustard is made from brown mustard seeds, or a combination of brown and yellow seeds, for a darker and zippier mustard. Some of the seeds' flaky bran is left on in the grinding process, adding texture and a distinct visual identity to brown mustard. Other spices, like cinnamon, are sometimes added to impart even more flavor and it is available in various levels of heat and graininess. Brown mustard is good on ham and used in delis, as it can hold its own in hearty sandwiches, like a pastrami on rye.

Dijon mustard: Famous, intense and hearty, Dijon mustard uses brown and black mustard seeds to give it a strong heat, but the real distinguishing twist is the substitution of white wine in place of vinegar. Alexandre Dumas dedicates a dozen pages to mustard in his *Dictionary of Cuisine*, writing at length about Dijon mustard: "If mustard was not invented there, at least Dijon restored it," he declared. "Understandably, imitators appropriated and exploited the name of Dijon mustard. But Dijon maintained its supremacy."[12]

Whole-grain mustard: More or less just macerated mustard seeds, broken down enough to bind the seeds together but not so much they lose their seedy shape and textures, this is an excellent ingredient to add mouthfeel to a dish. While whole-grain mustard can be made of any color seeds, it's usually brown and black seeds to

---

[12] *Dictionary of Cuisine*, 171.

make a strong, pungent flavor. This is a good option for thick sandwiches and for a charcuterie and cheese plate.

Mustard paste: Made from brown or black mustard seeds, which are ground up in vinegar, mustard paste is thicker than other prepared mustards. While coarse, whole-grain mustard spreads may be considered a "paste," the term *mustard paste* typically refers to a hotter version that adds chilis for a sinus-clearing heat.

A MUST

Mustard got its name from the ancient Greeks, who concocted a drink of ground seeds mixed with unfermented grape juice, which was known as *must*. But it was the Romans who introduced mustard to Gaul (in modern-day France) where it came into its own. Not only is mustard all over French cookbooks, but Dijon became the world's mustard capital and synonymous with the product.

The plant is hardy and able to adapt to new places easily, to the point that it can quickly go from easy-to-grow spice to impossible-to-get-rid-of weed. The Mission Trail in California is said to have mustard marking it due to seeds dropped by Spanish missionaries who traveled through hundreds of years ago. In order to make a trail marking where they went, they scattered mustard seeds to mark their comings and goings, like Hansel and Gretel leaving a trail of breadcrumbs.

Yellow mustard, seeds & powdered

PICKLING SPICES

Pickling was once a necessary method for preserving foods, though today we pickle mainly for flavor. Mustard seed is one of the most common spices in pickling mixes, which are added to the brine. Whole spices are usually best for pickling, but ground mustard is used for some kinds, especially the Piccalilli, a pickled relish of mixed vegetables. Nearly any combination of whole spices may be used in home pickling: black and white peppercorns, bay leaves, allspice, cassia buds, mace, cloves, ginger, star anise, dill seeds, juniper berries, coriander, cardamom, dried chili peppers, garlic, and turmeric all find a home in brine.

TEWKESBURY MUSTARD AND WASABI

Tewkesbury mustard is a mixture of mustard and horseradish that dates back to at least the 16th century. The mustard is famous for its use in the town's "mustard balls," a recipe of dried local mustard and horseradish formed into balls and dried out, so that bits could be shaved off when needed for a dish. Like eye of newt, it crops up in Shakespeare:

> **Doll**: They say Poins has a good wit.
> **Falstaff**: He a good wit! Hang, him baboon!
> His wit's as thick as Tewkesbury mustard;
> There's no more conceit in him than is in a mallet.[13]
> —*Henry IV*

If you love the wasabi you get at sushi restaurants, you actually love Tewksbury mustard (or something similar, at least). The BBC posited in 2014 that just 5 percent of "wasabi" is the real thing. True wasabi is expensive and hard to get, especially in the US. Even in Japan, it's expensive enough that mustard and horseradish, dyed green, is common. Wasabi also loses its flavor about 15 minutes after it's grated, so it's not practical for restaurants that need to dispense the condiment on a large scale.

Wasabi has a leafy, woody, *green* flavor that hits the tongue in a clean, brightly hot rush, which, to be fair, the imitation stuff does do a decent job of approximating. Wasabi,

---

[13] Translation: Him? Smart? Seriously? He's as thick as Tewkesbury mustard, which is to say, very dumb. Dumb as a sledgehammer.

mustard, and horseradish are, after all, part of the same botanical family (*Brassicaceae*), one that also includes broccoli, cauliflower, kale rutabaga, and Brussels sprouts.

Even powdered wasabi sold at high-end grocery stores is usually a combination of real wasabi, mustard, and horseradish. Some even tout that they're not "just" mustard and horseradish, but do have some real wasabi included. When buying freeze-dried or powdered wasabi, take a closer look at the ingredient list: if the first ingredient listed is wasabi, you know you have at least some legitimate wasabi in there. But (and this is frequently the case) if the order goes "horseradish, mustard, wasabi," you know there's probably very little true wasabi present.

HORSERADISH

Like mustard, horseradish is typically prepared with vinegar, as its distinctively sharp flavor begins to dissipate when the root vegetable hits air. It should be white; dark horseradish has absorbed air and won't give you the flavor you're looking for. It's most frequently paired with beef and roasts, as it pairs well with rich, fatty foods. Powdered horseradish is a handy shortcut; just add water for a pungent horseradish sauce. Don't cook horseradish, or you'll lose the sharp bite; only add it at the end.

CUMIN

Cumin is less religiously famous, but equally underrated. It did play some role in Ancient Egypt as early as 1550 BC, when it was included on a list of plants used medicinally.[14] Most commonly, cumin is associated with faithfulness, and Ancient Egyptian soldiers and merchants carried it as a reminder of home and those waiting there. Many stories associate cumin with happy marriages and fidelity, though that symbol goes beyond human relationships: cumin also was known to keep "poultry from straying beyond the farmland bounds."[15]

The word itself is of Semitic origin (*ku-mi-no*),[16] and today we pronounce it to rhyme with *summon*, *human*, or *lumen*. Outside Egypt, it was used in Ancient Rome and

---

[14] The Ebers Papyrus, per *The Book of Spices*, 218.
[15] *The Book of Spices*, 63.
[16] *Spice: The History of a Temptation*, 240.

Cumin, whole & ground

Greece and was popular in medieval Europe.[17] Pliny thought of cumin as the king of condiments[18] and he was right. In some parts of the world, cumin is the most popular spice after black pepper. Many people associate it only with Mexican cooking and chili, though it was only adopted in Mexico when introduced by Europeans. India, the Middle East, and North Africa all use an abundance of cumin. In modern Egypt, it's often found mixed with hazelnuts and coriander in *duqqa* (or *dukkah*).

Americans still have yet to catch on to cumin, too often treating it as just an occasional "secret ingredient." But it's good with other spices on poultry and in stuffing; in rice and lentil dishes; in sauces (especially hearty ones like tomato-garlic pasta sauce) and yogurt dips; and virtually any soup or stew. It's often a main spice in curries, and is a staple flavor in chili powders. It's good in hearty bread, adds complexity to cheese, and spices up eggs. It's absolutely necessary in guacamole. Cumin is a versatile, wide-ranging spice that deserves wider application and acclaim.

Much of the supply in the US comes from India, where it's so popular that India is both the world's largest producer of cumin and the world's largest consumer of it. If it's not Indian cumin, it's probably from Pakistan, Turkey, or Syria. If you're outside the US, you likely have access to Iranian cumin, which used to be prominent but can no longer be imported due to trade sanctions. You could, of course, grow cumin

---

[17] American Spice Trade Association, "What you should know about Cumin Seed."
[18] *The Book of Spices*, 63.

yourself. Superstition says that cursing at your cumin seeds while planting them will produce "a splendid crop."[19]

We mostly deal with cumin in its ground form, though you can easily find whole cumin seed, too. If you want to use your standard pepper grinder to grind cumin, grind some dried, stale bread in it first, to clean it out. I use a mortar and pestle for grinding cumin seeds; if you're just doing a little batch, it's not that much work. Lightly toasting before grinding will make your cumin even more delicious.

Kept whole, you can use cumin seeds as a garnish on soups and lentils, like tiny spicy croutons. Toasting them also makes the house smell amazing. Untoasted cumin seeds pack a strong cumin kick and I wouldn't eat them plain. But I do like to munch on roasted cumin seeds for a snack.

POPPY

The Jewish holiday of Purim comes with one prominent foodstuff: the triangle-shaped, *hamantaschen* pastry, which is laden with poppy seeds. The original name was *muntashen*; *mun* being Yiddish for poppy seeds.[20] Purim celebrates the deliverance of the Jewish people from Haman's planned massacre in ancient Persia, where his attempt to annihilate their population was thwarted by Esther, the secretly Jewish queen. It's possible that the German word for poppy, *mohn*, and pocket, *tash*, were combined to form *Mohntash* and then made into the pun name *Hamantash*.[21] In old illustrations of Haman, he was often painted wearing a three-cornered hat, perhaps translating to the triangle pastry.[22]

Other poppy seed pastries are popular across much of Europe, the Middle East, and India, and have been for thousands of years. In the first century AD, Pliny recorded the beloved Roman recipe of parched (dried) poppy seeds and honey. In the second century, Galen, in Greece, endorsed poppy seeds crushed and added to flour breads. Poppy seed was used in bread and as a condiment in medieval Europe.

---

[19] "A Glossary of Spices," 7.

[20] *Every Person's Guide to Purim*, 23.

[21] *The Purim Anthology*, 492.

[22] *Every Person's Guide to Purim*, 23.

Poppy seeds

Today, poppy seeds are used as fillings in cakes and breads, and their blue-gray color is an attractive garnish sprinkled on top of breads and biscuits. They show up in salad dressing recipes, giving oil and vinegar mixtures extra texture. Poppy seeds are also called for in some egg and potato dishes. To grind poppy seeds at home, always toast them first and use a hand grinder.

OPIUM

Poppy seed is harmless by the time it's dried and makes its way to your spice cabinet. But poppy's culinary use has always existed alongside opium. This dates back as far as 1400 B.C, with a poppy goddess in statue form at a sanctuary in Gazi, Crete, where the women are believed to have cultivated poppy specifically for opium production.[23] Opium is used to manufacture morphine, a pain-reliving sedative named for Morpheus, the Greek god of dreams.

SESAME

In *One Thousand and One Nights*, Ali Baba discovers a cave where treasure is hidden. "Open, sesame," he commands, and riches are his. The famous reference is thought to have used the word *sesame* because very ripe sesame pods will burst open and shower their seeds at the slightest touch. But sesame's history stretches back even farther.

---

[23] *The Book of Spices*, 354.

White Sesame seeds

Ancient Assyrians wrote of sesame on stone tablets, some of which are among the oldest written records known today. The tablets tell of gods drinking sesame wine on the night before they created the Earth. Sesame production began at least as early as 1600 BC, when it was cultivated along the Tigris and Euphrates rivers.[24] Sesame seeds were used to make wine and sesame oil, both of which seem to predate using sesame seed as a spice.

It is still used most in countries where it has a long history, being common in Arabic, Egyptian, East African, Chinese, Korean, Lebanese, and especially Indian and Japanese cuisines. Much of the world's crop goes into oil production, which is pervasive in Japan and China. Tahini, a sauce made from an emulsion of ground sesame seed, is popular in much of the world, notably as a base for halva confections.

Sesame seeds are mixed into or sprinkled onto all kinds of bread: loaves, rolls, bagels, crackers, biscuits, and cakes. In the United States, millions of sesame seeds are applied to the hamburger buns served in fast-food restaurants. India uses sesame seeds on baked goods too, and also in some rice pilaf dishes and the sweet *tilkuta* (or *til kuta* or *tilkatri*). In Japan, they're added to rice, tofu, and sauces, or toasted and mixed with salt for the *gomashio* condiment. Sesame seeds are often added to health food products, as the seed has good fatty acids, antioxidants, and protein.

Toasting sesame seeds brings out their richest, nuttiest flavor. If you're using sesame seeds on top of breads or other baked goods, though, the baking process does the toasting for you. To toast sesame seeds, simply add them to a pan, no oil, over

---

[24] *The Book of Spices*, 394.

a low heat. Shake every few minutes. They'll start to brown around the 5-minute mark, but they're so small that they burn easily, so keep a close watch. As with cumin, I wouldn't eat plain sesame seeds but I'll happily snack on toasted ones.

BLACK SESAME SEEDS

Black sesame seeds taste much like white sesame, though the black ones are slightly crunchier. I roast black and white together, since it's easier to see when the white seeds start to brown or burn. A mixture of black and white sesame seeds adds a nice crunch and texture to fish; adding them to an everything bagel or seed bread adds another layer of flavor. Black sesame seeds are called for alone in some Asian dishes, especially in Japan.

BROWN SESAME SEEDS

Oftentimes, *brown* or *golden* sesame seeds are simply toasted white sesame seeds, but a growing trend in health food stores is to sell unhulled sesame seeds, which are naturally light brown in color. Proponents claim there is more nutrition in the extra material of the hull. Unhulled sesame seeds are also called *whole sesame seed* (which is as redundant as *corn on the cob*).

OPEN SESAME PIE

The Pillsbury Bake-Off, a precursor to *The Great British Bake-Off*, started in 1949 to promote its Best Flour product.[25] Pillsbury staff sifted through thousands of recipes, inviting the writers of the top 100 to bake their recipes in front of a live audience. In 1955, the winning recipe was Open Sesame Pie. According to Pillsbury, there were sesame seed shortages soon after because so many people wanted to make the recipe.[26] Many spice companies began selling sesame seeds for the first time, bakers featured them more prominently in their breads, and their use in hamburger buns increased. Within five years, sesame seed imports to the US had doubled.[27]

---

[25] And the Pillsbury Bake-Off is the reason *The Great British Bake-Off* becomes *The Great British Cooking Show* when in the US; Pillsbury called copyright dibs on "Bake-Off."
[26] "History of the Pillsbury Bake-Off Contest," Pillsbury.com.
[27] "What You Should Know About Sesame Seeds," American Spice Trade Association.

Za'atar

Like fashion, food trends come in and out of style, the popularity of certain spices ebbing and flowing with the times. When the ban was lifted on imports from mainland China in the early '70s, star anise must certainly have seemed exotic to the American cook. The world has become smaller since then, with people and their foods crossing borders and bringing with them new flavors that get adopted, or co-opted, into other cultures.

Thus, I was not surprised to see *za'atar* listed among the other contextless foods at a trendy new restaurant in Chicago (the wait was long, the decor Spartan, and the menu items condensed past the point of clarity). The past few years have seen the seasoning branch out from Middle Eastern restaurants and land in the kitchens of chefs who set national food trends. But I *was* a bit surprised to see it had made its way into a pale ale craft beer at a Chicago brewery. Most of the beer descriptions were lengthy, more detailed than those for their food, but one was briefly noted: "brewed with za'atar spices." Too curious not to try it, I shelled out too much money for a beer and had a perfectly good, bland drink. Za'atar is wonderfully rich, but here it was just a gimmick.

Za'atar, in the United States, typically contains thyme, sesame seeds, and sumac. Sumac is an interestingly sour spice that, through za'atar, seems to be gaining traction in this country, with some restaurants using "za'atar spices" as a gateway to sumac.[1] In Middle Eastern countries, za'atar has been a staple for centuries; it is to some Middle Eastern countries what salt and pepper is to the United States: ubiquitous, required, reflexive. It's an all-purpose seasoning for meat and vegetable dishes, and often flavors hummus, *labaneh* (Greek yogurt), and eggs. Za'atar is prominent when seasoning breads like pita, or you can just mix it right into the dough for a hearty, flavorful loaf.

---

[1] You just do not need the word *spices* there. You don't.

THE COLUMBUSING OF SPICE

Having freshly appeared on culinary radars around the world, za'atar is also a lesson in the global appeal of spices and the unearned glory of Christopher Columbus. Inspired by the man whose search for spices led to European colonization of the Americas, the term *Columbusing* was recently coined to describe the phenomenon of a culture "discovering" something that has long existed in other cultures, which is a common occurrence when regional foods make their way to American table. The phenomenon isn't a problem in itself, but that the cultures for whom the food is traditional are too often erased in the new telling of the food. When food is specific to a place, it has a history and context that is ignored or even rewritten when appropriated this way. And so, two brief lessons in za'atar, the "it" spice of the moment.

First: While *za'atar* in this country mostly means a blend of spices, there's no strict recipe or ratios. Different variations of za'atar have existed across the Middle East for centuries. Similar to curries, it's a thoroughly American, modern phenomenon to merge all the diverse variations and varieties and reduce them down to just one restrictive definition. Americans know za'atar to contain sumac, thyme, and sesame seeds, but across Iraq, Syria, Saudi Arabia, Palestine, Jordan, Egypt, Morocco, and Turkey, the contents vary by region, ethnicity, and family, though they all contain a strong herbal element. There is no one single *za'atar*, just like there is no one single recipe for barbecue seasoning in the States. Za'atar frequently includes salt or cumin, for example, and other spices may be added to the basic blend as desired.

Second: *Za'atar* also refers to an herb. The word itself is the Arabic name for a family of related wild herbs used in cooking.[2] Rather than a specific herb, it refers to several varieties of oregano, thyme, and savory that grow wild or are cultivated in small plots and gardens. Based on translations by several prominent Jewish scholars, the name most properly applies to *bible hyssop*.[3] The za'atar herbs of Middle Eastern countries are not necessarily the same as the thyme or oregano produced in mass quantities and used in the US; these herbs are usually similar, but not grown in high enough quantities to be exported, so the generally available oregano is used in our blends.

---

[2] *The Oxford Companion to Food*, 863.
[3] Also called *Lebanese oregano* or *Syrian oregano*. It should not be confused with *Persian hyssop* (*Spanish oregano*) or *hyssop*, just.

Sumac, dried & ground

SUMAC

Sumac is the fruit of the sumac plant, dried and coarsely ground. It's unique for its tartness, bringing a sour and lemony tang wherever it's used. Sumac is also vastly underrated for its salt-like properties of bringing out the flavor in food. Its deep red color makes it attractive, too. It adds a pop of flavor and appeal to hummus and baba ghanoush. Sumac grows natively across Africa, East Asia, and North America, and is widely used in Middle Eastern cuisine, being especially popular in Palestine, where it's featured in the national dish, *musakhan*.

Foragers like to seek out sumac growing in the wild, but a bit of caution is required. In the Western United States, a species of poisonous sumac covers itself with a resin that gives passersby an irritating rash, and locals are careful not to burn it, as the resin can be deadly if inhaled. Native Americans were the first to identify nonpoisonous varieties of sumac that can be made into a sour but nutritious drink.[4] When lemon is added, some lazily call it "sumac-ade."

Sumac can be added to chicken and fish to bring a Mideastern flair. It pairs wonderfully with feta cheese and olive oil to dip bread in. You can use sumac instead of lemon in most recipes, which is what ancient Romans did before they were introduced to lemons.

---

[4] *The Burns Philp Book of Spices*, 55.

Garlic, Onion, Shallot & Chives

O f all the superstitious spices, garlic takes the (odiferous) cake. It's one of the best weapons against vampires, though it's not just about consuming massive quantities. In Transylvania, the birthplace of Dracula, garlic is the best way to sniff out a vampire: Anyone who doesn't enjoy garlic is immediately suspected to be undead. Not only can garlic reveal the vampires among us, but it can also be used to keep them away. As vampires can take many shapes, including snakes, bats, and vapor, garlic must be rubbed on keyholes, windows, and doors.[1] Even farm animals are not safe and must be garlicked up. Sheep seem especially susceptible and should therefore be well-rubbed.

Garlic was believed to safeguard you against many forms of death, including sickness, sorcery, and specters. In Eastern Europe's Middle Ages, poor health was sometimes thought to be the result of a bad spirit invading the body,[2] which garlic could ward off. Odysseus drank a brew of wild garlic to protect himself from Circe's enchantments,[3] and ancient Greeks offered it to Hecate, the goddess of magic.[4] Garlic was found preserved in the tomb of King Tutankhamen, possibly to protect him on his journey into the afterlife. It was eaten by the Egyptian slaves who built the tomb, too, perhaps to keep them alive long enough to complete the project.[5]

The protection afforded by garlic also linked it to a bolstering of courage, making it a good meal for soldiers. "Now bolt down these cloves of garlic," wrote the playwright Aristophanes in Ancient Greece. "Well primed with garlic you will have greater mettle for the fight." In his *Lysistrata*, the wives who seek to end the war promise not only to withhold sex from their husbands, but garlic, too: "Now just

Garlic, granulated & powdered

---

[1] *In Search of Dracula*, 120.

[2] *The Fanatic's Ecstatic Aromatic Guide to Onions, Garlic, Shallots and Leeks*, 59.

[3] *Odyssey.*

[4] *Glorious Garlic*, 8.

[5] *Chicago Tribune*, "Beer, Garlic Stoked Labor of Pyramids."

you dare to measure strength with me, old greybeard," the chorus of women sing to the old men, "and I warrant you you'll never eat garlic any more."

But garlic's popularity among soldiers and common folk drew the ire of the wealthy. When Don Quixote became governor, he warned Sancho Panza to stop eating garlic and onion, "for their smell will reveal that you are a peasant." As usual, Miguel de Cervantes' quip exposed a truth about the period he was writing in. Disdain for garlic by the upper classes stretches all the way back to Rome, whose nobility understood garlic and its consumption to be a sign of vulgarity.[6]

THE ALLIUM FAMILY

Is garlic a spice? *Allium* is the genus that includes garlic, onion, leek, shallot, scallion, and chive, and its members are often categorized as their own entity, one that may share counter space with spices but is closer to herbs in status.[7] Humble alliums are designated as non-spices by the aristocratic types who subscribe to the idea that being abundant or inexpensive is synonymous with being unworthy. Yet, garlic is one of the world's most popular flavors, and onions and shallots are the backbone of many a dish, the working class of the spice rack. For all the hard work these odoriferous bulbs do, their virtues are little celebrated, their contributions overshadowed by flashier ingredients. But woe betide the cook who doesn't appreciate the allium, for showing them a little respect will get you far in the kitchen.

Like herbs, alliums are used fresh and dried, though they're often referred to instead as *dehydrated*. For every use of the fresh plant, there's a use for the dried. Much like herbs, having dried onion and garlic on hand is essential.[8] You can even use both fresh and dried in the same meal, since the dried stuff carries a slightly different,

---

[6] *The Book of Spices*, 311.

[7] Even their names are related: Middle English *garlek* came from Old English *gārlēac*, built from the roots *gār* (spear) + *lēac* (leek). Garlic is a *leek spear*, but not a root (bulbs are technically stems).

[8] It's also an option for picky eaters who say they don't like onion in their foods—dried onion, spread throughout the dish, won't have any bits for the picky eater to pick out, and you still get the necessary onion flavoring.

Alliums: onion, garlic, shallot, leek

sometimes toastier flavor than the fresh. The greens of most alliums are also used as a foodstuff, usually picked while still immature, and contribute a milder version of the same flavor. Garlic, onion, leek, chives, and shallot are all alliums dried out and added to the spice rack.

GARLIC

If I had to choose three spices to have with me on a deserted island, I'd choose salt, pepper, and garlic. This triumvirate can season a huge array of meals by themselves, and they often do so in my kitchen. Garlic transforms eggs from bland to delectable, adds zing to vegetables, and brings extra interest and complexity to chicken and fish. Most of my favorite blends contain these three spices as a base, with additional spices to round out the flavor. It's rare for a savory dish to not be improved by the addition of garlic.

Garlic is familiar across the culinary spectrum. There's a whole showcase for it in garlic bread; it's a common starter in sauces, soups, and salad dressings; it's added to meat products and cheese to boost the flavor; many spice blends include granulated garlic. Garlic provides both a strong base on which to add other flavors and, when needed, can be called upon to provide the dominant flavor in a dish.

Garlic comes in more varieties than other alliums, ranging from powdered and granulated to dehydrated pieces in little and slightly larger pieces. Large chunks of dehydrated garlic are a good option for dishes that have leisurely cooking times, like sauces that will simmer for a while on the stove, soups and stews, and anything made in a slow cooker. Garlic lovers find an accomplice in these larger pieces of garlic. The smaller, minced dehydrated garlic is better for quickly made sauces, because it rehydrates faster and isn't as noticeable in your food (if that concerns you). But mouthfeel can be the point of garlic pieces in the first place.

Granulated and powdered garlic are what's called for when you simply want garlic flavor. Like sugar, powdered garlic is ground very fine, while granulated is a coarser consistency. Granulated is the standard, and even if a recipe calls for powdered garlic, granulated may be used. One-eighth of a teaspoon of granulated garlic is roughly equivalent to a medium-sized clove of garlic; one-half tablespoon is roughly equivalent to a whole bulb.

A general rule applies to all the above dehydrated garlics: the garlic flavor is only activated when it comes into contact with liquid. In the majority of cases this is never an issue, but if you're, say, wanting to add some garlic flavor to a salad that doesn't have dressing, you can reconstitute garlic in water. The amount of water should be equal to the amount of garlic. Let it sit for about 15 minutes, and then add to your dry dish.

You can grind dehydrated garlic, onion, and shallot pieces in a pepper grinder to make a seasoning.

BLACK GARLIC

Black garlic is a relatively recent addition to my spice rack (though I keep it in the fridge), but has been a staple in parts of Asia, especially the Korean peninsula, for a long time. Through a fermentation-like process, ordinary garlic is aged in a temperature-controlled environment for several weeks, allowing microbial reactions (the Maillard reaction) to take place. The sharp edge of garlic is softened as it caramelizes, fruity notes appear, and a chewy texture emerges. Black garlic cannot be used in place of white garlic, as its flavor is drastically different and much less potent. I like to combine white and black garlic with some simple sautéed vegetables.

GARLIC BREATH

Sith garlic then hath poure to save from death
Bear with it though it make unsavoure breathe.
—Robert of Normandy, 1100 AD

I have little patience for people concerned about the state of their breath after consuming members of the allium family—what point is there to eating enjoyably if you're more concerned with the status of your breath than the satisfaction of your stomach? A little garlic breath is well worth the price of admission to a garlic-forward meal. Besides, there are plenty of spices that naturally sweeten the breath—when you return your garlic to the spice rack, look no further for the cure. Fennel seeds, sometimes covered in candy, are familiar to people who frequent Indian restaurants. Mint and cardamom seeds also freshen the breath.

Garlic on your hands is another matter. Even after washing, the garlic odor persists on skin—and garlic odor out of the context of the garlicy meal isn't all that enjoyable. I recommend two methods that always work: lemon or fresh parsley. With a lemon, I simply squeeze the juice over my hands, rub them together for about a minute, focusing on getting the lemon juice to cover all the surface area of the skin on my hands, then rinse. The garlic smell will be gone. This method's downside is that if you have even one cut on your hand or, God forbid, a hangnail, the lemon juice is going to give you a terrific sting.

In this case, use fresh parsley. Roughly chop it and do your best to spread it all over your hands. You can also chew parsley to mask garlic breath. Since both lemons and parsley are fairly common mealtime ingredients, it's usually easy to save a little of one or the other to deal with that pesky garlic hand problem.

If you don't have either, one last solution is a salt paste. You should always have salt in your kitchen (if you don't, that's a more serious problem). Pour a generous amount of salt (two tablespoons or so) into a small bowl or ramekin, and add water, mixing with your finger, until a paste forms. Rub this paste all over your hands. Like the lemon method, this will not feel good if you have any cuts on your hands. But it'll work.[9]

WHAT'S BAD FOR DRACULA IS GOOD FOR YOU

For those of us who aren't Dracula (we who go out in the sunshine and see our reflections), garlic is a good thing. It's been used medicinally for as long as we've been eating it: Ancient Egyptians reached for garlic as a cure for headaches, tumors, and heart problems in 1500 BC and Dioscorides, the Greek physician living in the first century BC, prescribed garlic for internal diseases. A few hundred years later, in the second century AD, the Roman physician Galen went from prescribing garlic cures for certain ailments to recommending it as a cure-all *and* an antidote to poison. Pliny believed it to cure dozens of issues, from ulcers to asthma.[10] Alexandre Dumas wrote that "the air of Provence is saturated with garlic, which makes it very healthful."[11] The garlic variety that grows in the Americas is made into a tea by some tribes and is thought to have been used as a headache cure.[12]

Today, garlic is considered to be one of the best foods for disease prevention. One study (from Italy, unsurprisingly) shows garlic hurts some of the "bad" bacteria in our stomachs, allowing the good freer rein to grow.[13] The *allicin* compound, which is responsible for the garlic aroma, has been studied for its antifungal, antibacterial potential. While garlic pills are touted to prevent everything from the common cold to cancer, a meta-analysis from 2016 reviewed the available data and concluded that there are some "promising" results in these studies, but more work must be done to demonstrate the actual efficacy of allicin.[14]

---

[9] Yes, I've heard of and tried the stainless-steel method. This theory posits that rubbing your hands on stainless steel will get rid of the garlic smell, and there's even a small but steady cottage industry selling lumps of stainless steel for this sole purpose, as if your sink faucet wouldn't do the exact same thing. The truth: the stainless-steel method does not work.

[10] *Glorious Garlic*, 6.

[11] *Dictionary of Cuisine*, 129.

[12] *Glorious Garlic*, 6.

[13] "Effect of garlic powder on the growth of commensal bacteria from the gastrointestinal tract," *Phytomedicine*.

[14] Marchese, Anna, et al. "Antifungal and antibacterial activities of allicin: A review." *Trends in Food Science & Technology*.

It's never a bad thing to consume more spices, vegetables, and nonprocessed foods in general. Science may just be catching up with what people have long known about garlic. Or maybe it's all a placebo effect, and garlic is just a tasty, strong food that's been worked into traditional medicine exactly because its strong odor seems medicinal. I'm never convinced that eating foods out of their natural contexts is all that effective, so I opt to eat fresh and dried garlic on foods, instead of in pill form. At the very least, garlic generally isn't bad for you[15]; at its best, science may one day demonstrate its benefits.

SHALLOT

Freeze-dried shallot is seriously underrated. It's an even more efficient culinary shortcut than dried onion and garlic because freeze-dried shallot can be substituted for fresh shallot without losing the distinctive sweetness. Like other dried alliums, if you're not cooking freeze-dried shallots in a liquid, they should be reconstituted in equal parts water—or equal parts red wine, which complements shallot's unique flavor.

The difference between freeze-dried and dehydrated: Freeze-dried foods have nearly all the moisture removed (up to 99 percent), while dehydrated foods have around 90 percent of moisture removed. The more moisture that's removed, the longer foods last without going bad, which translates to freeze-dried foods lasting longer than dehydrated.

---

[15] Unless, of course, your doctor tells you specifically otherwise.

Shallot, freeze-dried

ONION

Dried onion—whether minced, chopped, ground, or granulated—is a shortcut to add onion flavor without the labor of peeling, chopping, and cooking onions. It's most useful in sauces, and is the obvious choice for adding onion flavor to dips. Onions that are grown to be dehydrated are different than the ones you buy at the supermarket to use fresh; ones destined to lose their moisture have less moisture to begin with and are bred to be consistently pungent and white throughout, to produce a consistent color once dried.

Dehydrated onion can be used in place of fresh onion, and you won't cry when you use it, either. Toasted granulated onion somewhat replicates a sautéed onion flavor. Like garlic, powdered and granulated onion should be rehydrated if they're being used in a dish with no liquid. One-half teaspoon of onion powder is the rough equivalent of a quarter-cup of minced onion.

CHIVES

It seems most people know of chives only through their association with loaded potato skins, where they accompany cheddar cheese, bacon, and sour cream. With a milder flavor than onion and garlic, the chive is a little brother of the allium family, giving a fresh, bright, earthy flavor wherever it falls. It pairs well with sour cream, as featured on the potato skins, and also mixed in butter, in scrambled eggs and omelets, and as a garnish on cheesy pasta dishes and on top of soups.

Chives, dried

Like the rest of the allium family, fresh chives are good but dried are useful when kept in the spice rack, to shake on as a garnish and add for a bright pop of green color and flavor. Chives are not as widely available as other alliums and herbs in supermarkets, making dried chives especially necessary to keep on hand.

Turmeric

If you're consuming any spice in pill form these days, there's a good chance it's turmeric. It hit co-op groceries and alternative health aisles around 2013, when it gained popularity as the next "superfood." If you weren't familiar with the bright orange spice already, you likely are now, seeing it widely available in pills, kombucha, and health food juices/smoothies. You may not know what the problem is, a friend recently observed, but the solution seems to be turmeric.

While more research is needed, there's some evidence that turmeric's active agent, *curcumin*, does offer health benefits, though the current fanaticism for turmeric is based on anecdotal evidence, at best.[1] Studies done on curcuminoids suggest they may "reduce the number of heart attacks bypass patients had after surgery," "control knee pain from osteoarthritis as well as ibuprofen," and "reduce the skin irritation that often occurs after radiation treatments for breast cancer."[2] Perhaps science will eventually demonstrate what many people claim to be true: turmeric improves indigestion; acts as an anti-inflammatory to alleviate joint pain and arthritis; and treats heart disease, ulcers, Alzheimer's, liver disorders, and cancer. It's become so popular that turmeric has emerged from health-food stores and specialty alternative medicines and into grocery stores and the mainstream. Even the woman at the pet food store suggested turmeric when my dog was ill.

Turmeric *is* good. It is tasty and nutritious. But it isn't a panacea. Even if it doesn't improve the full range of maladies hypothesized, it's always a good idea to eat a range of plant life, spices included, for they obviously contain beneficial nutrients. In India, turmeric has long been used in Ayurvedic medicine and is still used to treat colds.[3] It's possible, and even likely, that turmeric does have demonstrable health

---

[1] This is according to the National Institutes of Health's turmeric analysis on the existing studies.

[2] The National Institutes of Health.

[3] "What you should know about Turmeric," American Spice Trade Association.

benefits. But I sort of shudder at the idea of packing a bunch of dried turmeric into a pill capsule and swallowing it. That feels like a gut bomb waiting to happen.

I also subscribe to food writer Michael Pollan's concept of nutrients within their context: isolating a nutrient and eating large quantities of that is never going to be as good as consuming it in its natural form. It's better to get vitamins from eating a variety of vegetables rather than taking a multivitamin pill and calling it a day. We can't replace eating actual vegetables.

Because the thing about turmeric is that, on its own, it's not a particularly pleasant spice. *Bitter* is the adjective most people use to describe turmeric, though it's also earthy, rooty, and somewhat peppery. It's a spice best used in conjunction with other spices, which helps explain why it's a key ingredient in many curries. I think it would be best if everyone got their turmeric in their food, melded with other spices in some sort of fat and protein, tasting and digesting it all together.

Furthermore, its bright golden color, which ranges along the yellow-orange spectrum, adds a pleasant hue to sauces. Marco Polo wrote in 1289 of turmeric: "There is also a vegetable which has all the properties of the true saffron, as well as the colour, and yet it is not really saffron. It is held in great estimation, and being an ingredient in all their dishes, it bears, on that account a high price." He exaggerates: Turmeric bears none of saffron's flavor, but it does bear its color.

For most of its history, turmeric has been used as a natural dye, one of the earliest known.[4] Today, it's come back into vogue as a natural, plant-based dye, used to give food, fabric, and even hair a yellow glow. Only a small amount is needed to turn foods a brilliant golden color. Turmeric brings a vivid yellow to mustard and also adds color to relish, chutneys, and pickling formulas. It's called upon to brighten deviled eggs and to add a golden hue to butter, margarine, and some cheeses.[5] It's also been passed off as a fake saffron, as Marco Polo alluded to in his writings. In the Middle Ages, it was sometimes called *Indian saffron* or *Eastern saffron*, which is extra confusing since that's exactly where actual saffron comes from, too.[6]

---

[4] *The Book of Spices*, 64.
[5] *The Complete Book of Herbs and Spices*, 256.
[6] *The Lore of Spices*, 150.

Like ginger, turmeric is a rhizome and not actually a root. It's harvested, boiled in water or an alkaline brine, then left in the hot sun or cooked to dry out. It grows in India, Thailand, and the Pacific Islands, though its true origin is unknown; it isn't found growing in the wild, but has been cultivated for more than 2,000 years in Assyria, China, and India.[7] Some evidence suggests it is native to Cochinchina, Vietnam.[8]

TYPES OF TURMERIC

There is Indian turmeric and the rest of it. India produces most of the world's turmeric, and most of it stays in India, as it's used there far more than anywhere else in the world, in curries and other foods. The two main types of turmeric are *Madras* and *Alleppy*.[9] Alleppy is the higher quality of the two, and it's this type that is mainly exported and used in the United States. It is overall stronger in flavor and a darker golden color, and the curcumin (the property of medical and health relevance, and also an indicator of the color) ranges from 2.5–5.5%, while Madras has only around 2%.[10] If you're looking to get any health benefits from turmeric, you need the level to be *at least* 5 percent.

---

[7] *The Complete Book of Herbs and Spices*, 255.

[8] *Spices*, 422.

[9] The American Spice Trade Association reports that there are some 30 different types of turmeric that grow in India, though only the Madra and Alleppy are "commercially significant."

[10] "What you should know about Turmeric," American Spice Trade Association.

Curry

Turmeric is a key spice in many curry powders, responsible for giving orange curries their color, especially chicken tikka masala, a staple curry in the United States. But tikka masala is just one of many curries; using it as shorthand to speak of the diverse world of curries would be like reducing all the pasta and pasta dishes down to angel-hair spaghetti with tomato sauce.

Like the definition for *spice*, the definition for *curry* is necessarily broad. A lot of Americans have a specific idea of what a curry is, based on the curries they've had. It's a word that doesn't have a strict definition, but can mean any of thousands of spiced meat or vegetable dishes, or can refer to the mix of spices that goes into those dishes. *Curry* is a catchall term, as vague as the word *sauce*. Merriam-Webster defines it as "a food, dish, or sauce in Indian cuisine seasoned with a mixture of pungent spices; also: a food or dish seasoned with curry powder."

Indian curry mixes contain anywhere from a handful to a few dozen spices and are known by more specific names: rogan josh, garam masala, vindaloo, and korma, to name a few familiar to those who frequent Indian restaurants. In America, most curry powders contain a core set of spices, including cumin, turmeric, coriander, fenugreek, and chili peppers. Premixed curry powders were not traditionally used in India, where people mix their own spices (often roasting them whole and then grinding by hand) and this offers greater opportunity to adjust and improvise.

Making curries this way at home reveals a truth about spices: the sum of their combination is frequently greater than the flavors of each individual spice. Turmeric, ginger, and cayenne are three flavors that can be dominating or overwhelming on their own. But their flavors meld and improve in conjunction with other spices, brought together through heat and fats.[1] Contrasting flavors make a dish more complex, and more delicious.

---

[1] This is the opposite of many dishes in America, where a single ingredient or flavor is highlighted in a dish: dill on salmon, cinnamon on apples, etc.

The curry philosophy is a good one, and should be applied to cooking beyond a homemade curry, to any dish you season with spices. Foods like chicken, potatoes, and oatmeal—blank slate foods—are excellent for adding numerous spices to. My mom calls this philosophy her "Himalayan mountain range" style of cooking. In cooking a curry-type dish, for example, cayenne pepper is Mount Everest. Its heat is big and bold and stands above the rest. But it's only a single peak in a vast mountain range, and ginger is a large neighboring mountain, cumin is a little ways off, and so on, with all the peaks and valleys coming together to form the Himalayas, or the great, complicated flavors of a curry. Under this paradigm, "Is turmeric a good flavor?" is the wrong question to ask. A better one is "What other flavors will turmeric work well with?" Turmeric is an earthy, root-like flavor that tastes bitter and astringent on its own, but adds a unique, necessary component to flavor medleys. Curries can include ginger, cayenne, cloves, cardamom, cinnamon, mace, saffron, galangal, tamarind, peppercorns, chilis, caraway, aniseed, fennel, fenugreek, celery seed, mace, asafoetida, mustard, poppy seeds, sesame seeds, mint leaves, mustard seed, and curry leaves.[2]

SOME THOUGHTS TO CURRY FAVOR

Roasting whole spices is an excellent way to bring out even more of their flavor and add a rich, nutty aspect to your dish. The first step of making a truly great curry should involve roasting whole cumin, coriander seed, and fenugreek, and then grinding them and adding them to your other spices.

If you make a large batch, bottle the extra seasoning and save it for next time, because it is a labor-intensive process. It's a weekend activity. On weeknights, I use premade curry powders, and the appeal and time-saving aspect of using them is undeniable.

Tempering is important to bring out the flavors of the spices and bind them together. In tempering, the spices are sautéed in oil, butter, ghee, or an animal fat. At this stage, onions and garlic are often added to the fat as well.

---

[2] Curry leaves come from the curry leaf tree (*Murraya koenigii*) and are named after their use in curries, though they are prominent in other Indian and Sri Lankan dishes, too. The aromatic leaves are used fresh, as drying diminishes their flavor.

Hot chili peppers will get hotter the longer they cook. Capsicum peppers, like jalapeño, and their dried forms, like cayenne pepper, increase in heat the longer they're stewed. This typically isn't an issue in quickly cooked meals, but if a curry is simmered for hours, the heat levels will grow. This is especially important to keep in mind if you're doubling or tripling a recipe, as doubling or tripling the amount of hot peppers will create a dish far hotter than it's supposed to be. A dish like vindaloo, already hot to begin with, will be inedible if the hot peppers are tripled along with the rest of the recipe.

Hot curries are traditionally served with breads and lassi, and for good reason. Most people know that drinking water doesn't alleviate a burning mouth. Rice and a regional bread, like papadan, chapati (roti), parota, and the ubiquitous naan help cut the heat and cool your mouth between forkfuls of fiery food. Lassi, the cooling yogurt drink popular in India, is especially helpful for this: the widely available mango variety adds a sweet, cooling flavor.

You *can* build up a resistance to hot foods. Like any other food, you can slowly build up tolerance to heat and learn to enjoy spicy curries. Children are taught to like hot foods by starting out with softer, spicier flavors like cinnamon and ginger, to which hotter spices and foods are slowly added until it's just part of their palate. Adults can learn this too.

ASAFOETIDA

Asafoetida is known for its overwhelmingly strong sulfur odor when in raw powdered form, but when it's cooked down it mellows out into a very pleasant onion/leek-esque smell. It's also called *hing*, *jowani badian*, *ingu*, and, less politely, *devil's dung*. The name *asafoetida* is derived from the Persian word *aza*, their name for mastic resin, and the Latin word *foetida*, as in *stinking*.[3]

The substance comes from a species of giant fennel. The plant produces a gummy resin that can be dried into a form also called *asafoetida lump*. It's also available in paste and powdered forms. If powdered, it most likely contains extra substances to

---

[3] *The Oxford Companion to Food*, 37.

prevent lumping, often just wood ash. Some brands add other components simply to reduce the noxious odor that can be overwhelming in this form, especially in that first moment when the cap is undone but before it's melded into the dish. If your asafoetida is orangish in color, it likely has turmeric in it.

Asafoetida was used medicinally and culinarily in Ancient Rome and Greece. The Roman gourmand Apicius writes of an ingenious way to use and elongate the life of asafoetida by keeping a piece in a jar with pine nuts, which absorb the flavor; using those pine nuts in a dish imparts the asafoetida to the foods.[4] Asafoetida is primarily used in Jain cuisine, a religious tradition in India (though with small numbers elsewhere) that prescribes a vegetarian diet, sometimes including no root foods such as garlic or onion.[5]

Asafoetida substitutes for roots in vegetable dishes, adding an umami element of depth and deliciousness. It's typically added in the tempering stage of making a curry—mixing in the spices with the fat, be that butter, ghee, oil, or animal fat. Always be cautious when adding asafoetida to a dish: too much will overwhelm the food with its odor.

CURRY GETS AROUND

Curry's popularity outside of India is a lesson in the history of colonialism, a journey of traditional diets crossing borders, and a demonstration of the appeal a certain culture's food can have across oceans. The spice blend, dish, and catchall name most likely originate in Southern India, according to Colleen Taylor Sen, a food historian and author of *Curry: A Global History*. On the word:

> It probably derives from southern Indian languages, where *karil* or *kari* denoted a spiced dish of sautéed vegetables and meat. In the early seventeenth century, the Portuguese used the word *caril* or *caree* to describe broths "made with butter, the pulp of Indian nuts . . . and all sorts of spices, particularly Cardamoms and ginger . . . besides herbs, fruits and a thousand

---

[4] *The Oxford Companion to Food*, 37.
[5] Bulbs are not actually roots; bulbs are stems, though they do grow underground.

other condiments . . . poured in good quality . . . upon boiled rice." In English, *caril* became curry, which Hobson-Jobson, the great dictionary of nineteenth-century British-Indian English, describes as "meat, fish, fruit or vegetables, cooked with a quantity of bruised spices and turmeric, and a little of this give a flavor to a large mess of rice."[6]

Chicken tikka masala was called a "true British national dish" by the British Foreign Secretary in 2001[7] and, in the US, Indian and Thai curries are popular and regularly eaten dishes. In Germany, a ubiquitous street food is the currywurst: roasted pork sausage, onions, and green peppers, spread with ketchup and heavily seasoned with curry powder. In 2011, it was estimated that Germans ate 800 million currywursts per year.[8]

This influence worked the other way around, too, as foreigners who invaded India imparted their own traditional dishes onto the Indian curries. The best example of this is vindaloo, a fusion of Portuguese and Indian tastes: the name comes from the Portuguese words for wine (*vinho*) and garlic (*alhos*), and the dish combines European flavors with the Indian spices. In the US vindaloo on Indian restaurant menus is often accompanied by several chili pepper icons, signaling a warning to the patron: this dish is very hot. That's thanks to the Portuguese and their stint as the main movers of spice around the globe, which brought the spicier chili peppers to India, where they were quickly incorporated into the already spicy dishes.

---

[6] *Curry*, 10.

[7] "Chicken tikka masala is now a true British national dish," said Robin Cook, "not only because it is the most popular, but because it is a perfect illustration of the way Britain absorbs and adapts external influences. Chicken Tikka is an Indian dish. The Masala sauce was added to satisfy the desire of British people to have their meat served in gravy." ("Robin Cook's chicken tikka masala speech," *The Guardian*.)

[8] "Germany loves its currywurst—contradictions, calories and all." *The Seattle Times*.

Paprika & Cayenne

For a long time, the spice trade went more or less one way: out of India, China, and the Spice Islands in modern-day Indonesia, toward Europe. Then those same spices fueled the age of discovery, that seafaring era when Europeans set sail to discover a new path to the fragrant, faraway spice ports and instead stumbled on an entirely different land, with entirely different spices. Vanilla and allspice made their way back to Europe with these explorers, desperate to show their efforts were worth something in the end. But no New World spices made as much impact on the rest of the world as capsicums.

They quickly became ubiquitous in diets around the world, from spicy Indian curries and African sauces to the ones found on Vietnamese banh mi sandwiches and chili sauces in Japanese ramen. So thoroughly did these New World species get adopted into new homes and worldly cuisines that people forgot, if they ever knew to begin with, that the plants are native to Central and South America. Owing to their heat, capsicums were called *pepper* by many, a legacy that remains today, with English-speakers calling them *hot peppers* or *chili peppers*. The genus name *Capsicum* is the simplest way to distinguish this versatile group, though it's not a term in general culinary use.[1]

The *capsicum* family (fleshy, seeded peppers) is far cheaper and easier to grow than *piper* (peppercorn) and brings more heat. For thousands of years, peppercorn had no equal, but with the tireless march of capsicums around the globe, it had met its match.

PAPRIKA

There's perhaps no better example of this than paprika, the spice that is now practically synonymous with Hungary and its national cuisine. While numerous spices

---

[1] The word *capsicum* possibly comes from the Greek work *kapto*, "to bite," referring to the hot "bite" on the tongue. It might also come from the Latin *caspa*, meaning "container-like" and referring to the shape of the ovular and round fruits. *Top 100 Food Plants*, 158.

can be traced to antiquity, paprika didn't appear in Hungarian kitchens until the 17th century. Overlooked by Columbus while on his quest for peppercorn, cinnamon, and cloves, the hot capsicum plants were first noted by Columbus' ship's doctor, Chanca, who called them *Indian peppers*,[2] beginning a linguistic legacy of both calling anything spicy a "pepper" and calling New World plants "Indian," as they still thought they might have hit upon part of the subcontinent.

The European colonizers returned without the spices they sought, but carried pretty red capsicum fruits home as decoration. It wasn't until the late 16th century that capsicum was mentioned as a spice by Margit Széchy, referring to them as a red *Turkish pepper*.[3] It seems that the plant came to Portugal and Spain, brought from Mexico by the conquistadors, before spreading to Greece and the Balkan Peninsula. The Greeks called it *peperi*, which was already their name for peppercorns, following and reifying the confusing naming convention.[4] Turks and Bulgarians began to cultivate the capsicum plants, and the word morphed into *paparka*. When the Turks conquered Hungary in the mid-1500s, Bulgarian farmers settled there and cultivated the capsicum.[5] At last, the New World pepper had found a home in Hungary, where it was adopted, cultivated, and—over the course of the next 500 years—transformed into the highlight of their national cuisine under the name *paprika*.[6]

TYPES OF PAPRIKA

Capsicum peppers were able to proliferate around the globe because they grow in temperate climates, and because they can adapt to thrive practically everywhere. In the case of paprika, growers were even able to make the once-spicy pepper much more mild to suit unfamiliar palates. Demand for a milder spice led Hungary to cultivate a sweet paprika in addition to the standard *sharp*, or spicy, variety.

---

[2] *The Lore of Spices*, 174; *The Home Garden Book of Herbs and Spices*, 150.

[3] *Gourmet*, "Paprika," 45.

[4] Though it isn't only Greece's fault. Most everywhere in the world, when a new spicy condiment was added to the diet, it was called pepper or some derivation thereof.

[5] *Paprika Through the Ages*, 24.

[6] *Paprika Through the Ages*, 24.

Today, paprika, itself a subcategory of capsicums, is produced in even more varieties: sweet, smoked, half-sharp, and sharp paprikas from Hungary, with additional strains and styles produced in Spain and California.[7] *Sharp* simply means *hot* or *spicy*, while *half-sharp* denotes somewhat, but not terribly, spicy. *Sweet* means it has no heat, and smoked is self-explanatory: the capsicums, usually the sweet variety but sometimes a mix, are smoked as they dry, which imparts the ground paprika with a delicious smokiness.

WHICH, WHEN, AND HOW

I adore smoked paprika, and typically mix sweet and sharp or half-sharp together, depending on how much heat I desire. Besides using it in goulash-type stews, I like a mixed-style paprika on roasted chickpeas, lentil dishes, and on chicken, and smoked paprika in eggs. My spice-heavy recipe for mac and cheese uses paprika liberally, which also gives the casserole a wonderfully deep orange color. Paprika's naturally bright color can be used just for garnish, too: one of my favorite cookbooks from the '60s makes constant use of sweet paprika as a finishing spice, dusted over pale dishes like chicken and fish to impart a bright, beautiful red color.

Like curry, paprika should be tempered into a dish. My grandfather wrote of testing new paprika imports by adding each paprika to a pan of frying onions and lard, a traditional Hungarian preparation. It's important to remove the pan from the heat before adding the paprika, to keep it from burning.[8] Most home cooks in the US don't use lard; butter or oil is more typical. When tempering spices like paprika, the cooking fat should be hot but not smoking, or you'll burn the spice. Hungarian cuisine also incorporates paprika into *roux*, a lard-flour combination used to thicken sauces and goulash.[9]

---

[7] The most common cultivar used is "tomato pepper," which is only adding to the naming confusion. But tomatoes are in the nightshade family, as are all capsicums.

[8] *Gourmet*, "Paprika," 46.

[9] *Paprika Through the Ages*, 127.

Cayenne pepper

CAYENNE

Cayenne is another product made from various species within the *Capsicum* genus. The fiery red cayenne spice isn't sourced from one particular species, but rather from a variety of the small, extremely hot capsicums which range from yellow to red in color. In the past, cayenne came in different shades, from light orange to red to brown, but today the product has become more standardized, with the name *cayenne pepper* referring to a bright red spice that sits around 40,000 Scoville heat units[10]. In other words, what makes cayenne *cayenne* is the end result, not necessarily the specifics of the products going into it. To get the desired color and heat, cayenne is necessarily a blend of hot capsicums.

Cayenne is very hot, but it also imparts a unique flavor that goes beyond purely spicy. Still, little goes a long way. Like paprika, it's best to add cayenne to the fats in a dish, but cayenne gets hotter the longer it cooks, so be wary that a little used at the beginning of the dish will be amplified by the time it's done. I often add cayenne to take-out curry, if the "medium" hotness has barely a hint of heat or the "hot" just isn't hot enough. Similarly, a few shakes added to a vegetable recipe, along with a pinch of cumin, adds a pungency that enlivens even the most basic of dishes.

The capsicums used to make cayenne are not grown in Cayenne, the capital of French Guiana (in South America). There's confusion and speculation around how the spice got its name. One source stipulates that the word *cayenne* comes from the

---

[10] For details on Scoville units, see the chapter on chilis.

Tupi, an Indigenous people from what's now modern-day Brazil, whose term for the local "hot pepper" was *quiínia*. Europeans mistakenly associated the capsicum with a geographical spot on the northern coast of French Guiana and called it Cayenne.[11] In other words, the municipality was named after the capsicum, and not the other way around.

CRUSHED RED PEPPER

Crushed red pepper—also known and flake peppers and the kind you put on pizza—adds a pleasant heat to foods both during meal preparation and at the table. It's typically made from cayenne pepper varieties, but may include others to adjust the flavor or heat. It's a staple in Italian restaurants and pizza parlors, providing a medium-hot bite. Crushed red peppers are visually recognizable, with both the dried seeds of capsicums and the thin red shavings of the dried flesh. In addition to pizza, crushed red peppers are an excellent addition to vegetables and pastas that needs a pick-me-up, and can add zing to salads, stir-frys, and eggs.

---

[11] Top 100 Food Plants, 157.

Chilis

There are many more capsicums, and these fall under the umbrella of *chilis* or *chili peppers*. Chilis are typically considered spices when they're dried, after which they're usually shaved, ground, or powdered. In some cases, they were brought from the Americas and transplanted in Europe, Asia, and Africa, where their taste was altered as the plants adapted to new regions, climates, and soils. Five hundred years after their spread around the world, there are dozens of varieties of capsicums we know as chili peppers. Some, like banana and bell peppers, are consumed primarily fresh (powdered bell pepper versions do exist, though they aren't very popular), while others are more recognizable in processed states like sauces (the case with tabasco peppers) or dried and pulverized (like hot pequin peppers).

SCOVILLE SCALE

A chili's spiciness is measured on the Scoville scale. A pharmacist named Wilbur Scoville refined his testing technique in 1912, which depended on trained testers to detect heat in a diluted sample. It was subjective; a decent barometer but not a rigorous method. Scientific accuracy arrived in the 1980s with liquid chromatography, a test that determines the pungency of the capsaicin compounds that are responsible for giving capsicums their kick. Those results are converted into Scoville units, keeping Wilbur's legacy alive, if not his technique.

A bell pepper has zero units on the Scoville scale while a jalapeño, one of the most common chili peppers in the United States, normally ranges from 2,000 to 8,000 Scoville heat units (SHU). However, growing conditions and selective breeding produce drastically different heat levels in what's technically the same pepper, with some jalapeños reaching as high as 460,000 SHU. You might be served a jalapeño salsa with a mild or medium heat one day, and then, the next time you have a dish with jalapeños in it, be surprised with how fiery spicy it is.

Chipotle Chilis, dried

Mild: 0–5,000 SHUs
> **Bell Peppers:** 0 SHUs
> **Pepperoncini:** 100–500 SHUs
> **Ancho:** 1,000–3,000 SHUs

Sort of hot: 5,000–10,000 SHUs
> **Guajillo:** 2,500–8,000 SHUs
> **Chipotle:** 5,000–10,000 SHUs
> **Jalapeño:** 2,500–8,000 SHUs

Yep, that's hot all right: 10,000–100,000 SHUs
> **Pequin:** 40,000–58,000 SHUs
> **Tabasco Sauce:** 30,000–50,000 SHUs
> **Cayenne:** 25,000–60,000 SHUs

Oh no, this might be too hot for me: 100,000–500,000 SHUs
> **Habanero:** 150,000–325,000 SHUs
> **Piri Piri:** 100,000–300,000 SHUs
> **Scotch Bonnet:** 200,000–400,000 SHUs

I've burned my taste buds off and might be dead: 500,000+ SHUs
> **Bhut Jolokia:** 1,000,000 SHUs
> **Carolina Reaper:** 1,560,000–2,200,000 SHUs
> **Pepper Spray:** 2,000,000–5,300,000 SHUs
> **Pure Capsaicin:** approx. 16,000,000 SHUs

A common misconception is that the heat of a capsicum is held in the seeds. That's not true at all. The heat is actually in the ribbing or veins of the capsicums, which are the yellow or white parts running along the inside of the fruit, where the seeds cling to the inner placenta. When recipes tell you to reduce or omit the seeds to reduce the heat level, they're depending on the cook to remove the veins along with the seeds; in that sense, the advice achieves what it intends. When paprika farmers in Hungary first developed a method to reduce the heat levels in their product, they deveined their capsicums to make it milder, and thus sweet paprika was born.[1]

------

[1] *Paprika Through the Ages*, 45.

Jalapeños demonstrate this well: If you carefully devein a jalapeño, the remaining green flesh won't be hot; in fact, virtually all of the heat is in the white parts.[2] Some of the new, genetically modified capsicums, however, defy this rule. Removing the veins from the *Moruga Scorpion*, *Trinidad Scorpion*, and *Bhut Jolokia* capsicums, known as "super-hot chilis," only seems to decrease the heat levels a little bit, with a substantial amount of fire left in the flesh. Researchers in 2015 found that these burning capsicums store 40–60 % of their capsaicin compound in the flesh,[3] explaining why removing the veins won't save you from their intense, overbearing heat.

ALEPPO

Scoville Heat Units: 10,000
Aleppo pepper is tragically underrated. Aleppo pepper added to mayonnaise is a marked improvement, and adding Aleppo for a burst of sweet heat adds a pleasantness to just about anything. These chilis have a small amount of heat that comes and goes quickly, with an incredible, distinctive flavor that's more fruity than spicy. These peppers are good on anything you'd put crushed red peppers on: pizza, pasta, grain bowls, etc.

---

[2] "Novel Formation of Ectopic (Nonplacental) Capsaicinoid Secreting Vesicles on Fruit Walls Explains the Morphological Mechanism of Super-hot Chile Peppers," 253.
[3] Ibid., 255.

Aleppo, ground

Ancho chili, whole

ANCHO (POBLANO)

Scoville Heat Units: 1,000–2,000

While green and fresh, this chili is a *poblano*; after it's been ripened to a deep red color and dried, it's an *ancho*. Ancho has a touch more heat than the benign Aleppo, with just enough warmth to give your tongue a quick embrace before receding. This pleasantness makes it an asset in chili powders, Mexican sauces, and meat rubs. It's sometimes added to chocolate to give it a chili flavor without extreme heat.

ÁRBOL

Scoville Heat Units: 35,000–55,000

Chile de árbol peppers are close to cayenne in hotness. They're sold dried and whole, and are best used to add heat to a dish while it cooks—removing before serving—as in a soup or stew.

CHIPOTLE (MORITA)

Scoville Heat Units: 3,000–10,000

There are different varieties of chipotle pepper, but the most common, and the one mostly used in the US, is the *morita*. The morita offers a medium heat that brings some warming fire. Its smoky fruitiness brings a lot of flavor to a dish in addition to heat, and its appealing dark red-purple color adds a secondary benefit. Moritas are excellent in adobos, chilis, and barbecue seasonings.

Guajillo chili, whole

GUAJILLO

Scoville Heat Units: 2,500–10,000

If you like Mexican food, you probably like Guajillo peppers. Their bright, peppy flavor is found in salsas, moles, rubs, chilis, sauces, and soups, where they lend some nice but widely tolerable heat. Guajillos lie between cayenne and ancho in heat level.

HABANERO

Scoville Heat Units: 150,000–300,000

The habanero is the world's hottest naturally occurring pepper. In addition to its intense spiciness, the habanero is fruity, with a sweetish tang that pairs well with fruits and fruity salsas. But it's most commonly used for its scorching heat.

PERI PERI

Scoville Heat Units: 175,000

This African hot chili has many names, including *piri-piri*, *pil-pil*, and *pill-pill*, all of which may translate as *pepper pepper* or *spicy spicy*. All the names refer to both the pepper and the famous Mozambican sauce that features them. The peppers are simmered with lemon juice and made into a paste, which is spread over meat and fish. Their bright, hot flavor goes well with heartier foods and meat-based dishes.

GHOST PEPPERS

Twenty years ago, the habanero pepper was listed by Guinness World Records as the hottest. It's now several spots down from the top, but no one has discovered any new peppers. Instead, peppers are engineered in labs to have a heat far beyond nature. *Ghost peppers* and other hotter-than-hot chilis are little more than a series of never-ending one-upmanship, as scientists and hobbyists genetically engineer and crossbreed peppers to ever higher Scoville units. The *Carolina Reaper*, for example, was created by a hybrid of the a ghost pepper and a *Red Savina Habanero*. But to what end? At an insufferable 2.2 million SHU, the Carolina Reaper is too hot to use in the kitchen. These monsters seem to exist solely for hyperbolically labeled hot sauces and competitions at chicken wings restaurants looking to lure in the most susceptible type of person looking to prove himself by consuming hot wings. If you want hot, a habanero will do you just fine.

TIEN TSIN

Scoville Heat Units: 50,000–75,000

Though all capsicums are New World plants, Tien Tsin peppers are cultivated and used almost exclusively in China, demonstrating how thoroughly the chilis were adapted. At 50,000–75,000, SHU they're very hot, and often called for to bring heat famous in Szechwan cuisine. They're also called "Tianjin," "Chinese peppers" or "Chinese red peppers."

Tien Tsin chilis, dried whole

In the Kitchen

Chili powders and blends

Chili powder means a powder of dried, pulverized capsicums, while a chili blend is the dried capsicums plus other spices like cumin, oregano, and garlic. However, chili powders are often actually blends of capsicums and other spices, and today's chili blends can contain dozens of different spices. The capsicums can range from mild to hot, and while specific capsicums are called for in specific blends, there isn't any one capsicum required for all blends. Mild chili blends have the sweet and benign Aleppo as a base, while others can use extremely hot capsicums like piri piri or make use of fiery cayenne. Popular chili blends include chili con carne, used to make the basic chili stew with beef and beans; Cajun seasoning, which uses hot capsicums such as cayenne; and taco seasoning, a sweeter, milder blend that often makes use of sweet paprika and salt in addition to cumin, garlic, onion, and herbs.

Home cooks—especially those who enter chili competitions—love to make their own chili blends at home. The stews can range from a thinner soup to a thick sauce and have a variety of meats, beans, and garnishes, and recipes are painstakingly tinkered with, their ingredients guarded with care. While cumin, garlic, and a variety of dried capsicums are found in most chilis, some "secret" spice ingredients include clove, nutmeg, coriander, and non-spice ingredients like dark chocolate, ground coffee, and beer.

HARISSA

Harissa means many things: paste made from a certain red chili pepper; a blend of dried spices made of red chilis; a dish of green peppers and tomatoes; and a porridge soup of wheat and lamb.[4] The harissa that belongs on your spice rack is the North African paste or dried powder blend (or both). Harissa can be made with a variety of hot capsicum peppers, or a combination of sweet and spicy to bring a pleasant balance. Mild pimento peppers mixed with fiery serrano peppers is a common combination. What's important is that harissa bring some heat. Other spices are added to build flavor: coriander, caraway, garlic, and salt are common but harissa may also include cumin, paprika, onion, and more. To make the paste, the spice blend is combined with oil, and sometimes tomato paste.

I use dry harissa powder as I would a curry powder, adding to onions and garlic to temper at the beginning of a hot dish. The paste is good for drizzling over fatty meats and roasted vegetables; use it in place of a hot sauce for a rich, smoky flavor. It's also nice as a pungent spread on rich sandwiches, especially ones with lots of meat and cheese.

DO NOT TOUCH YOUR EYES OR . . . OTHER SENSITIVE PARTS

I spent a year working as a sous chef at a restaurant in Milwaukee. The head chef wore latex gloves when chopping jalapeños, and instructed me to do the same. He relayed the story of one cook's hubris that, as in Greek tragedy, led to man's downfall. The protagonist demonstrated his manliness by insisting he didn't need to wear gloves when slicing jalapeños. Upon completing the task with his machismo proudly displayed, he strutted to the bathroom. Almost immediately after the door shut, the rest of the kitchen heard him screaming. You see, he had touched a very sensitive body part with hands covered with fiery capsicum residue. He wore gloves after that.

Take this lesson to heart: If you touch hot peppers, the capsaicin—the active component in peppers and pepper spray—*will* rub off on your hands and stay there until it's removed. You might not notice until you rub your eyes, or repeat

---

[4] *The Oxford Companion to Food*, 371.

the chef's mistake. Rubber gloves are probably the most effective, efficient way to avoid the issue; when you're done chopping, you simply peel them off and throw them away. But if you don't want to buy them or produce the extra waste, wash your hands with lots of soap and, for good measure, add whatever oil you're using in the kitchen, too. Personally, I just dump a lot of dish soap directly on my hands and rub it all around, without water, for at least a minute, then rinse. Some people oil their hands *before* touching the peppers, which creates a barrier between the capsaicin and the skin. I find this method cumbersome, mainly because the oil makes your hands slippery, and it's not a great idea to have slippery hands when using a knife. Whatever you do, don't touch your eyes—or other sensitive parts—before thoroughly cleaning your hands.

Pepper

Out of all the spices available to us—and there are so many great choices—why do we reach for the pepper grinder reflexively, often before we've even tried our food? Pepper is called the king of spices. It rules over our plates and our palates. I wonder if my deep and unconditional love of pepper is the product of conditioning: I've trained my tongue to expect it, so I keep grinding it on. If I only just discovered pepper today, would I be equally enamored of it? If salt makes food taste more like itself, pepper gives it an edge; salt enhances the flavor already in our food, while pepper makes food a bolder version of itself.

There were times when pepper was one of the only products to connect distant places to each other, the growers meeting a need for people they had very little, if any, knowledge of. Pepper was once so valuable that it was used as a currency and to pay rent. Today, it's abundant and relatively cheap. And what a blessing, because it should be used on nearly every savory dish, and some sweet ones, too. I don't add it to plain fruit, and I don't want it on sushi, but pepper finds a place on virtually every other food I eat. I refill my average-sized pepper grinder about once a week, and I'm extremely grateful to have access to high-quality peppercorns. I love so many spices, but I use pepper as much as I use salt, which is to say: all the time, on almost every meal I make.

"True" peppers are all part of the *Piper* genus, though they take many forms. Black, white, and green peppercorns all come from the same vine, while long pepper and cubeb pepper are closely related. They get their pungency from the *piperine* alkaloid and other volatile oils. It's said that pepper increases the flow of both saliva and gastric juices, improving the appetite.[1] Perhaps the science explains the supreme appeal of pepper, perhaps not. Either way, its ability to improve food is demonstrated across millions of meals in households and restaurants around the world.

---

[1] *The Oxford Companion to Food*, 595.

Many "peppers," including Sichuan, Sansho, grains of paradise, and pink peppercorns, are completely unrelated botanically. Some are more closely related to citrus and others are kin to cashews. In each case, the seeds, hulls, or berries are dried and crushed to add their own flavor, distinct from true pepper but still good in their own right.

Types of Pepper

Green peppercorn: Like most fruits, young peppercorns are green. Once picked, they will continue to ripen, so green peppercorns were traditionally pickled to retain their youthful appearance and flavor. These days, more sophisticated dehydration methods are available, so pickling isn't necessary. Because green peppercorns are picked and processed before they're dried, they don't develop the depth of flavor found in black and white peppercorns. Instead, green peppercorns are fruity and zesty.

Black peppercorn: Waiting for it to mature allows the green berry time to turn darker, eventually becoming a deep red. The fully ripe fruit is picked and dried, where the color darkens and the skin gains its distinctive wrinkles. If you look closely at black peppercorns, you'll see colors ranging from dark reds to browns to black. Some pepper is picked while still green or freshly red; drying turns the green ones light brown and the red ones become dark brown (but not fully black).

Peppercorns grow on a spike, with the ones on top getting slightly bigger because they receive the most sunlight. The whole bunch is picked when the top ones ripen, meaning there's a range of sizes coming from the same vine. The bulk peppercorns are sifted through sized mesh/screens to sort out different grades. The bigger the peppercorn, the bolder the flavor, so the largest peppercorns get the highest grades. The top 10 pounds are usually designated as premium.

Malabar pepper: For centuries, spices were exported from India through ports on the Malabar Coast. Malabar peppercorns are brown and of good quality, with a mild flavor that a lot of people like to use for their all-purpose pepper needs. They're graded as *garbled* (blacker, higher quality) or *ungarbled* (browner, lower quality). *Malabar pepper* is a registered product of the region, so produce must meet specific guidelines to use the name.

Tellicherry pepper: These are the best peppercorns in the world. Tellicherry peppercorns are from the Malabar region, but the designation is more rigidly defined.[2] Within the Tellicherry designation lie further grades of quality: the premium peppercorns are called *Tellicherry Extra Bold* or Special Bold or similar.

Lampong pepper: Hailing from Indonesia, these peppercorns are quite good, with strong punchy flavors, though they lack the supreme depth of the Tellicherry peppercorn.

Sarawak pepper: The Sarawak state in Malaysia is better-known for producing white pepper, but their black pepper is a good mild option. It's best when used in conjunction with other spices, and especially for a hint of pepperiness without a strong single-note pepper flavor.

Vietnamese pepper: This pepper from Vietnam is sweet and mild, without the punch of Indian peppercorns.

Brazilian pepper: New World pepper is typically considered inferior, so is often used by bulk producers that require a lot of pepper for premade foods and who don't want (or need) to pay the premium price for premium pepper. Brazilian pepper has a flavor that seems to disappear into food more readily, providing just a quick bite before receding. The flavor is sharper and thinner than other, higher-quality options.

White pepper: White pepper is black pepper, left on the vine until ripe. Before drying, though, the berries are soaked or left under running water. Their skin dissolves and is easily rubbed off, leaving only the white seed, which further lightens during drying. White peppercorns are necessarily smaller than black peppercorns because those outer husks have been removed. If the process is done incorrectly, the seeds are at risk of molding. If they have, you'll know immediately by the smell. White pepper does naturally smell different than black pepper, but the smell is still appealing: sharply floral notes with a somewhat fermented trace imparted by the processing.

---

[2] It's a similar control/labeling system to the one used for wine in France and Italy.

White pepper is most common in Europe and parts of Asia, even more prevalent than black in some locales. It's viewed by much of the world as the more complex and refined pepper. Some recipes and chefs say white pepper is necessary for light-colored soups and sauces, where you don't want black to "ruin" the color palette. Perhaps this was beneficial on old coal-powered trains, where black specks would look like soot in your food. But the differences go deeper than color, so if you want black pepper flavor in your food without the specks, use whole peppercorns and remove before serving.

Muntok white pepper: Muntok peppercorns, from Indonesia, are left sitting in water until the skin/husk is soft enough to be removed, which makes them slightly more gray than white.

Sarawak white pepper: In Sarawak, Malaysia, pepper producers use running water to soften and remove the skin, resulting in bright white peppercorns. While Muntok white peppercorns are by no means bad, Sarawak is the superior product, with the export from the country generally consisting of larger, more flavorful peppercorns.

Penja white pepper: This white pepper from Cameroon is in such high demand that it was granted a protected geographical indication (PGI) label to protect its reputation against would-be counterfeiters. It's grown in a valley rich with volcanic soil, which gives the peppercorns an interestingly bright, hot, fragrant flavor that's retained when the outer hull is washed off to make white pepper. The export is relatively small, making Penja white pepper hard to find and very expensive when you do.

COMMODITY VS. VALUE-ADDED

Pepper raises the issue of *commodities* versus *value-added crops*. Indian pepper growers (and Madagascan vanilla growers) care about producing the best crop, which means it's value-added. These growers will try to make the highest quality spice possible, so it takes longer and involves more risk.[3] Their products ultimately sell at a higher

---

[3] Leaving peppercorns on the vine longer increases the risk for the grower. Ripe peppercorns are enticing to all sorts of critters and more time equals more opportunities for the berries to be snatched (and for the crop to be damaged by storms or other natural disasters).

Black & white pepper, cracked

price, with customers willing to pay more for the quality. Smaller spice shops are interested more in these crops, as they want the highest quality pepper and have the flexibility to adjust prices according to each year's crop. But big industry buyers that trade huge quantities of peppers and mass-production food manufacturers don't operate like that; they care most about the *amount* of product. They will contract for the volume they need and the date they need it, agreeing beforehand to pay so much money for so much pepper. Growers work to meet the demand/contract, with less attention on the quality. Under this practice, pepper is a commodity.

GRINDING

Pepper is best when ground directly onto food, or ground and used within a few hours. The flavor comes from the volatile oil, which is only released upon grinding. That's why whole peppercorns don't smell very strongly of pepper. While pre-ground pepper can still be very good if somewhat fresh, the flavor inevitably dissipates. Whole peppercorns, on the other hand, can keep for years if stored, like all other spices should be, in an airtight container, away from light, and in a place that doesn't get too hot or humid. When I know I'll be using a lot of pepper for a dish, I'll grind an ample amount in a small ramekin bowl beforehand, so it's still very fresh but I don't have to spend time grinding while cooking.

A wooden grinder is ideal, as it keeps out heat, light, and humidity. Some grinders allow you to manipulate the grind, from coarse and chunky to flowing and fine. Usually, grinders and ground pepper products list designations as *coarse*, *medium*, and *fine*, but occasionally you will spot the exact measurements. When pepper is ground, it's sifted through a wire mesh screen for sorting, just as the whole peppercorns were when graded. The wire screens are a bit like regular cloth, with the amount of wire acting like a thread count. More wires create a tighter mesh with smaller openings, letting only finely ground flakes through. A 6–10 mesh measures cracked peppercorn, 12–14 is coarsely ground, and 30–34 is finely ground. A basic home or restaurant grinder, without settings, is 18–28, right in the middle.

Does pepper really make you sneeze?

It plays out in *Looney Tunes* schtick: A whiff of pepper results in a massive sneeze, which subsequently sends the pepper everywhere. I sneezed plenty of times working at my grandparents' spice shop, but it was never specifically because I was inhaling pepper. It's possible this myth of pepper making you sneeze was born during a time or place when low-quality product abounded, for the lower the quality, the more likely it contains more components that make you sneeze. It's also possible that old pepper, full of dust, is the real culprit. Good fresh pepper has heat, and can certainly make your nose tingle, but it rarely results in a cartoon sneeze.

Pepper blends

European: This is a simple blend of black and white peppercorns. It's called European because Europeans tend to be on much friendlier terms with white pepper than Americans are.

French: A French-style peppercorn blend brings together green and black peppercorns, due to the popularity of the zesty green peppercorn flavor in French cooking.

Four peppercorn: As the name suggests, this blend combines black, white, green, and pink peppercorns for a royal mélange of colors and flavors. It's peppery, spicy, and somewhat floral, with a zing from the white pepper melding into a zest from the green and finished with a piquant surge from the pink, all on the base of a good black pepper. It's great for a complex and interesting flavor wherever you use pepper while cooking, but especially in stews and stir-fries.

Lazy man's shake: My grandfather talked of doing this, but I don't think he ever did: the idea is to combine ground pepper and salt into one, like two-in-one shampoo and conditioner.

PINK PEPPERCORNS

Pink peppercorns are not peppercorns at all, but an unrelated berry with a fruity, sweet taste.[4] They're also very close in size and shape to peppercorns, hence the name. They're occasionally called *rose pepper*. They are often added to dishes for color as much as for flavor. Pink peppercorns are good on fish and chicken, and the color/taste is a pleasant combination in ice cream.

Pink peppercorns are sold (and should be kept in) glass jars, because the whole berry is very fragile. Handling it through plastic will result in the berry crumbling. They cannot be added to pepper grinders, as they're too soft to go through the grinding mechanism. (In a four peppercorn blend, they should fall apart while jostling with the other colors before ever contacting the mechanism, so this shouldn't be a problem, though it might!) Sprinkle them onto a dish, pinching them between your fingers to crush them as you go.

A word of warning: the pink peppercorn shrub is in the cashew family. Though in a separate genus, the berries still contain some of the same enzymes and oils, so can activate tree nut allergies. Pink peppercorns are potentially poisonous to poultry and pigs, and records exist of children having severe gastrointestinal reactions. The United States banned pink peppercorn imports from France in the 1980s, but the FDA currently lists all species as "generally recognized as safe."

---

[4] If I were in the food business, perhaps a chocolatier or part of the cabal who decides what the next hot food trend will be, I'd go all-in on pink pepper. Its fruity, mild flavor could really go with anything; its bright pinkish-red color is attractive; and the fact that it's called *pink peppercorn* and isn't widely used gives it an allure of the special.

ALLSPICE

Another dried-berry-as-spice is allspice, which appears in dishes
from the Caribbean to the Middle East, from Poland to Cincinnati
(where it's a key ingredient in the local version of chili, an adaptation of
Mediterranean spiced meat sauce). Allspice may be called *pimenta*
(after the plant's genus) or *myrtle pepper.* Several unrelated shrubs are
called "*something*" *allspice* (*Carolina, Japanese,* and *wild,* among others)
even though their fruits are not commonly used culinarily. The *Pimenta
dioica* shrub was encountered by Christopher Columbus and brought
back to Europe, though it is still mainly grown in Jamaica.

GRAINS OF PARADISE

As a valuable spice, pepper had its fair share of imitators. One such spice was grains
of paradise, which does a decent job approximating the kick of true pepper, though
with less heat and a spicier bouquet that carries hints of cardamom (a related plant)
and a suggestion of nutty, buttery fatness.[5] Grains of paradise grow in West Africa,
and were named by crafty merchants to enhance the aura of mystery that surrounded fabulous spices from far-off places.[6] Grains of paradise were also called

---

[5] Juniper berries were also used to swindle: they would be dried and the ones that matched
peppercorns in size would be sold as the real thing. (*The Lore of Spices,* 102).
[6] *Spice: The History of a Temptation,* 45–46.

Grains of paradise, whole

Long pepper, whole

ossame or *Melegueta pepper*.[7] The spice has fallen out of use, though you can still find grains of paradise in specialty stores and online. If you do use them, they're good mixed with regular black pepper and ground onto dishes where you'd normally just use pepper.

LONG PEPPER AND CUBEB PEPPER

Long pepper and cubeb pepper belong to the true *Piper* genus, with black/white/green pepper, sharing their heated effervescence. Long pepper was far more common in the past than it is today; like the round peppercorns, long pepper was grown in India and exported to Ancient Greece and Rome. (Pliny mentions black, white, and long pepper.)[8] It may be due to the introduction of the hot chili peppers in the 16th and 17th centuries that long pepper is now little more than a curiosity: those plants were easily adaptable, cheap, and more noticeably spicy than long pepper.

Long pepper is very visually distinct, a long, thin spice that looks like many seeds clustered together. It's hotter than regular pepper, but sweeter, too, with an extra zing reminiscent of ginger or nutmeg. Long pepper is difficult to grind and

---

[7] *The Book of Spices*, 339. There is a similar spice sometimes called *African pepper*, *kimba pepper*, or *Grains of Selim* which is used for its similar flavor, mainly in Senegal, though it's neither a true pepper nor related to grains of paradise.

[8] *The Oxford Companion to Food*, 459.

Cubeb pepper, whole

easiest to use whole, added to roasts, soups, and vegetables during cooking, then removed.

Cubeb pepper (which goes by many names, including *Java pepper*, *Benin pepper*, and *tailed pepper*) is even more obsolete than long pepper. It's similarly hot and peppery in taste, with a tail coming off the round berry. It has a nice fragrance that's rather minty. Cubeb was used in Europe and China as a medicine and as a spice through the 17th century. Its downfall may have come from Portugal's desire to sell more black pepper: a source from 1640 reported that the king forbade the sale of cubeb so it wouldn't be competition.[9]

SICHUAN PEPPER

Sichuan pepper has a long history as a popular spice in China, where it was used, like so many other spices, as both medicine and seasoning. It is variably known as *Chinese pepper* and *flower pepper*, perhaps because it is extremely aromatic. Sichuan creates a very interesting sensation in the mouth; not truly hot but with a tingly numbness. Sichuan pepper was banned by the FDA for years because it can carry a bacterial disease that could damage citrus crops. (The bacteria is not harmful to humans.) Now, though, so long as the Sichuan pepper is heated so the bacteria is killed before entering the country, the FDA allows it. Rest assured that if you're buying Sichuan pepper in the US, it's been treated.

---

[9] *The Burns Philp Book of Spices*, 54.

Sichuan pepper, whole

SANSHŌ

These green seedpods make your tongue tingle in a most peculiar way. The orange berries are dried, and their inner seeds discarded. As they dry, they turn green, and can be kept whole or ground. The plant, a shrub, is part of the citrus family. Sanshō (also called *Japanese pepper* or *Korean pepper*) is used mainly in Asian cuisine, and goes especially well on fatty dishes, as the strange numbing heat cuts the fat.

A TIME LINE OF PEPPER

We live in a world abundant with spices, but pepper towers over them all. Books have been written about the history of pepper and its role in medieval trading and the Age of Exploration. Some stories grab the imagination, while others demonstrate the power and influence of the little peppercorn.

A long time ago: Pepper was likely one of the earliest spices used. More than 3,000 years ago, it was referenced in Sanskrit medical volumes.[10]

Fourth century BC: The Greek philosopher Theophrastus mentioned two different kinds of pepper in his *Enquiry into Plants*, likely meaning black pepper and long pepper.[11] Antiphanes, the Greek poet and playwright, wrote of pepper: "If a man should bring home some pepper he's bought, they propose a motion that he be tortured as a spy."[12]

---

[10] *The Book of Spices*, 339; *Spices: What they are and where they come from*, 13.

[11] *Spices*, 251.

[12] *Spice: The History of a Temptation*, 59.

64 AD: In *Periplus of the Erythraean Sea*, a Greek manuscript detailing sea navigation and trading, pepper is recorded as an export from the Gulf of Kutch (then called Baraca) on India's west coast.[13]

77 AD: Pliny noted that black pepper was 4 denarii per pound, while white pepper was 7 denarii.[14]

40–90 AD: Dioscorides speaks of white pepper, in a context that demonstrates the apparently common belief that black and white pepper were two different plants.[15]

176 AD: Under the Roman emperor Marcus Aurelius, trade between India and Rome flourished, and in 176 AD a customs duty was imposed on long pepper and white pepper, which were more expensive than black pepper.[16]

408 AD: By the beginning of the fifth century, pepper was so valuable it was used to pay off levies and taxes in place of currency. When Alaric, king of the Visigoths, besieged Rome in 408 AD, 3,000 pounds of peppercorns were part of the ransom paid for Rome's release.[17]

600 AD: Isidore of Seville believed that peppercorns gained their wrinkles because of the fire that pepper harvesters lit under the pepper trees, in order to drive out the snakes that guarded them.[18]

978 AD: The Statutes of Ethelred (who ruled English from 978 to 1016, with a little exile at the start of 1014) recorded that traders entering London were taxed 10 pounds of pepper (along with some cloves and vinegar).[19]

1000 AD: By the turn of the millennium, pepper was becoming commonplace across Europe, especially among nobility.[20]

---

[13] *Spices*, 251.

[14] *Spice: The History of a Temptation*, 73.

[15] *Spices*, 251.

[16] *The Book of Spices,* 339.

[17] "A Glossary of Spices," 12; *The Book of Spices*, 340; *The Complete Book of Herbs and Spices*, 201–202.

[18] *Spice: The History of a Temptation*, 87.

[19] *Spices*, 252.

[20] *Spice: The History of a Temptation*, 101.

1100s: Pepper was coming into Europe in such quantities, and had become so important, that England formed the Guild of Pepperers, a trade organization to manage and monitor the imports and labor of pepper.[21] It evolved into a spicers' guild, and in 1429 became the Grocers Company, which, under the name of the Worshipful Company of Grocers, is still present in London today. Merchants who dealt in spices beyond just pepper were still called *pepperers*, which was mirrored in France, where they were called *poivriers*, and in Germany, where they were *Pfeffersacke*.[22]

The Middle Ages: In the Middle Ages, pepper was a rare intermediary between Europe and India; though the people at each end of pepper's trade knew little of each other, pepper connected parts of the globe when little else did. So valuable, and apparently necessary, was pepper that at times in Europe it was used as a currency, to pay rent and dowries, and serfs could buy their freedom with pepper.[23] Whence the term *peppercorn rent*, which has come to mean a small amount of rent paid or a rent that's perfunctorily paid out of tradition rather than need for payment.[24]

SALT AND PEPPER

Like two people in love, salt and pepper meld their individual flavors to create beautiful music together. They stand beside each other on restaurant tables and kitchen counters across America. They season everything from roasted vegetables and potatoes to meat roasts and stews. Their lore even gets mixed up: pepper, not salt, may banish the devil from your table, and you can substitute pepper as the magic ingredient during exorcisms. In some tales, a mixture of salt and pepper, scattered outside your home, is the most effective method to turn away the devil at your doorstep.[25] Salt and pepper are the pillars of spice, though all the spices in between are valuable and important. At the end of it all, spices are always better when they're together, like salt and pepper.

---

[21] *The Home Garden Book of Herbs and Spices*, 164.

[22] *The Book of Spices*, 340.

[23] *Spice: The History of a Temptation*, 92.

[24] *The Book of Spices*, 340. The second meaning of peppercorn rent was still alive in 1973, when Prince Charles took possession of his Duchy of Cornwall and was given a tribute, which included a pound of pepper.

[25] *Cunningham's Encyclopedia of Magical Herbs* (*Salt & Pepper*, 21).

Afterword

My grandparents were undeniably experts in all things spice. After 50 years running their business, teaching their children and then their grandchildren the craft, they probably knew more about spices than most people in the world. Which is to say that by the time I came along, decades into their life's work, I would've thought they knew everything there was to know. But over the course of my childhood and young adult years working at their store, I saw them continue to learn from their customers, about how spices are used in other countries, how one complements another in an unexpected way. There is always more to learn on a subject. This book is but a first draft of spice knowledge, one I'm sure many other members of my family could have written with more breadth of knowledge. Theirs is a bottomless deep blue ocean of information; mine is a wide shallow inlet with scattered clam holes.

Yet, spices define who I am in a tangible way. My kitchen is cluttered with them and my desk at work has a drawer full of them (the smell wafts out when I open it). Coworkers ask for seasonings to add to delivery pizza and other lunches. Friends text me photos when they spot a Penzeys store in whatever far-flung state they're visiting, or when they spot my family's jars in a relative's kitchen. Before writing this book, I had never quite made the connection that when I talk about my love of spices, I'm really talking about my family. Writing my own ode to spices is really remembering all that I learned from them.

One of my favorite books is *A Treasury of Spices,* from the American Spice Trade Association. It was printed in 1956, a year before my grandparents got married and started the William T. Penzey Coffee Co., the progenitor of the Spice House. Tucked between pages 100 and 101, which contains spices starting with the letter C—cardamom seed, cassia buds, cayenne pepper, celery salt, and celery seed—is a piece of slippery paper torn from the roll of spice jar labels. On the blank side is my grandma's writing, in a thick red marker: "Happy Sept! Love you." The rosemary label on the other side proclaims: "Whole Rosemary: The herb of lovers since at least the time of Shakespeare, signifies love, trust, and remembrance." I wonder if my grandma purposefully chose the rosemary label. I wonder if my grandfather tucked it into this particular page from this particular book as a bookmark, or because he simply wanted to preserve the note and this book was at hand, embedding his life's love in the pages of his life's work.

There was something else between those pages, too: a photo of my sister Eva, and my brother Lucas, and me at work in the Spice House. In it, we're busy putting ginger into jars and the whole ginger is spread across a marble slab propped up on boxes used as a makeshift worktable. My grandma's handwriting on the back records the date as July 1994: Eva and I were 5 years old and Lucas was 3. Some families have home videos—I have a book called *A Treasury of Spices* that doubles as a treasury of family, kept by my grandparents, their grandkids foregrounded on a background of spice.

A life in spice: my siblings and I helping prep in the Spice House.

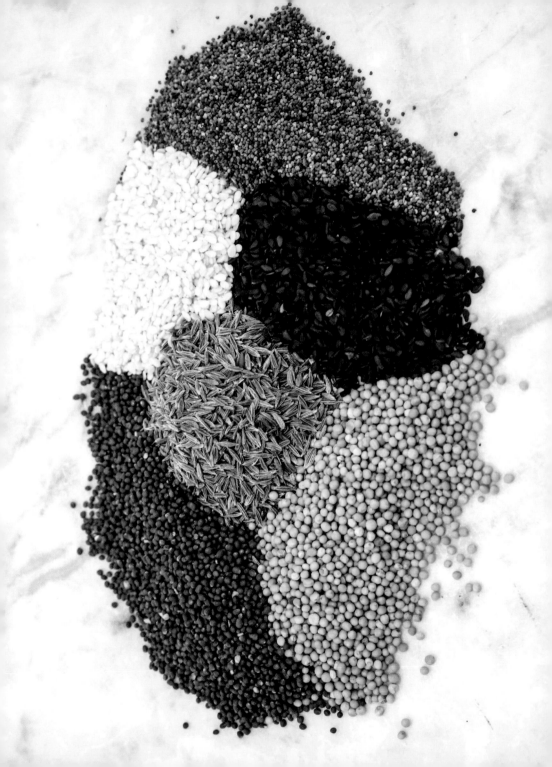

Appendix A
Spice Blends

"Never employ one spice if more can be procured."
—An old maxim on cookery from *The Herbalist*

Adobo

The name *adobo*, or *adobar*, is simply Spanish for *marinate* or *dressing*. In Iberia, it typically contains paprika, oregano, salt, and garlic, usually mixed into soy sauce and/or vinegar. It has been widely adopted throughout Latin America, where many countries employ both wet and dry applications. Additional ingredients may be onion powder, cumin, and all varieties of chili powders.

Advieh

Advieh means *spice* in Persian, and the mixture is primarily used in Iranian cuisine. Most recipes include cinnamon, cardamom, cloves, turmeric, cumin, ginger, and the distinctive rose petals/buds. Personal versions add all manner of further refinements: coriander, nutmeg, black pepper, mace, and more. It is often sprinkled on rice, chicken, and bean dishes. When used for stews (and thus called *Advieh-e khoresh*), it almost always includes saffron.

Berbere

A key ingredient in Ethiopia and Eritrea, the *berbere* mixture includes many ingredients little known elsewhere in the world, which often have borrowed names. *Ajwain* may be called *ajowan caraway*, *nigella* is sometimes *black caraway* or *black cumin*, and *korarima* is also called *Ethiopian cardamom* or *false cardamom*. In addition to ajwain, nigella, and korarima, *berbere* typically contains chili peppers, garlic, ginger, basil, rue (herb-of-grace), and fenugreek. When the native ingredients can't be found, it's

A medley of spices

207

common to substitute in sweet paprika, cardamom, allspice, cinnamon, nutmeg, and coriander. If making your own blend, there should be a decent focus on spicy heat.

CAJUN SEASONING

Your basic Cajun seasoning is just garlic powder, onion powder, sweet paprika, thyme, and cayenne pepper. Because the focus shouldn't just be on heat, many people add more herbs for complexity: oregano, parsley, and basil are good options. Remember that Cajun seasoning is a staple in both Cajun and Creole dishes; the only difference is that Creole cuisine uses tomatoes but Cajun food does not.

CHAAT MASALA

Chaat refers to all the common roadside snacks in India, fried dishes including samosa, aloo tikki, and papdi. *Chaat masala* is simply the seasoning applied (*masala* translates as *mix* or *ingredients*), which means it can vary greatly. The staples, however, are asafoetida, cumin, coriander, ginger, salt, black pepper, a selection of chili powder, and the distinctive *amchoor*, also spelled *aamchur*. This powder is made from unripe green mangos, which are thinly sliced and dried in the sun until firm enough to be ground. It adds a sour, tangy flavor to *chaat masala* and complements the various chutneys served alongside chaat.

DUQQA

Duqqa, or *dukkah* (pronounced doo-ka), is an Egyptian blend based around nuts. The name means "to pound," as the ingredients should be toasted whole and then crushed (or, more modernly, run through a grinder). Hazelnuts are the traditional base, though some recipe substitute or add almonds. This blend can be traced back to Ancient Egypt and the recipe has been in flux ever since. Sesame seeds (white and black), coriander, cumin, salt, and black pepper appear consistently. Texts throughout the ages have also listed fennel seeds, caraway, marjoram, mint, za'atar, chickpeas, nigella, paprika millet flour, pine nuts, pumpkin seeds, and sunflower seeds. It's most often served as a dip; just add oil.

Garam Masala

Probably the most well-known spice blend from the Indian subcontinent, garam masala is now easily found all over the world. *Masala* simply identifies a spice mix (from the Urdu and Arabic words for *ingredients*) and *garam* is Urdu for *hot* or *pungent*, though the meaning is less about spiciness and more about the supposed healing properties of elevating body temperature (as practiced in Ayurvedic medicine). Indeed, *garam masala* includes no truly "hot" spices, focusing on a base of black pepper, cardamom, cinnamon, coriander, cumin, and nutmeg. Customizing options include asafoetida, cloves, fennel seeds, garlic, ginger, mace, mustard seed, star anise, tamarind, and turmeric. Some versions include herbs as well, typically bay, fenugreek, or Malabar leaves. Garam masala is distinguished from curry powder by not containing any chili peppers and generally including fewer ingredients. Northern Indian cuisine usually uses the mix powdered while southern dishes first form paste by adding the spices to coconut milk, vinegar, or water.

Harissa

First things first: yes, *harissa* is a paste. But it's a spice paste, so it counts. It starts with grinding caraway, coriander, cumin, garlic, and salt. Chili peppers (serrano, Árbol, Guajillo, morita/chipotle, whatever you like) are boiled and then blended into a paste with the spices and some olive oil. For a dry version, use chili powder and omit the oil. You can experiment with cayenne and paprika to change the heat profile and add mint or cilantro to add some herbal cooling.

Hawaij

Because *Hawaij* is Arabic for mixture, the name covers two types of Yemeni spice blends. The first is largely used for soup though it can, of course, be used in stews and curries, sprinkled on rice and vegetables, or applied as a barbecue rub. This basic savory Hawaij mix should contain black pepper, cumin, turmeric, and green cardamom. More complex versions add caraway, cloves, cilantro (coriander leaves), and ginger. The other kind of Hawaij is mainly added to coffee (during brewing, not in the mug), though it has application in some desserts and meat-based recipes. This

Hawaij mix focuses on the licorice flavors of aniseed and fennel seeds, with ginger, cardamom, and cinnamon often present as well.

JERK

Normally applied to chicken or pork, *jerk* is an open-fire cooking style native to Jamaica with a dry-rub seasoning focused on allspice (called *pimento* in Jamaica) and hot pepper. If you love heat and have access to them, Scotch bonnet peppers, native to the Caribbean, are the prime pick, but other dried chilis, even crushed red pepper and cayenne, will work. The blend can be filled out with any number of additional spices including, but not limited to, cinnamon, cumin, garlic, nutmeg, onion, paprika, parsley, and thyme.

MITMITA

This Ethiopian mix goes for the heat with piri piri, or bird's-eye chilis (pequins or serranos work, too). Mitmita is rounded out with cardamom, cloves, cinnamon, cumin, and sometimes ginger. It is used both within dishes (especially the raw meat dish *kitfo*) and as a condiment (as with *injera* bread, the national dish).

MONTREAL STEAK SEASONING

As the name implies, *Montreal Steak Seasoning* is used to flavor steaks and other grilled meats. The mix is based on the pickling spices necessary for Montreal-style smoked meat, a brisket dish popular with the Jewish diaspora. A basic version contains salt, black pepper, red pepper (likely cayenne), garlic, paprika, and mysterious "natural flavors." Home recipes commonly add onion, coriander, and dill seed.

OLD BAY SEASONING

Developed by a German immigrant, *Old Bay Seasoning* is now a specific brand name marketed by McCormick & Company, still produced in Maryland near its name-sake Chesapeake Bay. Known ingredients are celery salt, black pepper, crushed red pepper, and paprika. The full flavor profile is emulated with some combination of bay leaves (ground), dry mustard, ginger, nutmeg, cloves, allspice, mace, and cardamom. Chiefly used with crab and shrimp, it can be added to nearly any seafood or chowder dish and, really, pretty much anything else: chicken, eggs, fries, corn, potatoes, salads, popcorn, and more.

Panch Phoron

Not widely known outside the Indian subcontinent, *panch phoron* is the five spices of Bangladesh and Nepal. All the ingredients are seeds: fenugreek, nigella, cumin, fennel, and black mustard (in Bengal, the mustard may be replaced with radhuni/wild celery). This blend is always used whole, never ground, often first frying the spices in mustard oil or ghee and then adding other ingredients.

Poudre-Douce

Poudre-douce is referenced in medieval and Renaissance cookbooks, though rarely are the ingredients defined. One 14th-century manuscript, however, lists grains of paradise, ginger, cinnamon, nutmeg, sugar, and galangal. Modern versions focus on the cinnamon and ginger. The name means "sweet powder" and it has a "strong powder" counterpart: *poudre-forte*. The strong version simply adds black pepper and maybe some cloves.

Qâlat Daqqa

Qâlat daqqa is Tunisia's version of a five-spice blend: cloves, nutmeg, cinnamon, peppercorns (any color), and grains of paradise. Like other national five spices, it rarely sees sweet applications despite the presence of cloves, nutmeg, and cinnamon. It works as a dry rub for meat (notably on lamb) and in vegetable dishes, especially ones featuring pumpkin or eggplant. It does occasionally show up in fruit crisps and pies.

Quatre Epices

French for "four spices," *quatre epices* is a standard counterpart to *fines herbes*, and contains ground pepper (white or black), cloves, nutmeg, and ginger. For less kick, use allspice instead of pepper; for more sweetness, use cinnamon instead of ginger.

Adding more spices contradicts the name, but the recipe can vary from an even mixture of all four to almost all pepper with the others are minor notes. It features, naturally, in French dishes (especially soups, strews, and charcuterie) but has also found a home in some Middle Eastern cuisines.

RAS EL HANOUT

Ras el hanout is a hard mix to pin down; the name is simply Arabic for "head of the shop" or "top of the shop" and it can be found throughout North Africa (though it is generally associated with Morocco). Each and every spicemonger creates their own top-shelf blend of the best spices they have with the goal being a savory mix for use on meats or sprinkled on rice and couscous. A dozen ingredients seems to be the bare minimum, but some mixes extend into the twenties. The most common ingredients are available worldwide: aniseed, cardamom, cumin, cloves, cinnamon, fennel seeds, nutmeg, mace, allspice, ginger, coriander, pepper (black, white, and several varieties of chilis), paprika (both sweet and hot), fenugreek and turmeric. Others are highly regional and can be difficult to source: ash berries (rowan), chufa (nutsedge), cubeb pepper, galangal, grains of paradise, long pepper, orris root, monk's pepper (vitex), and rosebud. Further differences are in whether or not any or all of the spices are toasted before mixed. Note: It is uncommon to add salt, garlic, or saffron to *ras el hanout*, as those are better added at the table (salt and garlic) or would be overwhelmed (saffron).

SHICHIMI

The full name for this Japanese blend is *shichi-mi togarashi*: "seven-flavor chili pepper" (it can also be called *nana-iro togarashi*: "seven-color chili pepper"). It must feature red chili pepper (coarsely ground), citrus peel (orange or tangerine, dried), Szechuan or Japanese (sansho) peppercorns, white *and* black sesame seeds, poppy seeds, and *nori* (seaweed). Hemp seeds, ginger, garlic, or *shiso* (*Japanese basil* or *beefsteak*) round out the mix. Adherence to the "seven-flavor" name depends largely on whether you count white and black sesame seeds as separate flavors.

Taco Seasoning

The vaguely referenced *taco seasoning* is as flexible as its namesake dish. You can't really go wrong with a base of garlic, onion, oregano, paprika, cumin, and some form of chili (many recipes simply reference *chili powder*, which unhelpfully adds only further vagueness). This is a great mix to experiment with, trying out different peppers, adding a secret ingredient (coriander is common), or adjusting ratios. The blend works whether your taco is soft or hard (or a burrito, fajita, or quesadilla) and on all manner of fillings: beef, chicken, pork, bean, and vegetables. It's less common in fish tacos, where citrus and cilantro flavors reign, but not unheard-of.

Vadouvan

A French derivative of an Indian masala is a curry with additional aromatics. *Vadouvan* starts with cumin, fenugreek, garlic, mustard seeds, and onion, with customization into various curry styles from there. Traditionally, it undergoes several drying stages, beginning with sun drying while whole and then multiple cycles of mixing with oil and redrying. Use anywhere curry spices are called for.

Appendix B
Recipes

Aleppo Eggs

Serves: 1   **Spices:** Aleppo pepper, garlic

Simple scrambled eggs are elevated with Aleppo pepper and garlic; the Aleppo pepper also adds a pleasant red color to the eggs.

2 eggs   2 teaspoons Aleppo pepper
1 tablespoon butter $\frac{1}{8}$ teaspoon garlic powder
1 tablespoon milk or cream   salt and black pepper, to taste

Whisk together eggs, milk/cream, Aleppo pepper, garlic powder, and salt and black pepper. Melt butter in a small pan over medium heat. When butter is hot and foamy, add egg mixture. Reduce heat to very low. Using a plastic spatula, continuously scrape the bottom of the pan, bringing the cooked eggs to the top, for about 5 minutes, or until eggs are cooked and reach desired texture. Remove from pan; further season with same spices if you wish.

Note: Eggs will continue to cook/firm up when removed from heat. Take them off just before they reach your desired texture and let them sit for a minute; then they should be perfect.

ALMOND-BLUEBERRY GRANOLA

Yield: 5–6 cups   **Spices:** salt, cinnamon, vanilla

Using olive oil increases the deliciousness of this granola—don't use any other type of oil.

4 cups dry rolled (old-fashioned) oats
1½ cups sliced almonds
½ cup brown sugar
½ teaspoon salt
1 teaspoon cinnamon

½ cup olive oil
½ cup honey
2 teaspoons almond extract
1 teaspoon vanilla extract
½ cup dried blueberries

Preheat oven to 325°F.

Mix oats, almonds, brown sugar, salt, and cinnamon in a large bowl.

Mix olive oil, honey, almond extract, and vanilla extract in a microwave-safe dish or in a pot. Heat in microwave or in a pot on the stove. For microwave, heat for two minutes. For pot, stir over medium heat until honey thins, 3–4 minutes.

Add the wet ingredients, still warm, to the bowl with the dry ingredients, mixing to coat evenly. Spread into a large sheet pan and cook until golden brown, about 1 hour. Open the oven and stir every 10–20 minutes with a spatula or large spoon, being sure to move the granola in the corners into the middle of the pan.

Once cool, mix in dried blueberries.

Note: After the granola comes out of the oven it will dry out a bit and become a little harder, so even if granola seems only lightly golden brown, it will become darker. To keep a lighter crunch, remove from oven earlier.

ALOO GOBI

Serves: 4   **Spices:** curry, coriander, mustard, cumin, cilantro, salt

Potatoes, cauliflower, and plenty of spices make for a relatively simple Indian dish.

6 medium red potatoes

2 cups cauliflower florets (~½ a head)

2 tablespoons curry powder

1 teaspoon ground coriander

½ cup, plus 1 tablespoon water

2 tablespoons butter or olive oil

1 small yellow onion, minced

1 teaspoon whole brown

   mustard seeds

½ teaspoon whole cumin seeds

2–3 tablespoons lemon juice

3 tablespoons fresh cilantro, chopped

1 jalapeño pepper, seeds removed,

   thinly sliced

salt, to taste

Bring 2 quarts water to a boil, then add red potatoes. Reduce heat to a high simmer and cook until fork tender but not mushy, about 20 minutes. Drain and rinse until cool to the touch. Peel skin off of potatoes and cube.

While potatoes are cooking, bring a second smaller pot of water to a boil for the cauliflower. Cut cauliflower into florets and mince the onion. Boil cauliflower for 3 minutes, drain, and rinse with cool water. Pat dry.

Combine curry powder and coriander with 1 tablespoon water; let stand for at least 3 minutes. Heat butter/olive oil in a skillet over medium-high heat. Add minced onion, brown mustard seeds, and cumin seeds. When seeds start to sizzle and pop, add the curry mix, stirring well to evenly coat onions for 3 minutes. Add lemon juice, potatoes, and cauliflower, stirring well to coat. Add cilantro and jalapeño, along with ½ cup water. Turn down heat and let simmer till the vegetables are heated through and the sauce is thick, about 10 minutes.

Add salt to taste and serve with saffron rice.

ANISE-ALMOND COOKIES

Yield: 36 small cookies   **Spices:** aniseed, vanilla

Try these even if you've never liked anise before. They're delicious.

1 cup sugar
1 egg, plus 1 egg yolk
1 teaspoon aniseed
1 teaspoon vanilla extract

¼ teaspoon almond extract
2 cups almond flour
⅓ cup coarse sugar

Preheat oven to 350°F.

Blend sugar with eggs. Add aniseed, and vanilla and almond extracts. Blend with electric beater on low. Sift almond flour into mix and stir to combine.

Form dough into small balls, then roll in or sprinkle with coarse sugar. Bake on parchment-lined or greased cookie sheets, 9 minutes for somewhat gooey cookies (they will look flat and crackly) to 12 for crispier ones (which will have a round top and be slightly browned).

BAKED CINNAMON APPLE

Serves: 1–2   **Spices:** cinnamon

Once fresh apple cider becomes available, it's time for a cinnamon apple, baked so soft it melts. I prefer to top mine with crumbly streusel and a cider-whiskey reduction. I especially like these treats as a single-serving dessert; like an apple pie for one (or maybe two).

¼ cup brown sugar
½ cup, plus ¼ cup butter, kept cold
¼ cup rolled (old-fashioned) oats
2 teaspoons cinnamon
¼ cup hazelnuts, roughly chopped
2 apples (preferably Braeburn)

2 teaspoons maple syrup
½ cup apple cider
vanilla ice cream or yogurt
optional:
   3 tablespoons whiskey

Preheat oven to 350°F.

Combine the brown sugar, butter, oats, and cinnamon in a large bowl. Using your hands, combine the ingredients in a bowl until you've produced crumbled chunks (cold butter actually makes this easier). Mix in hazelnuts. Set aside, away from heat, or in fridge if working in a warm kitchen.

Using a paring knife, core the apples, leaving an inch or so at the bottom. You're drilling a hole to hold the streusel, so you don't want to drill all the way through and make the hole wider at the top, an upside-down cone.

Pour 1 teaspoon of maple syrup into each apple, then fill with streusel. Place filled apples in an 8-by-8 baking dish. Pour the apple cider and whiskey into the bottom of the pan, around the apples.

Bake for 40 minutes. Apples should become extremely tender without falling apart, and streusel should be golden brown. Remove the apples from the pan and place into serving bowls. Cool for 5 minutes.

Meanwhile, pour the cider-whiskey mix from the baking dish into a small saucepan. Bring to a brisk simmer over medium heat, stirring frequently. The thicker the sauce gets, the sweeter it will be. I reduce until I can't bear to wait any longer to eat the apple.

Pour the sauce directly on top of the apple and top with a scoop of ice cream or yogurt.

Note: Leftover streusel will keep for 2 weeks in the fridge, so you can save it for other dishes or future apples.

BALSAMIC VINAIGRETTE

Yield: 2 salads worth   **Spices:** white & white sesame, poppy, salt, black pepper

This easy-to-make vinaigrette adds tang and crunch to virtually any salad. I use it on lettuce salads and over vegetables like roasted beets.

1 teaspoon white sesame seeds
1 teaspoon black sesame seeds
1 teaspoon poppy seeds
1 pinch salt

black pepper, to taste
1½ tablespoon balsamic vinegar
1 tablespoon olive oil

In a dry pan over a low heat, add white sesame seeds, black sesame seeds, and poppy seeds. Shaking every minute or so, cook until white sesame seeds are brown, about 5 minutes. Remove from pan and set aside.

Once cool, combine seeds, salt, and pepper in a small bowl with balsamic vinegar and olive oil, mixing with fork. The seeds make emulsifying the oil and vinegar much easier, and this dressing will be more like a slurry.

Note: Toasting the seeds is optional, but it adds a nice flavor, making the seeds taste nuttier and richer, subtly improving the overall salad.

BANANA CINNAMON OATMEAL

Serves: 1   **Spices:** vanilla, cinnamon, salt

Walnuts, bananas, and cinnamon are three flavors that go extremely well together, making for a tasty and healthy oatmeal.

1 cup water
½ cup dry rolled (old-fashioned) oats
½ teaspoon vanilla
½ teaspoon cinnamon
1 pinch salt

1 tablespoon walnuts, chopped
1 banana, halved lengthwise,
   cut into ½-inch pieces
1 teaspoon honey or maple syrup

Boil water in small pot. Add oats and vanilla, decreasing heat to medium. Stir until desired consistency is achieved; the oatmeal should have absorbed the water but not be paste-like. Remove from heat, add cinnamon, salt, walnuts, and chopped banana. Add honey or maple syrup until as sweet as you like.

Buttermilk Ranch Dressing

Yield: 1½ cups **Spices:** salt, paprika, mustard, black pepper, parsley, chives, dill

Making dressing at home is easier than you think. This recipe is from my dad, and better than anything I've bought in a store.

1 cup buttermilk

½ cup mayonnaise

¼ teaspoon mustard powder or ½ cup buttermilk, ½ cup sour cream

1 teaspoon lemon juice

½ teaspoon salt

⅛ teaspoon paprika

⅛ teaspoon black pepper

1 tablespoon fresh parsley, chopped

1 teaspoon fresh chives, chopped

¼ teaspoon dry dill, or 1 teaspoon fresh, chopped

In a medium bowl, stir together the buttermilk and mayonnaise until fully blended. Add all other ingredients, adjusting for taste. Keeps for a week, covered in the fridge.

Note: If you don't have buttermilk on hand or forget to buy it, there are several substitutes. You can add 1 tablespoon of lemon juice or vinegar to 1 cup milk (whole or 2%) and let stand at room temperature for 5–10 minutes to thicken. Alternatively, you can thicken 1 cup of milk with 1¾ teaspoons cream of tartar. Or you can thin yogurt, sour cream, or kefir with water to reach the desired consistency.

CANDIED GINGER OATMEAL

Serves: 2   **Spices:** ginger, cinnamon, salt

Small bits of candied ginger add texture and interest to oatmeal.

1 cup water
½ cup dry rolled (old-fashioned) oats
¼ cup candied ginger (small pieces), or
　large piece cut into smaller pieces

⅛ teaspoon cinnamon
¼ cup walnuts, chopped (lightly
　toasted, if desired)
honey or maple syrup, to taste

Boil water in small pot. Add oats, candied ginger, and cinnamon, decreasing heat to medium. Stir until desired consistency is achieved; the oatmeal should have absorbed the water but not be paste-like. Remove from heat, and stir in walnuts. Add honey or maple syrup to sweeten.

CARDAMOM CRISPS

Yield: 8 dozen little cookies   **Spices:** cardamom, salt

These crispy cookies are excellent in December, as there's something distinctly holiday-feeling about them.

1¼ cup sugar
1 cup butter
2 eggs
2½ cups all-purpose flour

1½ teaspoon baking powder
½ teaspoon ground cardamom
½ teaspoon salt
sugar & grated coconut, to taste

Preheat oven to 375°F.

Blend sugar with butter. Beat in eggs. Sift together flour, baking powder, cardamom, and salt. Gradually stir into butter mixture.

Drop ½ rounded teaspoon dough at a time on ungreased cookie sheets. Flatten to ⅛ inch thickness using a glass covered with damp cloth. Sprinkle tops with granulated sugar and coconut.

Bake 8 to 10 minutes; cookies should be lightly brown around edges. Cool on pans for 30 seconds, then remove to wire cooling rack.

CINNAMON-AND-MORE FRENCH TOAST

Serves: 2 **Spices:** cinnamon, nutmeg, allspice, cardamom

Warming spices make this French toast recipe more interesting than the usual very sweet recipes. I sometimes add even more warm spices to my cinnamon sugar, like ginger.

6 eggs	½ teaspoon allspice
1 tablespoon whole milk or half-and-half	¼ teaspoon cardamom, ground
2 teaspoons, plus extra cinnamon	6–8 slices of hearty bread, thickly cut
cinnamon sugar	2 tablespoons butter
½ teaspoon nutmeg	butter and maple syrup, to taste

In a medium bowl, beat eggs well. Mix in milk, 2 teaspoons cinnamon, nutmeg, allspice, and cardamom. Dip both sides of each bread slice into the egg mixture, letting eggs soak in for a few seconds before turning. Lightly sprinkle one side with more cinnamon and the other side with cinnamon sugar.

Heat butter in a large pan over medium heat. When butter is hot and foamy, add bread and toast for approximately 3 minutes per side, until lightly brown and crisp. Serve warm with butter and maple syrup, and more cinnamon sugar if desired.

Note: The extra cinnamon and cinnamon sugar sprinkled on the bread after it's dipped in the egg mixture highlights the sweet cinnamon flavor by adding it to the outside, where the hot pan and butter can fry it, along with the egg, into a cinnamon crust. I love this, but for a less pronounced cinnamon flavor, skip this step.

GARLICKY SCRAMBLED EGGS

Serves: 1 (double for 2)   **Spices:** garlic, onion, oregano, black pepper, salt

An easy way to make your scrambled eggs savory.

3 eggs
1 tablespoon milk or heavy cream
¼ teaspoon garlic
1 dash onion powder

⅛ teaspoon oregano
⅛ teaspoon black pepper
1 pinch salt
3 teaspoons butter

Crack eggs into bowl. Add milk/cream, garlic, onion powder, oregano, black pepper, and salt, and whisk together. Put butter in a small pan over medium heat. When butter is hot and foamy, add egg mixture. Reduce heat to very low. Using a plastic spatula, continuously scrape the bottom of the pan, bringing the cooked eggs to the top, for about 5 minutes, or until eggs are cooked and reach desired texture. Remove from pan; add more spices if you wish.

Note: Eggs will continue to cook/firm up when removed from heat. Take them off just before they reach your desired texture and let them sit for a minute; then they should be perfect.

HEARTY GREENS BREAKFAST (OR DINNER) SALAD

Serves: 2   **Spices:** garlic, black pepper, white & black sesame, poppy

This is a favorite breakfast in my house, but can be made and eaten for any meal.

2 strips bacon

1 tablespoon olive oil

1 cup bread (I like an Italian loaf)

¼ teaspoon garlic

¼ teaspoon salt

⅛ teaspoon black pepper

1 teaspoon white sesame seeds

1 teaspoon black sesame seeds

1 teaspoon poppy seeds

1½ tablespoon balsamic vinegar

¼ cup white vinegar

2 eggs

1 pound spring mix

¼ cup goat cheese, crumbled

Fry 2 strips of bacon. Set aside on paper towel to drain. Remove about half of the bacon grease from pan, leaving the rest. Add 1 tablespoon olive oil to pan.

Cut bread into half-inch cubes. When bacon fat and oil are hot, add cubed bread to pan. Sprinkle garlic, salt, and black pepper over the bread and shake pan to mix. Fry bread, shaking every minute or so, until bread is golden and crisp, 5–7 minutes. Set aside on paper towel.

In a separate, dry pan, toast white sesame seeds, black sesame seeds, and poppy seeds over low. Shaking every minute or so, cook until white sesame seeds turn brown, about 5 minutes. Remove from pan and set aside. Once cool, move to a small bowl and stir in balsamic vinegar and olive oil.

Bring a medium pot of water to a steady simmer, then add white vinegar. Carefully break two eggs into a shallow bowl. If a yolk breaks, set aside and crack a new egg into bowl. Carefully dip bowl with eggs into simmering water, slowly transferring eggs to water. Cook until poached, approximately 4 minutes. Using a slotted spoon, carefully remove from water and pat dry with paper towel.

Divide spring mix and croutons between two roomy bowls. Crumble in bacon and goat cheese. Give the dressing a quick stir if it has separated, then pour over salad and stir to coat spring mix. Add egg to top, splitting open.

Lazy Tomato Basil Soup

Serves: 6–8   **Spices:** basil

Using canned tomato soup and crushed tomatoes, this recipe adds some oomph with vegetables and basil to improve the canned products without spending the time of making soup from scratch.

2 tablespoons olive oil
1 medium yellow onion, diced
1 red or yellow bell pepper, chopped
2 8-ounce cans condensed tomato soup

1 16-ounce can crushed tomatoes
1½ cups half-and-half
2 tablespoons dried basil
  or ¼ cup fresh, chopped

Heat oil in a large pan over medium heat. When oil is shimmering, add onion. Cook until tender, about 5 minutes. Add pepper and cook until tender. Add soup, canned tomatoes, half-and-half, and half of the basil. Bring to a boil, then reduce to simmer 1 one hour, stirring regularly. Serve with remaining basil sprinkled on top.

Note: This soup ages especially well. You'll probably be making more than you need, so will have delicious leftovers for the next day or two. Microwave if necessary, but better to reheat on the stovetop over low heat.

Paprika-Leek Mac and Cheese

Serves: 6   **Spices:** yellow mustard, paprika, red pepper, nutmeg, salt

Box mix mac and cheese has its place and time, but nothing compares to homemade. I highlight paprika, along with leeks and a few other spices, for my personal flair. Breadcrumbs on top add a nice crispiness.

1 tablespoon, plus ⅓ cup unsalted butter	1 teaspoon dry yellow mustard powder
4–5 leeks	1 tablespoon smoked or sweet paprika
2 tablespoons, plus 1 teaspoon salt	¼ teaspoon nutmeg
1 pound penne	1 teaspoon crushed red pepper
3 tablespoons all-purpose flour	2 eggs
3 cups whole milk	*optional*:
1 pound sharp cheddar cheese, grated	3 tablespoons breadcrumbs

Grease 9x13-inch pan with unsalted butter. Remove dark green part of leeks and cur remainder into ¼ inch cubes.

Put on water to boil for pasta. When boiling, add 2 tablespoons salt and penne. Cook until tender but still firm. Drain and return to pot.

In large pan, melt butter over medium-low heat. When foamy, add leeks and stir for a minute, then cover pan, cooking 10–15 minutes until soft. Stir once after five minutes and lower temperature if the bottom leeks are browning. Remove cover and add flour, stirring to combine. Add milk and stir until simmering. Add cheese, mustard, paprika, nutmeg, crushed red flake pepper, and salt.

Whisk eggs together in bowl. Temper in ½ cup sauce, gradually, so eggs don't scramble, then pour eggs into saucepan and combine.

Add cheese mixture to pasta pot and stir to coat. Pour into prepared baking dish. If using, top with breadcrumbs. Bake until cheese bubbles and edges are brown, about 30 minutes. Let cool for at least 10 minutes before digging in.

Paprika Potato Pancakes, with Applesauce

Serves: 2   **Spices:** sweet paprika, garlic, thyme, black pepper

Wisconsin fish fry is so much more than fish. A brandy old-fashioned cocktail and an appetizer of pickled vegetables, which we call a "relish tray," whet the appetite for the fish to come. The fish isn't served alone, though: crispy potato pancakes, dipped in applesauce, are a must.

½ pound potatoes (~3 medium russets)
1 teaspoon salt
1 teaspoon black pepper, freshly ground
1 teaspoon sweet paprika
½ teaspoon garlic powder
¾ teaspoon thyme

1 egg, beaten
1 yellow onion, diced
1 tablespoon all-purpose flour
¼ cup butter
1 cup applesauce

In a large pot, bring water to a boil. Add potatoes and cook until tender when pierced by a fork, about 20–30 minutes. Meanwhile, mix salt, black pepper, paprika, garlic, and thyme into beaten egg.

When potatoes are cool, grate into a large bowl lined with a thin dish towel. (Do NOT do this while the potatoes are hot. If you're impatient, put the potatoes in ice water to help them cool faster.) Gather up the towel, creating a little sachet of potatoes within, and squeeze out excess moisture. Do your best; the less water in the potatoes, the crispier they can get.

Dump out water, dry potatoes with towel, and place back in the bowl. Add onions and spiced egg; combine with your hands. Mix in flour. The mixture should now be easily formed into patties, but if it feels too loose, add in more flour, a little at a time, until it comes together.

Shape mixture into two discs, 5–6 inches across and about ½ inch thick. Melt butter in a large frying pan over medium-high heat. When butter is hot and foamy, place potato cake in pan. Cook about 5 minutes, until bottom is brown and crisp, then turn over and repeat for other side. While one pancake is frying, get the next one shaped and ready. Add more butter between rounds as necessary. Serve hot and top with cool applesauce.

Note: Mix or pancakes may be prepared ahead of time; put in airtight container or in a bowl with plastic wrap pressed down onto the surface of the mixture.

Restaurant-Style Dipping Sauce, for Toasted Baguette

Serves: Several (or just 1)   **Spices:** rosemary, crushed red pepper, black pepper, salt

This is nice for an extremely easy dinner; all you need to pick up is a fresh baguette, and the dipping vinegar can be made at home. I'll also add any good cheese I have at the time, or pick up a wheel of Brie while I'm buying the baguette.

1 baguette	¼ teaspoon crushed red pepper flakes
¼ cup olive oil, divided	¼ teaspoon black pepper, freshly
3 tablespoons balsamic vinegar	cracked
1 teaspoon cracked rosemary	¼ teaspoon salt

Preheat oven to 400°F.

Slice baguette into one-inch thick pieces. Drizzle 2 tablespoons olive oil over bread slices. Place slices on sheet pan, then cook in oven until tops are light golden brown, about 10 minutes.

Combine balsamic vinegar, 2 tablespoons olive oil, rosemary, crushed red pepper, black pepper, and salt in a small bowl, whisking with fork to combine.

Dip crusty bread into spicy balsamic oil.

Note: This is also good paired with Brie cheese. I like to heat the Brie up in an oven-safe crock, and alternate dipping the bread into the cheese and the balsamic dip.

Rhubarb Pie

Serves: 6–8   **Spices:** salt, vanilla

When rhubarb is in season, late spring through midsummer, make this tasty pie with a crumble top.

1 cup sugar

1 tablespoon, plus 2 tablespoons all-purpose flour

1 pinch salt

2 eggs

2 cups rhubarb, cut into quarter-inch pieces

1 pie shell or crust, unbaked

½ cup brown sugar

1 tablespoon butter, cold

Preheat oven to 425°F.

For pie filling, beat together sugar, 1 tablespoon flour, and salt in a roomy bowl. Beat in eggs, one at a time. Fold in rhubarb pieces, combining until just mixed. Pour mixture into pie shell.

For pie topping, mix together brown sugar, cold butter, and 2 tablespoons flour in a bowl. Using your hands, mix together until it combines and is crumbly, like gravel. Sprinkle over the pie mixture.

Bake for 15 minutes, then turn oven down to 350°F and bake for another 30 minutes.

ROASTED CHICKPEAS

Serves: 1–2   **Spices:** cumin, za'atar, black sesame, salt; optional: curry, cayenne

This is one of those extremely simple recipes to make at home when you don't really feel like cooking, but still want a healthy meal.

1 15-ounce can chickpeas

1 tablespoon, plus ½ teaspoon olive oil

1 teaspoon cumin

1 teaspoon za'atar

¼ teaspoon black sesame seeds

¼ teaspoon, plus a pinch salt

½ teaspoon white wine vinegar

juice of ½ lemon

⅛ teaspoon honey

Preheat oven to 450°F.

Drain can of chickpeas into a sieve or strainer and rinse under cold water. Pat dry with paper towel. In a medium bowl, combine chickpeas, 1 tablespoon olive oil, cumin, za'atar, black sesame seeds, and ¼ teaspoon salt. Spread on a baking sheet, separating chickpeas apart from each other so they'll get crisp and brown instead of clumping together and steaming. Roast in oven for 15 minutes. Chickpeas should be brown and crunchy.

Meanwhile, mix ½ teaspoon olive oil, white wine vinegar, lemon, honey, and a pinch of salt into a small bowl. When chickpeas are finished, add to bowl with oil and spices. Toss to coat.

Note: If your za'atar seasoning has cumin or salt already in it, omit or reduce cumin and salt. For a spicy version, add ½ teaspoon cayenne pepper, or 1½ teaspoons hot curry powder.

ROSEMARY BREAKFAST POTATOES

Serves: 4   **Spices:** salt, black pepper, rosemary

Rosemary potatoes are a classic breakfast dish. Serve alongside eggs for a hearty start to the day.

2–3 russet potatoes, or 4–5 red potatoes	2 teaspoons salt
1 small yellow onion	2 teaspoons black pepper
2 tablespoons butter, olive oil, or bacon fat	2 teaspoons rosemary

Peel potatoes and chop into one-inch cubes. Boil potatoes until tender when pierced by a fork, about 10 minutes.

Coarsely mince onion. In a large skillet, heat cooking fat over high heat, then add onion, stirring until brown, 4–5 minutes. Add potatoes to pan, along with salt, black pepper, and rosemary. Let them sit for a minute or two in the hot pan, without disturbing, so they get nice and crisp. Shake every few minutes. The potatoes are already cooked, so you're really just browning and incorporating flavors. Remove when they reach desired crispiness; I like my potatoes nearly burnt so leave them in for a long time.

Note: You may add vegetables to the potatoes. Chopped bell peppers are especially good; cut into one-inch pieces and add with potato.

SAFFRON RICE

Serves: 4, as a side dish or mixed into curry dish   **Spices:** MSG, saffron, salt

This beautiful rice has flavor, too, from the faint floral aroma of saffron and the MSG enhancement.

1 tablespoon water, for saffron	½ teaspoon salt
1 pinch saffron (20–30 threads)	1 teaspoon MSG
2 cups chicken or vegetable stock	1 cup white rice, short or long grain

Boil 1 tablespoon water. Put saffron in a small bowl, then pour over 1 tablespoon boiling water. Let stand for 15–30 minutes, or longer if you have the time.

In a medium, heavy-bottomed pot combine the saffron water, stock, salt, MSG, and rice. Bring to a boil, then reduce heat to medium. Cover pot, and simmer until liquid has been absorbed into rice and rice is tender, 15–20 minutes.

SAFFRON SHORTBREAD SQUARES

Yield: 30 squares **Spices:** saffron, cardamom, cinnamon

The dominant flavor is saffron; the cardamom and cinnamon are very much in the background.

1 cup unsalted butter

¼ teaspoon saffron

1 cup, plus ½ cup sugar

1 egg, separated

1 teaspoon vanilla

1¾ cups all-purpose flour

2 teaspoons baking powder

½ teaspoon cardamom seeds

¼ teaspoon Ceylon cinnamon

1 tablespoon water

⅔ cups pistachios, chopped

Make ahead: In a small pot, melt butter and saffron over low heat. Stir to combine, cook butter for two minutes, then remove from heat. Put in jar or Tupperware and leave in fridge for a minimum of 8 hours (several days works too).

Preheat oven to 350 degrees Fahrenheit.

Cream saffron butter and 1 cup sugar. Add egg yolk and vanilla, mixing well. In a separate bowl, combine flour, baking powder, cardamom, and cinnamon. Gradually add dry ingredients to wet ones; mixture will be crumbly. Spread in an even layer in a greased 9 x 13 inch pan.

In small bowl, mix egg whites and water. Pour over dough. Sprinkle ½ cup sugar and pistachios over top. Bake 25–30 minutes.

Note: To bring the cardamom and cinnamon notes to greater prominence, add ⅛ teaspoon of each to the sugar sprinkled on top.

SAFFRON YOGURT

Serves: 1   **Spices:** saffron, salt

This yogurt is truly beautiful, and brings a refined flavor when added to other dishes.

½ teaspoon dried orange peel, or 1½ teaspoons fresh orange zest

1–2 pinches saffron (30–50 threads)

1 tablespoon water

1 pinch salt

1 cup plain, full-fat Greek yogurt

optional:

¼ cup sliced almonds, toasted

¼ cup pomegranate seeds

Boil water. In small bowl, combine orange zest and saffron. Pour over 1 tablespoon boiling water, mix, and let stand for at least half an hour. (If using fresh zest, add after 15 minutes.) After 30 minutes, add pinch of salt, stir, then add to 1 cup yogurt, stirring until mixed in. Add toasted almonds and pomegranate seeds for more flavor.

Note: Leave the saffron in the water for up to three hours before adding to yogurt. The flavor and color will be best if the yogurt is left overnight, as the saffron flavor deepens the longer it infuses.

SAVORY CURRY OATMEAL

Serves: 1   **Spices:** curry, salt

A savory oatmeal is excellent for breakfast or dinner.

1 cup water

½ cup dry rolled (old-fashioned) oats

2 teaspoons curry powder

1 pinch salt

2 tablespoons golden raisins

¼ cup sliced almonds (toasted, if desired)

honey or maple syrup, to taste

Boil water in small pot. Add oats, decreasing heat to medium. Stir until desired consistency is achieved; the oatmeal should have absorbed the water but not be paste-like. Remove from heat; stir in curry, salt, golden raisins, and almonds. Taste; add honey or maple syrup to sweeten.

SICK SOUP

Serves: 2   **Spices:** MSG, curry powder, garlic, salt, pepper, oregano

This is a hydrating and simple base that heartier foods can be added to, depending on how much the sick person in question wants. I find when I'm feverish, the last thing I want is heavy foods, so I favor a version some might find too watery. I also like to use a hot curry powder or add cayenne to give it enough heat to clear out my sinuses. Chicken, noodles, and crackers can be added to this if one wishes to make it a more substantial meal.

3 cups water	½ teaspoon salt
2 tablespoon chicken stock,	1 teaspoon oregano or other herbs
or 1 chicken bouillon cube	*optional:*
½ teaspoon curry powder (sweet or hot)	¼ teaspoon cayenne pepper
½ teaspoon garlic powder	1 pound egg noodles, cooked
½ teaspoon MSG	1 pound chicken, cooked & shredded
½ teaspoon black pepper	2 cups oyster crackers

Combine all ingredients over medium heat, simmering until warmed through, about 10–15 minutes.

Note: If adding chicken, you can cook and shred chicken breasts (seasoned as you like) or save time by buying a rotisserie chicken from the grocery store and just shredding it off with a fork.

Spicy Pita, for Hummus

Serves: 4   **Spices:** za'atar, garlic, rosemary/oregano, salt

Here's another recipe that makes for a super simple dinner in. Buy (or make, if ambitious) a tub of hummus, carrots, and pita for a lazy dinner at home. Make the pita delicious with some oil and spices.

4 pitas
3 tablespoons olive oil
2 tablespoons za'atar
2 teaspoons granulated garlic

1 teaspoon rosemary or oregano
1 teaspoon salt
1 teaspoon black pepper, freshly ground

Preheat oven to 400°F.

Leaving pita rounds whole, brush on olive oil, covering surface in a thin layer. Sprinkle on za'atar, garlic, rosemary or oregano, salt, and pepper. Slice pita rounds into quarters for a soft middle or eighths for a crispier finish. Spread on a sheet pan, and bake until edges are golden brown, or longer, if you like them crisper, 8–10 minutes. Remove and serve with hummus.

Spicy Shoestring Potatoes

Serves: 2   **Spices:** caraway, salt, garlic, thyme, black pepper, cayenne pepper

These are like homemade potato chips, but better.

2 russet potatoes
1 teaspoon caraway seeds
½ teaspoon salt
¼ teaspoon granulated garlic
¼ teaspoon dried thyme

¼ teaspoon black pepper, freshly ground
⅛ teaspoon cayenne pepper
1 tablespoon olive oil
1 tablespoon butter

Peel potatoes. Using a mandoline or a knife and some patience, julienne the potatoes into the size of matchsticks. Place on paper towel–lined plate, and dry the best you can. In a small bowl, mix caraway, salt, garlic, thyme, pepper, and cayenne.

In a large pan, heat oil and butter. When hot and simmering, add potatoes, cooking about 5 minutes, until brown. Use tongs or a slotted spoon and place potatoes once more on paper towel to drain off grease. Sprinkle seasoning mixture over while potatoes are still hot.

Summer Fruit Tart

Serves: 6–8   **Spices:** vanilla

This is a fantastic way to use abundant fruit available in summer. When a neighbor drops some off, the fruits stands appear, or you go out berry picking, this is the best way to use up your supply.

2 cups graham crackers, crushed
½ cup butter, cold
½ cup sugar
1 cup cream cheese
1 cup powdered sugar

1 teaspoon vanilla
4+ cups fresh fruit, thinly sliced as
    necessary: strawberries, blueberries,
    raspberries, blackberries, kiwi

Preheat oven to 350°F.

Grease an 8-inch round pie dish with butter or cooking spray. Cut cold butter into chunks. Combine crushed graham cracker crumbs, butter, and sugar in a roomy bowl. Using hands, work butter into crackers and sugar, combining until you can work it into a pie dish. Move crust up sides of the dish, but don't worry about going all the way up. Bake for 8–10 minutes.

Whip cream cheese with a fork or beat with a beater for a few minutes, until the cream cheese is aerated and fluffier. Add sugar and vanilla and whip for a minute more.

LET CRUST COOL. If you don't, the frosting will melt into the crust. Once crust is completely cool, fill evenly with cream cheese mix. Decorate with strawberries, and other fruit as desired.

TACO BROCCOLI

Serves: 2–4 **Spices:** taco seasoning

Taco broccoli is delicious, even for people who say they don't like broccoli. The vegetable gets crisp and unrecognizable in the hot oven.

1 head of broccoli (~4 cups)
3 tablespoons olive oil

¼ cup taco seasoning (see Appendix A)

Preheat oven to 450°F.

Cut broccoli into florets. In a large bowl, combine broccoli, olive oil, and taco seasoning, mixing well until broccoli is evenly coated with oil and seasoning. Spread on a sheet pan, spacing the broccoli so there's space between florets, using two sheet pans if necessary. (You want the broccoli to roast, not to steam.) Roast until edges are brown and charred, about 25 minutes. Scrape into bowl and enjoy.

WISCONSIN FISH FRY

Serves: 4 **Spices:** cayenne pepper, paprika, salt, black pepper

Though Friday fish fry is a year-round staple in Wisconsin Supper Clubs, you can make it at home any day of the week.

1½ cups all-purpose flour
½ cup cornstarch
³/₈ teaspoon cayenne pepper
½ teaspoon paprika
⅛ teaspoon black pepper
2 teaspoons salt

1 teaspoon baking powder
12 oz. beer, cold (light, malty beer is preferable; avoid hoppy, bitter beers)
4 pieces yellow perch (or other freshwater fish)

In a bowl, whisk flour, cornstarch, cayenne pepper, paprika, black pepper, and salt until combined. Transfer ¾ cup of mixture to a rimmed baking sheet and set aside. Mix baking powder into remaining mixture. Add 1¼ cups of the of beer (10 oz.) and stir until mixture is just combined; the batter will be lumpy. Add remaining beer as needed, 1 tablespoon at a time, whisking after each addition, until batter falls from the whisk in a thin, steady stream.

Dry fish with paper towel or kitchen towel. Dredge fish in reserved flour mixture, patting excess off, and place on wire rack. Then, dip dredged fish in the beer batter, letting excess drip off. Placed battered fish back onto baking sheet with flour mixture and turn to lightly coat each side. Immediately fry in 375°F oil until fish is cooked through and batter is a golden brown. Drain fish on paper towel or paper bag. Serve immediately.

World's Easiest Baked Sweet Potato

Serves: 1   **Spices:** Cajun seasoning

This really is the ultimate in easy cooking.

1 sweet potato

2 tablespoons butter

2 tablespoons Cajun seasoning
(see Appendix A)

Preheat oven to 450°F.

Wash sweet potato, dry, then chop in half, lengthwise. Place flat-side down, then smear butter over skin. On that, sprinkle a healthy dose of Cajun seasoning, about 1 tablespoon per side. Place 1 tablespoon of butter in the center of sheet pan and put in over for about 3 minutes, to melt. Spread the butter out and place potatoes flat-side down, making sure butter coats entire surface. Cook until potato is cooked through and skin is brown and crisp, around 20–25 minutes.

Note: Depending on the size of the sweet potato, cooking times can vary. A small one might only take 10 minutes to cook through; a large one might take 30. Check with a fork every five or 10 minutes if you're unsure.

Appendix C
Beverages

CASSIA TEA
Serves: 1

water
cassia chunks

Heat water to 200°F, or boil and let cool for one minute. Put 2 teaspoons cassia chunks in a tea strainer or in the bottom of a mug. Pour hot water over and infuse anywhere from 3 to 20 minutes. The cinnamon flavor will start off mild and grow in strength the longer it sits; even after 20 minutes the flavor remains delicate.

Note: The cassia chunks will sink to the bottom of the mug, so a strainer isn't necessary. It doesn't get very strong, so I typically leave the cassia, allowing it to continue extracting while I drink. It is very sweet. Is it basically just hot cinnamon water? Technically yes. But it's warming and calming.

GRANDPA'S GINGER TEA
Serves: 1

1 cup water
½–1 teaspoon ginger, powdered or freshly grated
optional:
    5 peppercorns, whole, any color

Add water, ginger, and peppercorns (if using) to a small pot. Bring to a simmer and simmer for 10 minutes. Pour through sieve or pick out peppercorns.

My grandpa wrote that he used this tea to open his lungs when he was suffering from allergies, and also to give himself a boost before a meeting.

Mulled Wine

For a Night In

Serves: 1–4

4 small pieces candied ginger

3 whole cloves

3 cardamom seeds from a pod
(any color)

1 quarter of a nutmeg piece, broken
from a whole nutmeg

1 Korintje cinnamon stick and 1 Ceylon
cinnamon stick (or 1 tablespoon

cinnamon chunks, if you have no
cinnamon sticks)

1 bottle (750mL) robust red wine

2 tablespoons brown sugar

optional:

1 inch of vanilla bean

1 allspice berry

Combine all spices except cinnamon sticks in muslin bag. (If you have no muslin bag, simply add loose spices to pot.) Break cinnamon sticks in half. Add red wine, brown sugar, cinnamon sticks, and spices to medium or large pot. Bring to a simmer over a medium heat, being careful to not let it boil. Keep at a low simmer for 10 minutes.

Note: Don't break the cinnamon sticks down too much; you'll start to get cinnamon powder, and you don't want that in your mulled wine.

For a Party

Serves: 4–8

5 whole cloves

5 cardamom seeds from a pod
(any color)

2 bottles red wine

1+ cup brandy

1 orange, sliced into rounds

2 Korintje cinnamon sticks

¼ cup sugar

optional:

3 allspice berries

Combine all spices except cinnamon sticks in muslin bag (or let loose in pot). In large pot over medium heat, combine wine, brandy, orange slices, sugar, and all spices, snapping the cinnamon sticks in half. Like a rowdy party, this mulled wine can get sloppy; orange seeds will need to be picked out, too much brandy may be added. Adjust as necessary.

Saffron Spice Tea

Serves: 1

1 cup water

1 cinnamon stick (3–6 inches),
   or 1 teaspoon cassia chunks

1 piece dried ginger, or 2-inches fresh,
   cut into half-inch chunks

1 small pinch saffron (15–20 threads)

3 green cardamom pods, crushed to
   expose seeds

optional:
   honey, to taste

If using dried ginger, reconstitute by sitting in water for at least 30 minutes prior to making tea.

In a mug: Heat water to 200 °F, or boil and let cool for one minute. Place cinnamon stick and ginger directly in mug. Combine saffron and cardamom pods in tea strainer. Pour water over and infuse for 6–8 minutes. You may want to add a little honey to sweeten.

On the stove: In a small pot, bring one cup water, saffron, cardamom, cinnamon stick, and ginger to a simmer. Simmer for three minutes. Place a sieve on top of a mug and pour the tea through.

SMOKING BISHOP

Serves: 8

Save the good port for sipping and use a decent quality, but not expensive, bottle of port to go in your Smoking Bishop. This is an excellent dish to make during frigid weather, as the aroma the oranges produce when baking, combined with the drink, makes a satisfying answer to a cold day.

3 oranges

20 cloves, whole

1 bottle (750mL) port, medium quality

½ cup or more brandy or cognac

¼ cup brown sugar

¼ teaspoon nutmeg, ground

¼ teaspoon allspice, ground

1 cinnamon stick

juice of two oranges, or ⅔ cup orange juice

zest of one orange

Preheat oven to 350°F.

Wash the oranges. Using a thumbtack, toothpick, or sharp meat thermometer, pierce skin 20 times. Push cloves through holes. Place on baking sheet in oven until toasted and brown, at least one hour. Remove and cool.

Pour whole bottle of port into a large, thick-bottomed saucepan over high heat. Once simmering, lower heat to medium, add brandy or cognac, brown sugar, nutmeg, allspice, and cinnamon. Add orange juice and zest. Cut clove orange into wedges and add to pot. Stir together, taste, adding more spices or brandy if desired, and serve in small mugs or punch bowl. Sit back, exhale contentedly.

SPICED EARL GREY TEA

Serves: 4–6

This is a lightly fruity, lightly spiced mild black tea. Probably because of the orange juice, I like this tea when I'm sick. It's sort of like a hot toddy, but minus the alcohol and with more citrus and spices.

1 chunk nutmeg (broken from whole nutmeg)

2 medium oranges

1 lemon

1 quart (4 cups) water

¼ cup sugar

10 whole cloves

2 small or 1 large cinnamon stick, broken up

5 black peppercorns

4 bags (or ~4 teaspoons loose) Earl Grey tea leaves

To break nutmeg: Place whole nutmeg in paper towel or kitchen towel. Smash with heavy pan. One good pound should do it. For this recipe, a chunk that's about a quarter of the nutmeg is preferable.

Slice rind off one of the oranges, then juice both and the lemon. You want a minimum of ¼ cup orange juice and 2 tablespoons lemon juice.

In a medium pot, combine water, sugar, cloves, cinnamon, nutmeg, and peppercorns. Bring to a boil, then remove from heat and add tea. Steep for 4 minutes, then remove tea and spices, straining through sieve into a large measuring cup or pitcher. Removing spices from then pot, then pour the tea back in.

Add orange rind, orange juice, lemon juice. Bring to a low simmer, then remove from heat. Serve in small mugs. Garnish each mug with one cinnamon stick.

Bibliography

Acton, Eliza. *Modern Cookery, in all its Branches: Reduced to a System of Easy Practice for the use of Private Families*. London: Longman, Brown, Greek and Longmans, 1845.

American Spice Trade Association, Inc. *Spices: What They Are and Where They Come From*. New York: American Spice Trade Association, 1951.

———. *A Treasury of Spices*. New York: American Spice Trade Association, 1956

———. "A Glossary of Spices." New York: American Spice Trade Association, 1966.

———. "What You Should Know About Ginger." New York: American Spice Trade Association, 1980.

———. "What You Should Know About Basil." New York: American Spice Trade Association, June 4, 2000.

———. " What You Should Know About Cumin Seed." New York: American Spice Trade Association, August 8, 2000.

———. "What You Should Know About Nutmeg & Mace." New York: American Spice Trade Association, August 8, 2000.

———. "What You Should Know About Sesame Seed." New York: American Spice Trade Association, August 8, 2000.

———. "What You Should Know About Turmeric." New York: American Spice Trade Association, August 8, 2000.

Associated Press, "Hazardous materials unit called after horseradish spill," February 14, 1995. http://www.apnewsarchive.com/1995/Hazardous-Materials-Unit-Called-After-Horse radish-Spill/id-567df7bbaf8d6afb00098386a62bc32b

Barnett, Richard. *The Book of Gin*. New York: Grove Press, 2011.

Bitterman, Mark. *Salted*. Berkeley: Ten Speed Press, 2010.

Bomgardner, Melody M. "The Problem with Vanilla," *Scientific American*. September 14, 2016. https://www.scientificamerican.com/article/the-problem-with-vanilla/

Booth, Martin. *Opium: A History*. New York: St. Martin's Press, 1996.

Bosland, Paul W., Coon, Denise, Cooke, Peter H. "Novel Formation of Ectopic (Nonplacental) Capsaicinoid Secreting Vesicles on Fruit Walls Explains the Morphological

Mechanism of Super-hot Chile Peppers." *Journal of the American Society for Horticultural Science*, pages 253–256, 2015. https://www.researchgate.net/publication/279564263_ Novel_Formation_of_Ectopic_Nonplacental_Capsaicinoid_Secreting_Vesicles_on_ Fruit_Walls_Explains_the_Morphological_Mechanism_for_Super-hot_Chile_Peppers

Braida, Charlene A. *Glorious Garlic: A Cookbook.* Pownal, Vermont: Storey Communications, Inc., 1986.

Broomfield, Andrea. *Food And Cooking In Victorian England.* Greenwood Publishing Group, Inc., 2007.

Chicago Tribune, "Beer, Garlic Stoked Labor of Pyramids," April 25, 1993, Chicago Tribune: http://articles.chicagotribune.com/1993-04-25/news/9304250206_1_tombs -zahi-hawass-great-pyramids.

CDC. "Sodium and Food Sources." March 28, 2017. https://www.cdc.gov/salt/food .htm

CNN. "Larry King Live: Interview with Julia Child." August 15, 2002. http://transcripts .cnn.com/TRANSCRIPTS/0208/15/lkl.00.html

Coe, D. Sophie, and Coe, D. Michael. *The True History of Chocolate.* London: Thames & Hudson, 1996.

Cook, Robin. *The Guardian*, "Robin Cook's chicken tikka masala speech," April 19, 2001. https://www.theguardian.com/world/2001/apr/19/race.britishidentity.

Davidson, Alan. *The Oxford Companion to Food.* Oxford: Oxford University Press, 1999.

Day, Harvey. *The Complete Book of Curries.* New York: A.S. Barnes and Co., 1966.

Dickens, Cedric. *Drinking With Dickens.* Goring-on-Thames: Elvendon Press, 1980.

Dumas, Alexandre. *Dictionary of Cuisine.* New York: Simon and Schuster, 1958.

Elliot, Paul, and Brown, Ian. "Sodium Intakes Around the World." World Health Organization. http://www.who.int/dietphysicalactivity/Elliot-brown-2007.pdf

Eriksson, Nicholas, Shirley Wu, Chuong B. Do, Amy K. Kiefer, Joyce Y. Tung, Joanna L. Mountain, David A. Hinds, and Uta Francke. "A genetic variant near olfactory receptor genes influences cilantro preference" September 10, 2012. ArXiv.org. https://arxiv.org/ abs/1209.2096

European Union, Regulation No 110/2008 of the European Parliament and of the Council, Annex II, *Spirit Drinks*, "Gin," no. 20, "Distilled Gin," no. 21, and "Aniseed-flavoured spirit drinks," no. 25.

Ewbank, Anne. "Building a Life-Sized Gingerbread House Takes Over 10,000 Cookie Bricks." *Atlas Obscura*, December 14, 2017. https://www.atlasobscura.com/articles/life-size-gingerbread-house-san-francisco-fairmont-hotel

FDA. "Inspections, Compliance, Enforcement, and Criminal Investigations" CPG Sec. 525.750 Spices—Definitions. https://www.fda.gov/ICECI/ComplianceManuals/CompliancePolicyGuidanceManual/ucm074468.htm

Filocamo A., Nueno-Palop C., Bisignano C., Mandalari G., Narbad A. "Effect of garlic powder on the growth of commensal bacteria from the gastrointestinal tract." *Phytomedicine.* 2012 Jun 15. https://www.ncbi.nlm.nih.gov/pubmed/22480662

Gelles, David. "Now at Saks: Salt Rooms, a Bootcamp and a Peek at Retail's Future." *The New York Times*, August 4, 2017. https://www.nytimes.com/2017/08/04/business/saks-salt-room-bootcamp.html?smid=tw-nytnational&smtyp=cur&_r=0

George, Andrew. "How the British defeated Napoleon with citrus fruit," *The Conversation*: May 19, 2016. https://theconversation.com/how-the-british-defeated-napoleon-with-citrus-fruit-58826

Gibbs, W. M. *Spices and How to Know Them.* Buffalo, New York: Matthews-Northrup Works, 1909.

Goodman, Philip. *The Purim Anthology.* Philadelphia: The Jewish Publication Society of America, 1952.

Halász, Zoltán. *Paprika Through the Ages.* Budapest: Corvina Press, 1963.

Hayes, Elizabeth S. *Spices and Herbs: Lore & Cookery.* New York: Dover Publications, 1961.

Heth, Edward Harris. *The Wonderful World of Cooking.* New York: Simon and Schuster, 1956.

Humphries, John. *The Essential Saffron Companion.* Italy: Ten Speed Press, 1998.

Humphrey, Sylvia Windle. *Spices, Seasonings and Herbs.* New York: Collier Books, 1965.

"Ice Creams Were Produced." Monticello.org. https://www.monticello.org/site/jefferson/home-activity-0

Isaacs, Ronald H. *Every Person's Guide to Purim.* Jerusalem: Jason Aronson Inc, 2000.

Isaacson, Andy. "Meet One of the Last Pennsylvania Families Growing American Saffron." *Saveur.* January 18, 2016. http://www.saveur.com/pennsylvania-gold

Jacobs, Jennifer. "Rendezvous at the Legend Wholesome and holistic Culpeper." http://www.culpepperconnections.com/archives/uk/places/house.htm. January 2, 2015.

Bibliography

Jordan, Michele Anna. *The Good Cook's Book of Mustard*. New York: Skyhorse Publishing, 1994.

———. *Salt & Pepper*. New York: Broadway Books, 1999.

Keoke, Emory Dean and Porterfield, Kay Marie. *Encyclopedia of American Indian Contributions to the World*. New York: Checkmark Books, 2002.

Kiniry, Laura. "Where Bourbon Really Got Its Name and More Tips on America's Native Spirit." Smithsonian.com, June 13, 2013. https://www.smithsonianmag.com/arts-culture/where-bourbon-really-got-its-name-and-more-tips-on-americas-native-spirit-145879/

Knaapila, Antti, Liang-Dar Hwang, Anna Lysenko, Fujiko F. Duke, Brad Fesi, Amin Khoshnevisan, Rebecca S. James, Charles J. Wysocki, MeeRa Rhyu, Michael G. Tordoff, Alexander A. Bachmanov, Emi Mura, Hajime Nagai, and Danielle R. Reed. "Genetic Analysis of Chemosensory Traits in Human Twins," *Chemical Senses*, Volume 37, Issue 9, 1 November 2012, Pages 869–881, https://doi.org/10.1093/chemse/bjs070.

Landry, Robert. *The Gentle Art of Flavoring*. Translated by Bruce H. Axler. New York: Abelard-Schuman, 1970. Originally published in French as *Les Soleils de la Cuisine*, 1967.

Lewis, Y.S. *Spices and Herbs for the Food Industry*. Orpington, England: Food Trade Press, 1984.

Livingston, Kathryn. "Paprika." *Gourmet*, September 1980.

Loewenfeld, Claire, and Back, Phillipa. *The Complete Book of Herbs and Spices*. New York: G.P. Putnam's Sons, 1974.

Marchese, Anna, et al. "Antifungal and antibacterial activities of allicin: A review." *Trends in Food Science & Technology*, Volume 52, 49–56. June 2016.

Merriam-Webster.com. Merriam-Webster, 2011.

Meyer, Joseph E., and Clarence Meyer. *The Herbalist*. Meyerbooks: Glenwood, Illinois, 1986. (Revised; original 1918.)

Miloradovich, Milo. *The Home Garden Book of Herbs and Spices*. Garden City: New York, 1952.

National Geographic. *Edible: An Illustrated Guide to the World's Food Plants*. National Geographic Society: 2008.

National Institutes of Health. "Turmeric." https://nccih.nih.gov/health/turmeric/ataglance.htm

The New Straits Times Press. "Business Times," 29 July 1998, page 3. Accessed July 16, 2017. http://www.culpepperconnections.com/archives/uk/places/house.htm.

Norman, Jill. *The Burns Philp Book of Spices.* London: Dorling Kindersley, 1990.

Owen, Bill, and Alan Dikty. *The Art of Distilling Whiskey and Other Spirits.* Quarry Books, 2009.

Parry, J. W. *The Spice Handbook: Spices, Aromatic Seeds and Herbs.* Chemical Publishing Co., Inc: Brooklyn, New York, 1945.

Pendergrast, Mark. *For God, Country, and Coca-Cola.* Charles Scribner's Sons: New York, 1993.

Pillsbury.com, "History of the Pillsbury Bake-Off Contest." https://www.pillsbury.com/bake-off-contest/history-of-the-pillsbury-bake-off-contest

Poti, Jennifer M., Elizabeth K. Dunford, and Barry M. Popkin. "Sodium Reduction in US Households' Packaged Food and Beverage Purchases, 2000 to 2014." *JAMA Internal Medicine,* June 2017. http://jamanetwork.com/journals/jamainternalmedicine/article-abstract/2629447

Prabhakaran Nair, K. P. *Agronomy and Economy of Black Pepper and Cardamom.* New York: Elsevier, 2011.

Ramsey, Dom. *Chocolate.* New York: Penguin Random House, 2016.

Ridley, Henry N. *Spices.* London: MacMillan and Co., Limited, 1912.

Rosengarten, Frederic Jr. *The Book of Spices.* Pyramid Communications: New York, 1969.

The Salt Institute, "Iodized Salt." July 13, 2013. http://www.saltinstitute.org/2013/07/13/iodized-salt/

Sen, Colleen Taylor. *Curry: A Global History.* London: Reaktion Books Ltd., 2009.

Shulman, Martha Rose. *Garlic Cookery.* New York: Thorsons Publishers Inc., 1984.

Singer, Marilyn. *The Fanatic's Ecstatic Aromatic Guide to Onions, Garlic, Shallots and Leeks.* New Jersey: Prentice-Hall, Inc., 1981.

Slackman, Michael. "Germany loves its currywurst—contradictions, calories and all." *The Seattle Times.* January 29, 2011. https://www.seattletimes.com/life/food-drink/germany-loves-its-currywurst-8212-contradictions-calories-and-all/

Small, Ernest. *Top 100 Food Plants.* Ottawa, Canada: NRC Research Press, 2009.

Smithsonian Institution. "Egyptian Mummies." 2012. https://www.si.edu/Encyclopedia_SI/nmnh/mummies.htm

Spice-work.com, via the Wayback Machine. https://web.archive.org/web/20060816070915/http://spicehousebrand.com:80/shdj5.htm

Swahn, J. O. *The Lore of Spices*. New York: Crescent Books, 1991.

Tucker, Arthur and Michael J. Macciarello. "Oregano: Botany, Chemistry, and Cultivation," in *Spices, Herbs and Edible Fungi* (ed: G. Charalambous). Elsevier: Science BV, 1994.

Turner, Camilla. "Rosemary sales double during exam season after study suggests it boosts brain power." *The Telegraph*. May 17, 2017. http://www.telegraph.co.uk/education /2017/05/17/rosemary-sales-double-exam-season-study-suggests-boosts-brain/

Turner, Jack. *Spice: The History of a Temptation*. New York: Knopf, 2004.

Vanilla Bean Association of America, Inc. *The Story of Pure Vanilla*. New York: Vanilla Bean Association of America, Inc., 1955.

Westland, Pamela. *The Book of Spices*. New York: Exeter Books, 1985.

Wildman, Frederick S. *Spice Notes*. New York: 1960.

Willard, Pat. *Secrets of Saffron: The Vagabond Life of the World's Most Seductive Spice*. Boston: Beacon Press, 2001.

Wondrich, David. "Whiskey for the Winter." *Esquire*, December 17, 2010. https://www. esquire.com/food-drink/drinks/a9129/winter-drink-recipes-0111/

Wynter Blyth, Alexander, and Meredith Wynter Blyth. *Foods: Their Composition and Analysis*. C. Griffin & company, 1903.

Conversion Charts

METRIC AND IMPERIAL CONVERSIONS

(These conversions are rounded for convenience)

Ingredient	Cups/Tablespoons/Teaspoons	Ounces	Grams/Milliliters
Butter	1 cup/ 16 tablespoons/ 2 sticks	8 ounces	230 grams
Cheese, shredded	1 cup	4 ounces	110 grams
Cornstarch	1 tablespoon	0.3 ounce	8 grams
Cream cheese	1 tablespoon	0.5 ounce	14.5 grams
Flour, all-purpose	1 cup/1 tablespoon	4.5 ounces/0.3 ounce	125 grams/8 grams
Flour, whole wheat	1 cup	4 ounces	120 grams
Fruit, dried	1 cup	4 ounces	120 grams
Fruits or veggies, chopped	1 cup	5 to 7 ounces	145 to 200 grams
Fruits or veggies, puréed	1 cup	8.5 ounces	245 grams
Honey, maple syrup, or corn syrup	1 tablespoon	0.75 ounce	20 grams
Liquids: cream, milk, water, or juice	1 cup	8 fluid ounces	240 milliliters
Oats	1 cup	5.5 ounces	150 grams
Salt	1 teaspoon	0.2 ounces	6 grams
Spices: cinnamon, cloves, ginger, or nutmeg (ground)	1 teaspoon	0.2 ounce	5 milliliters
Sugar, brown, firmly packed	1 cup	7 ounces	200 grams
Sugar, white	1 cup/1 tablespoon	7 ounces/0.5 ounce	200 grams/12.5 grams
Vanilla extract	1 teaspoon	0.2 ounce	4 grams

OVEN TEMPERATURES

Fahrenheit	Celsius	Gas Mark
225°	110°	¼
250°	120°	½
275°	140°	1
300°	150°	2
325°	160°	3
350°	180°	4
375°	190°	5
400°	200°	6
425°	220°	7
450°	230°	8

Index

This book of *spice* is filled

With *magic* good and willed,

But if you take by *force*,

Steal or *deface* or worse,

Upon you be this *curse*:

Forever be you illed